PRA
THE QUEST

RELAX AND
RETREAT

THE NOTEBOOKS OF PAUL BRUNTON
(VOLUME 3)

PRACTICES FOR THE QUEST

RELAX AND RETREAT

PAUL BRUNTON
(1898–1981)

An in-depth study of
categories two and three
from the notebooks

A Larson Publication
for the
PAUL BRUNTON PHILOSOPHIC FOUNDATION

International Standard Book Number (cloth) 0-943914-15-9
International Standard Book Number (paper) 0-943914-16-7
International Standard Book Number (series, cloth) 0-943914-17-5
International Standard Book Number (series, paper) 0-943914-23-X
Library of Congress Catalog Card Number: 88-81030

Manufactured in the United States of America

Published for the
Paul Brunton Philosophic Foundation
by
Larson Publications
4936 Route 414
Burdett, New York 14818

Distributed to the trade by
Kampmann and Company
9 East 40 Street
New York, New York 10016

87   89   90   88   86
2   4   6   8   10   9   7   5   3

Photograph of Dr. Brunton reproduced
by courtesy of Arthur Broekhuysen

CONTENTS

EDITORS' INTRODUCTION

This third volume in *The Notebooks of Paul Brunton* is an in-depth presentation of the second and third (of twenty-eight) categories in the personal notebooks Dr. Paul Brunton (1898–1981) reserved for posthumous publication.

Part 1, *Practices for the Quest*, goes directly to the heart of the various disciplines, exercises, and techniques useful at various stages of spiritual self-discovery and self-development. It explains what qualities must be developed, why they must be developed, how they can be developed, and how that development will be tested by life itself.

The previous volume, *The Quest*, concerned itself with the *discovery* of the quest for self-realization and the general principles involved in spiritual seeking. Part 1 of this volume concerns itself with an overview of actually *living* the Quest insofar as its goal can be approached through our own daily efforts. Many of the themes treated in these paras are developed further in the next eighteen categories of *The Notebooks*: this category presents the interrelationship of the various facets of the work. It makes clear the extent to which every element of our being must eventually be turned to that greatest of goals.

Dr. Brunton offered less by way of structure for this category than for any other in his overall outline of *The Notebooks*. He provided only the main title (*Practices for the Quest*, which he later subtitled "An Overview of the Practices") and two principal subdivisions: "Ant's Long Path" and "Work on Oneself." Those of us working on this material found these two divisions—particularly the second—much too broad to give the reader an adequate notion of the details this category involves, so we devised the structure and titles of all but the first chapter in this section. We have structured this section as follows.

Chapters one through three are primarily for the person about to enter or newly entered upon the Quest. They examine what kind of development is necessary, and how to evaluate one's progress. These issues are somewhat abstract and theoretical, but an understanding of the perspective they offer is indispensable for the person trying to get a clear idea of what he or she is trying—or is about to start trying—to accomplish.

Chapter four begins a second level of approach to the practices: an approach that is relevant to all questers, no matter how long they have been practicing, no matter what experiences they have acquired or what development they have achieved. This chapter and the remainder of those in Part 1 deal with issues that confront both the novice and the proficient—both the person who has yet to experience any reliable inner illumination and the one who has achieved an abiding measure of success. Dr. Brunton makes eminently clear that while character development may not appear relevant at all stages of the Quest, it becomes—in the final stages—one of the most important deciding factors in the passage to permanent enlightenment.

Most importantly, this category as a whole distinguishes, clarifies, and begins to reconcile two fundamentally different attitudes underlying and preconditioning stages of spiritual development: the "Long Path" of self-improvement and character development, and the "Short Path" of ego-renunciation and illumination. It shows the relative usefulness of each of these attitudes at appropriate stages of self-development. As Dr. Brunton clearly considered a certain amount of Long Path development as an indispensable prerequisite to fruitful use of Short Path techniques, this section emphasizes the techniques and developments of the former. The Short Path attitude and its corresponding techniques, touched upon only briefly here, are fully developed in section twenty-three.

Part 2, *Relax and Retreat*, lays the cornerstone for a modern life of inspired sanity. Addressing the urgent need in our times to neutralize the hectic pace and mounting tensions of contemporary life with a deliberately cultivated spiritual equilibrium, it is a practical course in balancing periods of extroverted activity with recuperative periods of creative inner stillness. The category title and the broad general divisions serving as chapter titles in this section are from Dr. Brunton himself. Only the tertiary divisions have been devised by the editors.

As was the case with the first two volumes in this series, the selection and placement of the material in this volume has been done by students following Dr. Brunton's general guidelines. We acknowledge the arbitrariness of some decisions. Beyond beginning and ending sections with selected paras, no attempt has been made in either Part 1 or Part 2 to sequence the material within sections for "readability." We have, in fact, tried to avoid "coloring" a given para through its possible associations with what precedes and follows it. As stated in the introduction to volume two, we would like this series to be viewed as an open-ended, rich resource drawn from inspired notebooks rather than to try and present the individual volumes as highly structured, continuous works.

In preparing this volume, we set ourselves the twin goals of (1) bringing together *all* the principal ideas Dr. Brunton offered on these two topics, and (2) eliminating thematic redundancy wherever important nuances would not be sacrificed by doing so. Our aim has been to provide the reader with a comprehensive and comprehendable text of Dr. Brunton's "seed thoughts," one that is neither too structured nor too amorphous to deliver their essential spirit and relatedness.

In the interest of our first goal, we have repeated a few paras from *Perspectives*, the survey volume introducing this series. Such paras are indicated by a (P) at their end. In the interest of the second goal, we have had to leave unpublished, for the time being, those paras that we consider either to be less well written than or to contain statements adequately covered by material published in these pages. While this volume does not contain every "para" Dr. Brunton wrote on these issues during his last thirty years, we have tried to err on the side of including too much rather than too little. In having done so, we are certain that this volume is a thorough presentation of his valuable insights on these two important topics. For the present, earnest students may study the remainder of the unpublished material in the library of Wisdom's Goldenrod Center for Philosophic Studies in Valois, New York, 14888. If there is sufficient demand, this remaining material will be made available in a small subscription-only edition after the main series has been published.

Once again, we would like to acknowledge our profound gratitude to the many friends at Wisdom's Goldenrod without whose dedicated work and financial support this project could not be accomplished. We are particularly pleased to be able to announce with this volume that *The Notebooks* series will now proceed with the additional support and guidance of a new non-profit organization, the Paul Brunton Philosophic Foundation. This organization, incorporated in March of 1986, exists for the purpose of publishing, maintaining in print, and internationally disseminating the works of Paul Brunton and those of other individuals who further the interests of philosophy in Dr. Brunton's sacred sense of the term. More information about either forthcoming publications or the foundation itself may now be obtained by writing to the

Paul Brunton Philosophic Foundation
P.O. Box 89
Hector, New York 14841

Part 1:
PRACTICES FOR THE QUEST

Through establishing the correct inner attitude of faith and devotion, through correct methods of study both of general laws and of one's own weaknesses, with constant determination to correct these weaknesses through the pursuit of the ideal of a balanced psyche, and through the regular practice of prayer and meditation, one will be doing all that the ego can do by itself to establish the required conditions for the advent of help from higher sources.

1

ANT'S LONG PATH

What is the Long Path?

His first effort is to find the obstacles which retard the enlightenment; his second, to remove them. This constitutes the Long Path.

2

He who feels the inner urge to seek always for the Soul, the Hidden, who longs to be quite consciously united with it, first will have to undergo a long process of being separated from his baser attributes, of having the larger part of his imperfections washed away.

3

The mind is prevented from knowing the truth by its own defects limitations or deficiencies, by its own passions self-centeredness and possessiveness. The philosophic discipline sets up as an objective the elimination of these hindrances. Such disciplines are physical, mental, and emotional.

4

For the man or woman who truly desires to follow the Quest and who wonders how to begin, the present course should be to read and study the exercises given in my earlier books, going over them carefully again and again until all the basic concepts are familiar. At the same time, one should find a few minutes out of every day when it is possible to be alone, undisturbed and unobserved. Meditation should be opened by silent prayer, formulated to express spiritual yearnings for the higher way of life. This may be followed by concentrating on a chosen spiritual theme. Every endeavour should be made to keep thoughts from wandering and to bring them back whenever they do.

5

If we want certain knowledge, instead of vague hope, that the answer to this question "Who am I?" is "I am of godlike essence," we must follow the Quest into its disciplines and practices.

6

How can the influx remain if the negative elements of the man's character are still there and contradict its presence? One or the other has to go. If the man cannot remove those elements at once—and who can?—then he must do so by degrees and through the years.

7

It is a paradox whose truth the world has failed to realize, despite the repeated efforts of Jesus to point it out, that we best attain a happy worldly life when we seek a happy spiritual life, and that we least attain the first goal when we neglect the second.

8

Those who advise us to become saintly in character before we attempt to travel the mystic path, confuse cause with effect. No one can make himself a saint to order, but anyone who will patiently pursue this path will naturally become elevated in character, because he will come closer to divinity.

9

The Long Path principle is that enlightenment must be earned by his own labour.

10

The ego must become conscious of its guilt in blocking the light of the Overself and must perform the necessary penance to expiate that guilt. But this is merely another way of saying that it must enter on the Long Path and purify itself.

11

Those who pass through this phase when they see life as holding little that matters, and life's joys as being mostly empty, are marked out for philosophy: nothing else can serve them successfully after this experience although religion may help them for a time.

12

The doctrine of a gradual evolution through successive steps belongs to the Long Path.

13

Let him bring himself, through the Long Path, into the condition which may invite the approach of Grace.

14

If he is not insincere, sooner or later the quest will force his lower nature to throw up its hidden evil, so that he may face, fight, and conquer it.

15

He will try to put into practice what is sensible and worthy, without being overawed by environment, habit, or popular prejudice.

16

He will undertake them not as a penance to expiate his sins but as a training to fit him better for the reception of Grace and the practices of the Short Path.

17

Although the heroic way of abrupt harsh reform is the only way suited to certain temperaments, the easier way of gradual gentle change is the only way suited to most other temperaments. Few men can bring themselves to abandon the small comforts and daily routines to which they are accustomed for the purpose of plunging straightway into a rigorously ascetic regime.

18

The discipline cures the emotional nature of its faults, purifies the intellectual nature of its prejudices, cleanses the egoistic nature of its resistances. Thus it brings the mind into a state where it may understand truth without error and with clarity.

19

He will try to avoid all exaggeration and distortion in his thought and speech, certainly all falsehood.

20

It is useful to put a desirable quality into practice outwardly so that it may in time, by the body's influence on the mind, be acquired inwardly.

21

It is thoughtless of the poor to say that practice of philosophy is only for those who have the money, the leisure, and the freedom to spare. It is equally thoughtless of the rich to say that the practice is for those who need philosophy's consolatory service in their squalor and poverty. The truth is that neither the millionaire nor the pauper, nor even all those classes in between, can escape from the need of philosophic practice; without it, as Buddha pointed out, they are doomed to suffer.

22

Men lack the needful perceptions and therefore they accept the substitute whilst passing by the reality. This is why a preparation, a self-improvement, is prescribed to seekers after truth.

23

No narrower ideal, no height lower than sagehood is to be set up as his goal.

24

Always there is this image in front of him—what he could become and what life wants him to become in the end.

25

They tell us to lose our personal identity, to let it become absorbed in the universal self. What is prescribed in a few words could take up a whole lifetime.

26

The transformation of the whole inner man may happen slowly and imperceptibly or through a series of experiences brought on by crises. With it comes the purification of his character, the maturation of his intelligence, and the self-discipline of the ego.

27

Truth is open to all, if only all can receive it. But they cannot—until a preparation and purification open the way.

28

The first steps on the path call for an awareness of the aspirant's failings and for a determination to eradicate them.

29

Bring again and again into remembrance the fact that you are a pilgrim, that this world is but a camp, and that the situations in which you find yourself, or create for yourself, should be regarded not from the worldly point of view only, but still more from that of this quest of the Overself.

30

The period of preparation and discipline will be a long one. Few have even the desire, let alone the patience, to undergo it.

31

Whatever impedes the entry of spiritual lights must be removed. That is the Long Path's work.

32

It is essential to reject negative thoughts, to accept and hold only the affirmative ones.

33

Let him be vigilant about the way in which he reacts to experiences and circumstances, to men and women. Let him be on guard against the attractions and repulsions which they engender, the emotions which they excite, and the desires which they arouse.

34

He will have to correct and complete the materialistic evidence of his senses as he will have to discipline and overcome their animalistic outgoing tendency.

35

If he can do little to bring on the advent of Grace, he can do much to remove the obstructions to it.

36

The way must begin with a general quietening down of your mind, calming of your emotions, an overcoming of your passions, and a regular practising of meditation.

37

He fails to perceive that after all his work has removed some old weaknesses, new ones have been created in their place.

38

Whether he identifies his faults or fails to do so, he will still have to come to the point where he tries to build the virtues opposite them (if he knows them) or where he concentrates on the Overself-thought and forgets them.

39

It is the work of the Long Path to achieve a large measure of self-control but only the work of the Short Path can finish it.

40

The Quester cannot imitate the conventional lives of other people. He has to make some changes, and particularly some sacrifices, if he is to follow a path whose goal is different from theirs. He has to find some time for meditation and study, some time when he can fully and truly be himself, and this requires, however short, a daily period of solitude. He has to arrange his diet so that it will not provide more difficulty for his inner work. He has to be careful of what company he keeps, so that he will not be constantly responding to their auras, either in struggle or in defense.

41

The Long Path is one where the seeker criticizes himself as a prelude to the attempt to conquer himself.

42

The Long Path is an extended self-criticism. The Long Path cannot of itself bring him to God, but it can remove obstacles, straighten warpings.

43

The rays of light would enter every man's conscious mind even now, were they not prevented by the extroversion of his attention, the upheavals of his emotion and passion, the narrow rigidities of his logical intellect, and the attachments of his ego. This is why the removal of these obstructions—which is the Long Path's special work—is indispensable to his progress.

44

A certain educated taste for truth is needed, a development of heart and mind which brings about the ability to discriminate between appearance and reality, between lower and higher values, between personal opinions and impersonal facts. This education may come through life itself, or through the self-training processes of the Long Path.

45

Who would not welcome receiving the Short Path's exemption from having to pass through the long and tedious course of training of the Long one? But such an exemption exists only for the well-developed few, who have already done much or most of this preparatory work. All others will find, both in practice and in the end, that no amount of claiming it will avail them.

46

What hope is there of attaining the Long Path's goal? Even if it remains unattained, he can get nothing but benefit by the mere approach to it. All his efforts will be compensated in some way.

47

The Overself is a fact as actual as any other. Its discovery will make life more worth living, not less. But this must be found through personal experience, as others have done. Then one discovers that he is not deprived of anything by this Quest—unless it be defects of character which he wishes to be rid of—but he can keep all those things still which humans cherish. He needs much patience, of course, to go on with meditation practice and a little study when results seem slow in coming, but he will at least know that the time is not being wasted; every effort in this direction counts. For if it does nothing more, it prepares him to receive and benefit by the help which others may wish to bestow on him.

48

When he becomes dissatisfied with himself, when he feels that what he is doing, thinking, achieving is either not enough or too inferior or even too misguided, he may be ready for the Long Path of self-improvement.

49

Entangled in his animal nature, his attempts to live in his spiritual nature consist of constant approach followed by withdrawal—a rhythm which torments him for years. This is his history on the Long Path.

50

To break an old and undesirable habit, two things are helpful. First, take a vow, make a pledge before someone whose spiritual authority you respect or someone who is spiritually more advanced than yourself. Second, let yourself be carried as far as possible on the momentum of the first great tide of enthusiasm for the new resolve, into doing something about it, into visible and practical result.

51

There are no practices that will reveal the meaning of life. The latter can come only from experience and reflection. But practices have secondary uses, such as helping to develop concentration, which is needed for right reflection.

52

Although the Long Path is preparatory, for beginners, to the Short Path and should be attempted first, for intermediates it is better to make them twin quests. It might be said that the Long Path belongs to yoga and the Short Path to advaita—that is, to mysticism and to philosophy. Thus, when he is better prepared, the same person can cultivate both paths and there is then no antagonism between them, for they then complement and balance one another.

53

The tensions set up in his inner life by this struggle against the ego, the emotions, and the thought-habits will not be resolved until he has gone a long way on the quest.

54

The preliminary self-training ordinarily covers a few years if the effort is continuous, more if it is not.

55

There are inherent differences in people, differences of character, energy, intelligence, and temperament. For the quester to succeed, he must recognize this fact and not let himself become the slave of a system which is unsuited to him, or of a method which conflicts with his external circumstances.

56

We know that no two persons are wholly the same whether in outer form or inner status. We ought not demand that there should be—let alone is—a single fixed way of approaching truth or even describing it.

57

The Long Path votary lives a divided existence, ascribing reality to two powers—the ego and the Overself. If he is persistent he fluctuates between occasional glimpses of the one and long stretches of consciousness in the other.

58

The eventual aim of all this human evolutionary experience is to make us love the soul more than anything else; therefore all personal attachments have to be slowly purified in character. We may still hold them in our hearts, but they should be held inside the larger attachment to this divine Quest.

Purification and development of character

59

The quest of truth by a mind deformed by hate, anger, bias, bitterness, or greed, or deficient in concentration, calmness, or aspiration must end in a failure which will be partial or total to the extent that these negatives are partial or total. This is why the Long Path is needed.

60

Two processes are called for: a cleansing of the body and a cleansing of the character.

61

Illumination is certainly a joyous thing, but the way to it involves harsh discipline at times and hard sacrifices at other times.

62

It is not enough to practise these disciplines, controls, and denials of the self. He must also practise them cheerfully.

63

The inner work of mental purification, the travail of emotional cleansing will constantly go on. Many times in a single day he will be called on to reject wrong thoughts and to repel lower feelings.

64

The first stage is negative and preparatory. It is to get out of the animal-passional forces and lower emotional complexes which make him so largely a creature of this earth. Caught in the meshes of his lower nature as he is, he must free himself from them sufficiently to safeguard the work in mystical meditation from becoming a source of self-injury and social danger.

65

No one can deny that a proper methodical training is a highly valuable factor in achieving effective results in any sphere. This must also be true of the spiritual sphere.

66

He is not asked to be a saint, but he is asked to be sincere.

67

The instincts are to be purified, the passions calmed, the feelings refined, and the thoughts concentrated.

68

He must be brave enough to rid his thinking of enervating falsities and his emotions of their devastating egoisms.

69

The life of an aspirant must necessarily be an ever-recurring combat against his egoism, his passions, his desires, his extroversion, his attractions and repulsions. Hence it can be neither an easy nor a smooth one.

70

He has to undergo a self-discipline which is integral, total, and comprehensive.

71

Are you prepared to devote many years and much concentration to such studies? Enlightenment is no simple matter but rather a work of profound labour.

72

When the first transitional period of creating, pioneering, and establishing a new habit has been passed, it becomes no harder than holding on to a bad one.

73

He will not hesitate to acknowledge his personal frailties and to confess his personal limitations. For this is a part of the Long Path. He need only do so silently and secretly—except in the case of an interview with a spiritual adviser.

74

Only after passing through the prescribed cleansings can an aspirant be sufficiently ready and prepared to unfold the intuitive mystical side of his nature without blockage or bias interfering from the animal side.

75

Certainly he must be eager to seek the truth, willing to give time for the search since it requires study and meditation, but equally he must be prepared to practise some self-discipline. This is partly because the quest of truth succeeds to the extent that he disengages himself from the ego and from the thoughts, the passions, and the moods it produces.

76

Before a man can absorb truth he must render himself fit to do so. Otherwise, the violent intrusion of passion will cloud his vision, the sway of personal emotion will unbalance his understanding, and the working of attachment or aversion will affect the correctness of his knowledge.

77

Not having set out to seek truth, but only the verification of their own prejudices and superstitions, naturally they do not find it. This is why mental purification and emotional discipline are necessary at the beginning.

78

He should be deeply ashamed of his failures, deeply repentant of his sins.

79

He who follows the Quest will have to attend to his inferiorities of intellect, fill in gaps of personality, fight weaknesses of will, and develop needed virtues by self-training.

80

His first task is to dig up and uncover mercilessly and impartially the hidden roots of his character, and especially of his attachments, weaknesses, and repulsions.

81

It is easy and human to project our wishes on the universe of our experience and think our fancies into the universe of our ideas. Therefore, the quest of the Overself must begin with a discipline of the underself.

82

The aim of this discipline is to cleanse the heart of negative and obstructive emotions, to clear the mind of false and distorted thoughts.

83

What he has hitherto accepted—from heredity, tradition, and society— as normal, correct living habits will have to be severely questioned and, in a number of cases, altered and reformed. He will have to give up some familiar things and take up some new regimes.

84

The healthy life, whether of the body or the mind, calls for a certain amount of self-discipline, self-exercise, and self-training. We must give in effort a price that will entitle us to receive a benefit, although it need not be commensurate with the benefit. Indeed the *Bhagavad Gita* declares: "A little attention to this yoga produces great results."

85

Those who are willing to endure the unconventional disciplines and stiff rigours of such a daily schedule practise a self-denial which will bring them markedly closer to the goal than those who are not.

86

Such self-discipline is unattractive to, and unwanted by, those who have settled in comfortable ruts. Yet unless the lower nature is put under a yoke and made to obey the higher nature, the experiences of life fail to fulfil the purpose of life.

87

The candidate who stands before the Sphinx must be prepared to part with illusions long and dearly held, with passions which give strength to those illusions, with egoistic pettiness.

88

Because he has put himself under special obligations by the mere act of putting himself on this quest, he must freely and quickly confess his weaknesses, as a preliminary to setting about their correction. Condonation, justification, and alibis may be left to those who are uninterested in the quest.

89

His practical work will begin by entering the stage of self-purification, by repudiating little by little or, if he finds sufficient strength within himself, all at once, those elements of animalism which clog his upward movement and keep his mind physically immersed.

90

One of the most difficult but necessary lessons to be learned in life is the understanding and control of one's own emotional nature. It must be constantly observed, understood, and its energies should be redirected to produce that condition of inner calm and stability which is indispensable to progress. A very necessary part of this study is to observe how the emotional conditions of others impinge upon, and affect, one's own, as well as the reverse process.

91

If he is to put himself into a properly receptive attitude for the enlightenment which Truth brings, there are several corrections he must make in himself and by himself. He must discard the intolerance, the narrowness, the littleness which rejects any persons or condemns entire nations because of their appearance or their religion or their past history or their social condition. He must cast out all malevolence and enmity toward others. He must put a stop to the endless urges which covet more and more possessions, which stimulate stronger and stronger ambitions.

92

The quest's practical work seeks to rise above infantile attitudes, adolescent emotions, and animal passions.

93

Self-mastery is a personal duty for every man who wants to make something of his life, and much more so for every quester. Whatever method he uses to purge himself of blemishes and stains in his character, or errors and delusions in his mind, whether by positive effort of will or by constant contemplation of the ideal, he must withdraw from the old man to a substantial extent if he is to put on the new man.

94

The disciple's inner work is manifold, but sincere striving for self-improvement is the most important part of it.

95

Correct social behaviour is not necessarily an expression of spirituality: it may vary from one country, people, tribe, or century to another. But as part of the preparation of the way to spirituality it has its value so far as it calls for considerateness toward others, discipline of speech and action, curbing of selfishness, desire, and greed, and control of the passions.

96

It may be thought that being a gentleman has nothing to do with being spiritual. But, if the term is used in its ideal sense, then the belief is wrong. He who has been indoctrinated as a child with high ideals and inculcated with good habits, taught refined manners and speech, encouraged to seek the general welfare alongside of his own, and educated to practise self-discipline, has been well prepared for the Long Path if he comes to it later.

97

If he is to gather experience he can hardly help making mistakes. For they are often the heavy cost of inexperience. But he can certainly help repeating those mistakes. And this depends first on how ready he is within his own heart to admit them as such; second on how ready he is to search for weaknesses of character or capacity which may lie behind them.

98

His goal is to take these responsibilities upon his own shoulders, to develop his own courage and knowledge wherewith to meet them and not attempt to evade them in the name of spiritual surrender.

99

Although most persons do spend several lives on this quest, there is no rule which condemns them to give so much time. What they seek is close enough, within themselves, but it is they who must bring the mind, heart, and will into a condition necessary to find it. "He is a happy man," says the *Bhagavad Gita*, "who *during his lifetime* is able to conquer the passions."

100

All these energies which drag men into attachments that impede progress toward a higher level can be transmuted.

101

If one cannot predict with complete certainty when the hour of realization will arrive, one can at least prepare those conditions which are essential to its arrival. Let us do that, therefore, and then humbly await the fruit of one's labour. Whoever can instill into himself this kind of patience, which is far removed from slumbering inertia, will go far upon this path.

102

He will study his own character and other people's with the utmost impartiality.

103

So long as a man stays on the Long Path alone he is clinging to the idea of his ego, which embarks on the Quest to save *itself* by methods and processes of purifying *itself.* This idea is never let go, only refined and purified. For it starts the Quest as an imperfect and low ego, finishes it as a perfectly pruned and improved one. Its own reality is not questioned, for if it were regarded as the nonexistent fiction that it is, there would be no need to purify or save it.

104

Keep what is worth keeping in past ways of thought and life, custom and character: it took so long to come into being.

105

He is saved from spiritual snobbishness by the practice of humility, and from spiritual priggishness by a sense of humour.

106

The acknowledgment of evil done in the past and the confession of weakness experienced in the present are indispensable preliminaries.

107

He must put down the lower emotions every time they rear their heads. The ordinary unquesting man may allow resentment, jealousy, anger, lust, hate, and greed to appear and act without restraint on the scene of his life, but the disciple cannot. Self-purification is both his need and his duty.

108

His quest will not only have to take him out of the body's toxicity, negative feelings, lustful desires, and aggressive passions of the lower nature, not only out of the intellect's curiosity and restlessness, but also out of the ego's vain and disorderly imagination. It is from this source that so many false psychical experiences and hallucinatory revelations, so many prophetic messages and deceptive visions arise. The prudent aspirant will not blindly accept any self-flattering intimation or prediction, but will check it against the appraisals of informed persons, against the nature of his own conduct or the egolessness of his own character.

109

He may well weep over the muddled nature of his efforts in the past and over the wasted time spent in bypaths and sidetracks.

110

He should hold fast to the principles of the Quest, especially those of self-cleansing, reason, balance, and stability, because only after this preparation of the right inner conditions is it possible for illumination of a more lasting character to be safely received.

111

He can make a determined practice of ruling his feelings, dominating his reactions, and controlling his reflexes. This will not be easy but with time it could become a habit, that is, second nature.

112

He will obey such disciplines not as duties imposed from without but as expressions of the need to re-educate himself within.

113

Society (that is, other people) needs reform. Yes, certainly! But oneself needs not less, possibly even more reform.

114

A deeply shaming past cannot be pushed aside, but it can be transcended by learning to live on a superior level.

115

Equilibrium is a necessary part of the qualities to be developed on the Long Path. It is corrective against wrong ideas and protective against base emotion.

116

The ordinary man does not feel himself to be under any special constraint to correct his faults or remove his weaknesses or eradicate objectionable qualities; the Long Path man feels this every day.

117

They resent the fact that they are called to a *work* and prefer the delusion that they are to benefit by a miracle.

118

During the years between the times of knowingly starting on the Quest and that of meeting a Teacher, one should work especially hard at improving his whole general character and getting rid of any faults of whose existence he is aware. It is most important, for instance, to discipline temper, to develop self-control, and to learn how to overcome the temptation to give way to anger. Lesser faults, such as impulsiveness and carelessness, must also be checked and balanced by the deliberate cultivation of discrimination and prudence.

119

Looking at his past on the Long Path, a man who is honest with himself may experience feelings of dismay; but he ought to remember that all those events, thoughts, and actions were steps in his instruction and therefore productive. When examining and analysing it he should bear this in mind and therefore take it more calmly. At the same time the instruction must be taken to heart and used as a base contributing towards the future. The lessons are not to be ignored but they need not weigh him down.

120

Most persons live in an atmosphere which mixes the negative tendencies with the positive. The resulting mish-mash obscures their way. Even if the glimpse comes, visibility is very quickly blotted out again. There is necessary a cleaning-out work.

121

It is a serious step to take a vow, whether it be denying satisfaction to the sexual instinct or denying the craving for alcohol, or any other of the purifications. A vow of this kind is a promise made both to oneself and to the Overself. It is an unwritten contract.

122

We must begin self-reform by facing ourselves in our little human existences. Are we failing in our relationship with others? Are there negative elements in our lives, making us melancholy, dissatisfied, unhappy?

123

We take our little selves even into this analysis of the past and present. We do not see them with really impersonal eyes. The perspective is still egoistic. We do not care to accept the truth about ourselves. The task is impossible to our present stage of development. It cannot be done. But this does not mean it is not worth trying. It is. For though we shall come nowhere near to adequacy and to perfect honesty, we shall certainly move somewhat nearer.

124

Those who regard this regime as too austere to accept voluntarily give their lower nature an advantage.

125

It is open to question which leads to more mistakes in life, human frailty or human foolishness. The miseries appearing out of the first point to the need of practising self-control. The misfortunes coming out of the second say plainly that more intelligence must be developed.

126

He himself has sought this self-cleansing. He must be prepared to witness the rising up to the surface of negative qualities that have lain inert or only half-active, as well as the throwing into focus by outer events of those which have already been fully active. He will now have to deal with these qualities, usually one at a time, and to deal with them repeatedly so long as they are not thoroughly transmuted. It is all a part of the work of purification, resulting from the co-operation of his own higher self. As such it is not to be regretted but expected, not to be deplored but to be calmly dealt with.

127

If, instead of warding off the recognition of his own shortcomings, he confronted and surmounted them he would benefit. For one source of inner conflict would then disappear.

128

He must show his difference from the beast in the field by showing self-discipline, self-denial, and self-training. When a man begins to look at himself with horror, he begins to bring his sleep-walking to an end.

Confronting the obstacles within

129

He will meet with obstructions on the road. There they will lie until he uses enough energy and exertion to remove them.

130

The lazy disinclination to meditate and the emotional resistance to selflessness which obstruct his advance obstruct all other aspirants, too. It may console him to know that they are general.

131

He proposes to reorder his ways, to engage in the work of self-control, but finds that he has an intractable ego to deal with and obstinate passions to contend with.

132

On this path haste and impatience will not help him, however much they may do so on the worldly path. They will only dissipate his strength and obstruct the opening of the bud of intuition.

133

If the aspirant takes personal pride in the results of *his* endeavours, if he regards mystical experiences that come with meditation as favours special to him, then vanity and self-conceit have crept in on a higher level and block his path. He imagines himself to be far advanced on the path and swells with complacency at his achievement. In all this self-flattery, it is his ego who really benefits.

134

The danger of the Long Path appears after it has been travelled for a sufficient period of time. The utter novice is not exposed to it, but the experienced aspirant is. It consists in the egotism which is bred by the belief that progress depends on the efforts he puts out, on what he *personally* does. For the ego cannot transcend itself, and whatever it does will still remain within its own self. Indeed, the more successful the aspirant is in developing his willpower and virtue, as well as in overcoming his faults and weaknesses, the more he is likely to develop this spiritual pride which fixes him more subtly than ever in the ego. Only resort to the messianic practice of "being still" can save him from this impasse. Only this practice will let the Overself work on him and in him, whereas every other one keeps it out by keeping him in the ego.

135

Doubts will come to him at times, hesitations will paralyse him, and consummation of the distant goal will seem quite inachievable. Such moods will leave wretched depressions and frustrating despairs in their train. If he is to overcome them he must call in the help of reason and clearly understand, first, that the quest by its very nature is a matter of multiple lifetimes and, second, that a calm acceptant patience is the prime condition of engaging in it at all and that progression through its different stages will come in its own time and way, and not his.

136

If the advances in understanding, the glimpses of higher states, and the improvements in mental attitudes are regarded egoistically, that is, with the smug complacence that it is "I" who has brought them about, then their value is only preparatory. For they still leave him self-enclosed and he still remains outside the Overself. The Long Path merely takes him to another part of the ego, even though it is the higher part.

137

However commendable pity toward other persons may be as a trait of character, it is worse than useless to the student on this path when directed to his own person. It merely feeds his weaknesses and nourishes his ego. It prevents him from facing himself and from looking into his real problems. Self-pity stops him from uncovering the true causes of some of his troubles.

138

He must beware of being sidetracked into something seemingly significant but relatively unimportant, something in which he may get so engrossed that he eventually loses sight altogether of his original objective. The quest of the Overself is then deserted and the quest of some side-show takes its place.

139

It is one of the hardest things in the world to get men to change a course of thinking or living which is harmful to them if that course is long established by themselves and everywhere sanctioned by society. For custom has made them habituated to it until in the efflux of years it has become second nature.

140

If the quest is to make little difference to his outer life, if he is to continue living, eating, and spending his time much as he did before, then it is still a theoretical matter with him. His intellect may be converted but his will and heart are still among the unbelievers and dwell apart. His position is spiritually still precarious. For that which ruled his conduct before conversion was the lower nature and the darkened mind, the body's miscalled natural appetites, and the ego's worldly desires, ambitions, or attachments.

141

There are too many people who put forth brief efforts and then expect undisturbed possession of spiritual heights for the remainder of their lifetimes. They want to buy success too cheaply and therefore fail to buy it at all.

142

It is easy to put off the purificatory self-training, as so many put it off, for no better reasons than inertia, shiftlessness, or inconvenience.

143

To regard these regimes as being uncomfortable and irksome, unnecessary and depressing, is to miss their purpose and misunderstand their nature.

144

There is no danger that the average Western aspirant will indulge in excesses of asceticism, will lacerate his body and torment his humanity. That danger existed only in the medieval and earlier period, and is even fading away today in the Orient. On the contrary, the present danger is that the aspirant wants the way made all too easy for him, with its disciplinary regimes and reform of habits removed.

145

He must not judge himself with too much leniency, or he will fail to fight his weaknesses or to fight them sufficiently, or with too much severity, or he will be so easily discouraged as to bring on unnecessary mental suffering.

146

Do not get so compulsively attached to your own little ways that you automatically reject all new ones.

147

The more he tries to justify his shortcomings, the less is he likely ever to get free of them.

148

If occasions exist when he is unable to curb the animal in him, that is no reason for abandoning the quest altogether.

149

If he finds in the end the ideal to be impossible of realization, if he feels the longing for it to be doomed to perpetual impotence, if he sadly accepts the fact of his incapacity to attain it, then his attitude may change to bitter cynicism.

150

We are not always eager to improve ourselves, overcome ourselves. The enterprise is a tiring one. So we get lazy and neglectful, showing that we are inconsistent.

151

Worse is the belief that this futility must go on forever, that his quest is defeated at the start.

152

When a man never tries to turn his dreams into realities, never proceeds with the effort to realize ambitions, he is either suffering from a vacillating character or from lack of willpower.

153

The time may come when he will bring in a long bill of indictment against the quest, and turn away in disappointment or frustration. Or he may do the same against God. All this is a misdirection of mental energy. It would be more profitable, in the one case, to indict himself and, in the other, to revise his notions of what constitutes Wisdom.

154

Those who recur often to thoughts of their past get trapped by it and kept prisoner of the ego. Remorse for sins committed and self-pity for being the victim of other people's sinning—both are soon overdone and create more obstacles to be overcome on the quest.

155

Not only are the lusts and passions enemies to his inner tranquillity but also ambition and curiosity, even the wish to influence, sway, or persuade other men.

156

These spiritual longings are not easily capable of fulfilment. It is hard to find the strength to overcome egoism, thwart desire, and disturb apathy. These are torments of frustration and stagnation when travelling the road to spiritual perfection.

157

Every negative thought which may arise within himself or be picked up unconsciously from others becomes an aggression against this quest.

158

The fear of losing their fixed ground in the worldly life causes some to withdraw from the quest. They sense danger to those things on which they depend for security, or else danger to the values which they believe necessary to maintain survival in the worldly struggle and competition.

159

He becomes afflicted with doubts. What is the use of adopting an ideal which is not realizable in life as it is? Or perhaps the truth is that there is no Truth. If he is mentally adolescent or emotionally unbalanced, he may push his scepticism to extremes. The Quest's values may then seem quite spurious, the tranquillity it promises quite bleak.

160

If a man falls away from the true quest because of worldly trouble or spiritual dryness, it is because he is seeking to keep within his ego rather than to get out of it.

161

To get despondent and unhappy about one's inner progress is to exhibit a lack of patience. It is as if the builder of a house got despondent because after he had laid the foundations and put up half the frame, the house was still useless for living in.

162

Alas! there is always plenty of time in the future for taking up the quest in real earnest and so it is often comfortably postponed, while the familiar egoistic life is always immediate and urgent.

163

Spiritual pride will become harder to conquer the more he advances, for it will nourish its own strength by such advancement. The conquest of his animal nature will only intensify the power of this foe which lurks in his human nature; the upbuilding of his intellectual understanding of truth will only make him more abjectly its victim. At no stage should he let go of his chief protection against such a dangerous attacker, which is humbly to refer everything accomplished to the Overself and, secondly, prudently to measure his progress by the distance still to be travelled.

164

We readily give our thought and strength to negotiating and overcoming the obstacles to earning a livelihood, but we become fatalistically defeatist when confronted by the obstacles to deepening spiritual life.

165

Why not accept the fact of your own imperfection instead of tormenting yourself about it?

166

At no stage of this quest is he to show pride in what he has attained, for then he obstructs the way to stages beyond.

167

Too often spiritual aspiration is simply worldly ambition transplanted to a higher but subtler level. The aspirant is not necessarily deceiving himself, for a mixture of motives is quite common.

168

It is not enough to plead that times are different and circumstances have changed so that unworldly ways of thought, action, and life are inappropriate. This is really a defense mechanism of those who want their quest made easy.

169

Too many questers are too extravagantly earnest. All this solemnity is inspired by, directed towards, and activated through the ego. That it presents itself in the Overself's name makes little difference. This excess of seriousness betrays the egotism behind it and becomes self-defeating. Better to let go. But one may feel sad without appearing lugubriously solemn. There are times when no quester can miss mourning the transiency of things, can avoid the melancholy air which surrounds recognition of the insubstantiality of life, fortune, friends, and human happiness. Yet if he is faithful to his course of meditations, the sadness should not last long nor weigh him down. It will pass as his peace revives.

170

The obsession with self-improvement on the Long Path may run to such an extreme as to become morbid. The most trivial weakness will then seem a great sin, and even nonexistent imperfections will then be brooded over remorsefully.

171

When the emotions stand between him and situations as they are, when his passions cripple judgement and obstruct intuition, how can he reasonably demand to have truth conveyed to him—whole, complete, and instantaneous?

172

Too much preoccupation with his own spiritual advancement, too much of self in his thoughts and too little of the Overself—this only binds him tighter to the ego.

173

If the Quest becomes a source of stress and worry, then its precepts and injunctions, its promises and workings, have not been clearly understood. This condition may be traced back to not enough or not correct knowledge, or both together; but other causes could exist such as inborn temperamental fears. A less negative, more positive attitude toward it will help here.

174

However lofty his aspirations may be, they are all-too-often thwarted by the weakness of his will or the direction of his tendencies.

175

Although we must cease to blame others for our troubles, or conditions for our misfortunes, and assume responsibility for the self which we have created and the actions it has done, we need not push our sense of guilt to the point of morbidity. Although we have attracted so many of our misfortunes by our own thoughts and feelings and actions, we need not feed pessimism until it becomes despair. Too many persons on the Long Path fall into these errors through expecting more from themselves than they actually realized.

176

It is possible to run to such extremes on this Long Path as to lose all sense of humour, all need of lighter entertainment, all capacity to relax—looking only for meaning in outer life, for progress in inner life—to lose, in short, the art of being serious without becoming too solemn.

177

Of what use is Long Path self-reproach about one's faults if carried to excess so that one becomes disturbed to the point of neuroticism, or sad to the point of morbidity? Does he think that he alone, of all human beings, is expected to be free of weaknesses? Such excessive preoccupation with his faults is not a truly spiritual activity but, on the contrary, a highly egoistic one. The recognition of his own faults should make a man humbler, when it is beneficial, not prouder, which the thought that he ought to have been above these faults makes him.

178

When spiritual seeking becomes too complicated, its exercises too elaborated, its doctrines too esoteric, it becomes also too artificial and the resulting achievements too fabricated. It is the beginners and intermediates who carry this heavy and unnecessary burden, who involve themselves to the point of becoming neurotics.

179

Too much intellectual dissection of the personal ego done too often merely nourishes neuroticism; and the same result follows too much emotional preoccupation with it. This is a Long Path danger.

180

The followers of the Long Path are likely to form attachments to its ideals, practices, and aspirations. This is good. But if these attachments cause them to lose their equilibrium, to become over-anxious emotionally, or over-argumentative intellectually, then it is not good but bad.

181

Some things inside his own being are blocking his way to the Overself. An effort—determined, continuous, and daring—is needed to clear them. They are emotional and passional in appearance, egoistic in essence.

182

To overcome difficulties does not mean to overlook them, to be careless about them.

183

A condition may come when the appraisal of all that he has so far achieved is diminished in his own mind, and all that he has yet to achieve is grossly exaggerated.

184

There are those who feel, after a trial, that they are too limited in their capacities for this quest and give up the effort. In going so far as this abandonment they show a lack of patience.

185

Their fixed preconceptions of truth stand in the way of most persons when opportunity presents them with it. In the result, they fail to recognize it and so lose it.

186

Most men imply by their hidden attitude that they know truth; some men even openly assert it. From this they take the next logical step which is always to regard the habits they have established in the past, or allowed to become established, as right ones. Thus the ego justifies its self-indulgences and supports its weaknesses. A habit is accepted by a man only because it is his own habit, even though it is an evil, bad, or unwise one.

187

When we add to the oppositions offered by lifelong habit, family, and environment those which are offered by the innate sensuality and inherited gluttony of the race, we see what a hard struggle there will be before men will take to and follow scrupulously the stricter regime which will bring out all that is best in them.

188

If he fails in his Long Path efforts, he suffers in misery from frustration. If he succeeds, he tends to become smugly self-righteous.

189

They put too much stress on external methods, on physical techniques. But spirituality cannot be engrafted from the outside in, alone. The greater stress should be laid on an approach from the inside out.

190

The Long Path, so far as it is also a painful untangling of knots, is useful in the sense that surgical operations and castor oil are useful. But were a man to live only to be operated on, or only to drink castor oil, we would regard him as crazy. Yet, there is a type of aspirant who wants to live only in preoccupation with his knots! He is everlastingly preoccupied with shaking off his shortcomings, is unable to get away from them, and ends by becoming obsessed with them. His life, which should flow naturally and serenely, moves instead artificially and jerkily. His self-discipline, which should be rooted in hygiene, becomes rooted in hysteria.

191

The seeker on the Long Path tries to eliminate his baser feelings and to cultivate his nobler ones. But in all this effort he is looking at himself alone, purifying and improving his ego but still his own ego.

192

It gives a man no pleasure to perceive at last how much he has contributed toward his own troubles. It is indeed a grim awakening. But it need not be so grim if, alongside, he puts a positive attitude toward the future, if he adopts the Short Path.

193

The idea that what we like most and enjoy best has to be given up, seems an ugly one. But such an idea is not at all the basis of this discipline.

194

The continuing strain of the Long Path comes to a climax one day, to a revolutionary crisis.

195

If a scheme for progress, such as the Quest, remains intellectual alone and does not come down to the heart, and move it, the aspirant will continue to remain outside the precinct of the Overself.

196

If the Long Path does not lead him to the Short Path, either at some point along its course or in the end, it is not leading him aright.

197

The more he examines himself the more he is discouraged or horrified at what he finds just below the surface. This mood will continue only as long as he remains on the Long Path. For by going deeper still he will find his best self. To make this discovery he must cross over to the Short Path, itself a paradox of passivity and non-effort, a movement of sight to insight, of faith and identification.

198

The Long Path cannot be evaded. The man who wants to shift on to other shoulders the work he ought to do himself, will fail. The man who, calling on a God or a guru, imagines he has relieved himself of personal responsibility, will be deluded.

199

Of what use is a spiritual training, revelation, progress, or experience which keeps the aspirant's identification with his ego quite intact? None at all from a narrow, short-term, rigid, extreme point of view. But from a broader, philosophic, tolerant, and long-term point of view it is the beginning of a process which will indirectly lead to disidentification in the end. For the Long Path must ultimately show up its own futility, for truth, and thus bring about that turning over of the mind which opens up the Short Path.

200

The Long Path is concerned with techniques, how to practise and apply them. But techniques can only improve the human instrument, make it better able to receive enlightenment; they cannot of themselves give enlightenment.

201

Man, fascinated by his own ego, is always gazing at it, just as Narcissus was fascinated by the image of his own body reflected in the water. Even when he takes to the spiritual quest, the fascination persists: it is only the things and desires that preoccupy the ego which change their names; from being objects of the physical senses they are transferred to emotional, intellectual, and/or psychical fields. These may be praiseworthy and noble in themselves, but they are still within the circle of the ego, although on its finest and highest levels. This is why the Long Path cannot yield enlightenment.

202

Since the mastery of his lower nature must take priority, the Long Path is always prescribed for the beginner. Whether and when the Short Path is to be added to it, depends on his individual character and inner need.

203

The arc of his development usually begins with the Long Path and rises to the Short one, but theoretically it should begin with both together in harmonious combination.

204

Some fear to give themselves to the Quest because they fear terrifying demands will be made on them in the way of self-discipline. But this dread of what they may be commanded to do is much exaggerated. For they will be directed inwardly only toward what is within their capacity, even if it is spectacular and sacrificial.

205

The reader is warned that the first part is to be regarded only as preparatory and intermediate, that its point of view mostly belongs to the practical category and that its special function is to act as a transition to the far higher ultimate one. The second part carries the student upward to the mountain top where he will be able to see that the ideas and practices which served him well heretofore, were really only convenient and useful steps cut in the mountain side. They are not to be dallied on if he seeks truth as it is in itself and if he will be satisfied with nothing less than reality. The change of outlook which comes at the top will necessarily change his earlier evaluations.

206

The Long Path man becomes in time too egocentric because too filled with inner conflicts.

207

Efforts on the Long Path are efforts in time; as such they cannot touch the timeless.

208

Since the entity which is travelling on the quest is itself none other than the ego, it is hardly likely that the termination of the quest will end in the termination of the ego. But without the latter how is enlightenment possible? The ego may lead him from one spiritual advance, experience, or initiation to another, but it will not lead him to egoless being nor could it even if it wished to. What is the way out of this impasse?

209

Tirolean Talk by P.B., June 1965: *Short Path and Long Path*

All ways of spiritual seeking divide into two classes. The first is basic, elementary, the second for more advanced people. The first for beginners is the *Long Path*. It takes a long time to get results, and a lot of work has to be done on it; much effort is necessary for it. The second is the *Short Path*. The results are more quickly got; it is an easier path, and requires less work. To the Long Path belongs the methodical yoga. It takes a lot of work to practise daily: building of character and removing of weaknesses and overcoming of faults, developing concentration of attention to stop the distraction of mind and to get control over thoughts, strengthening of willpower, and all the activities for the beginners. These are the earlier stages of meditation.

Meditation has two parts. The lower one belongs to the Long Path. Also, the religions are for the beginners and popular masses. They, too, belong to the Long Path. To the Short Path belong Christian Science, Ramana Maharshi's teachings, Vedanta, Krishnamurti's teaching, and

Zen. They all say You Are GOD. The Long Path says instead: You are only a man. The one says that you are man and the other says that you are also really rooted in God.

Long Path—here is working through the ego. The student thinks he is the ego and develops concentration, aspiring to improve himself, getting more and more pure. He says: "I am doing this work." He is thinking that he is purifying himself and improving the quality of the ego. But it is still ego. He is rising from the lower to the higher part of the ego and becoming a spiritualized ego. He is looking for the Gurus (spiritual teachers).

Short Path—it is different because the idea "ego" does not come in, only the Overself, not the longing (which belongs to the Long Path), but the identification, not even aspiration.

Long Path has to do with progress and takes a time for it and therefore means moving in time, and it is the ego who is working.

Short Path is not concerned with time and therefore not with progress. Thinking only of the timeless Overself. No idea of progress, no desire, it does not matter. Real Self is always changeless. Progress implies change. All questions and problems disappear because the questioning (ego) intellect is not allowed to be active.

Now you understand the question of the Guru. On the Long Path the aspirant wants the Guru, he looks for a Guru, is depending on him, and the Guru helps him to progress. On the Short Path the Overself is the Guru and the aspirants depend directly only on the Overself. On the Short Path the Guru question does not come into consideration. Guru is outside themselves, but God is inside on the Short Path stage. The aspirants on the Short Path need not depend on a Guru. Intellectually they have freedom from the Guru. If a guru dies or disappears, they do not worry about it. There is a real reliance on God—no human being, but your Spirit.

Long Path—the aspirants are moving in shadows, there is not life but darkness, they are not in the light but in ignorance. Their reason is not enlightened. Because they are living in the ego they are living in spiritual ignorance, which is darkness.

Short Path—he lives in the Sunlight, because he lives in *Truth*, the only reality—like looking, being in the sun. As in Plato's story, he comes out of a cave, walking to the opening with his back turned to the opening of the cave, moving and seeing only the darkness. The other way is turning around to the mouth of the cave, seeing a little light, then more and more light. Even from the beginning there is still some light.

A question will be asked: Why does not every teacher teach the Short

Path? The answer is: Because people have not got enough strength of character to give up the ego and are not willing to turn at once to the light. It is a sacrifice. To make this possible, the Long Path teaches them to make the ego weaker by graduated stages. In the Long Path the progress comes in, just to prepare them to reach a point where it is easier for them to give up the ego. This is one of the most important of the reasons. It makes the aspirant ready to benefit by the Short Path; otherwise he would not be able to travel on it. The second reason is because they have not the strength of concentration to keep the mind on the Overself. They may be able to keep it for one or two minutes, but they then fall back. Therefore it is necessary to develop the power of sustained concentration. Even if one sees the Truth, one must get the power to stay in the Truth and to be established in it.

Most people have strong attachments and strong desires for worldly things. These are in their way, obstructing their way on the path to Reality. This means that they want to keep attachments and desires that are coming from the ego, which they do not want to lose. Therefore the teacher gives first the Long Path, because most aspirants are not able to follow the Short Path. The Long Path exists to prepare them for it. There is no use for them to go on the Short Path if they have not got the philosophical understanding to practise it. Even if they were shown the Truth in the Short Path, they may, if unprepared by study and thinking philosophically, fail to recognize it. They have not learnt what Truth is and might not value it. They have no philosophical knowledge to see the difference between Truth or Reality and illusion or error. They have to understand Truth even intellectually. That is a part of the Long Path.

Another very important matter related to the Long Path: when people follow the Long Path and spend years working on it, many such persons after several years find they have not made the progress they have expected. In the beginning they have enthusiasm. They expect inner experiences giving power, knowledge, and self-control; but after many years they have not gained these things. On the contrary, tests, hard trials of the life come, death in the family, for instance, changes of the outside life, and so on. They are disappointed and say: "Why has God chosen me for suffering even when I follow the Path? Troubles come to me." They are disheartened. At this point one of three things may happen:

(1) They may give up the Quest altogether, for one year or many years, or all life long, and turn back to materialistic living.

(2) They may think they have taken to the wrong path, or are using wrong methods, or have the wrong teacher, and they look for another

teacher and another way. But with the new teacher the results are the same because they are still within the circle of the ego. The ego prevents them from sufficiently deepening their state of light and wisdom.

(3) The third possibility may happen to them. When they themselves have tried so hard and did not succeed and feel too tired mentally and exhausted emotionally, they give up trying but they do not give up the Quest. They just sit passively and wait. Those who are in this last or third category are completely ready to enter the Short Path and should do it. Even beginners may enter the Short Path, but in practice they find it too hard.

The best way is from the beginning to make a combination of both. But this combination must be varied and adjusted to each person, because people are different. There is not one fixed rule for everyone. One person is suited for a little of the Short Path and more or longer of the Long Path; with the other person it is vice versa. With most people the combination is the best way. It depends partly on their feelings, their intuition, and advice given by teachers. In the end, everyone must come to the Short Path.

Contradictions between the two Paths: one is the ego and the other the Overself without ego. The Short Path is without plane, intuitive, like Sudden Enlightenment. On the Long Path they are looking step by step to get out of the darkness of their ignorance. The next important point: on the Long Path many students want experiences—mystical, occult, psychical ones. It is the ego wanting them and the satisfaction of progressing. The ego feels important. In the Short Path there is no desire for inner experiences of any kind. When you are already in the Real, there is no desire any more. For experiences come and go, but the Real does not. Now you see why the popular religions are only attempts to get people to make a beginning to find God, but are not able to go too far and too quickly. For those who are more developed and less bound to attachments, the teacher gives the Short Path. In the teachings of Jesus and Buddha we find both Paths. People have different stages of evolution and can therefore take what suits them. The teacher gives them what they understand from their level of understanding.

Popular religions are mixtures of the Long and Short Paths. But unfortunately they sometimes lead to confusion. In the Biblical sentence, "Before Abraham was, I AM," there are two meanings. The lower one means the reincarnation, the higher one means: I AM the Reality.

On the Short Path we do not care about reincarnation matters, we do not give them much importance. On the Short Path the aspirants need the philosophical study to understand only one point: What is Reality. It is necessary to understand the difference between the Illusion and the Reality. Every teacher's biggest difficulty is to get the students to understand that not only the world but also the ego is illusion. The aspirants do not know what the ego is. Therefore Jesus said: "If you want to find your true Self you have to deny yourselves," meaning deny the ego. Buddha said: "This is not I." The Buddha taught his monks to practise saying and thinking this mantram. There is much confusion about the two points if there is not the knowledge that all teachings fall into these two classes and if there is no understanding of the difference between them.

It is necessary to publish a new book. Even among people who have studied for many years, there is this confusion.

A very important point: because the ego lives in its own darkness, it cannot give light. The light may come only from the Overself, which is the Sun and Light of human existence. With the reason we can control the ego to some extent, but it is not possible to control the Overself. As regards Enlightenment, this is not coming from self-willed effort; it is coming only by what the Overself does to him. It is a matter of Grace—unpredictable—and it is the last secret. It is like the wind that comes you do not know where from and goes you do not know where to. It is a mystery. At the end we have to be like little children and leave our Enlightenment to the Father and give up our lives to him. On the Long Path the aspirant tries to improve himself. He experiences successes and failures, ups and downs. When he is disappointed, he gets melancholy. On the Short Path such a situation cannot arise, because he has faith like a little child. He has given up all his future to Overself-God and he has enough faith to trust to it. He knows he has made the right decision and therefore is always happy. He depends on this GRACE, he knows It, that It comes from the wisest being behind the world. Whatever will come, it will be the best. He is always relying on the Overself and having the joy in it.

The Short Path is a cheerful Path, a Path of happiness. Just before this begins, the aspirant may experience the Dark Night of the Soul. He feels utterly helpless, has no feeling of spiritual Reality. It is a melancholy time—no feeling of spirituality or longing for it. He is neither worldly nor spiritual. He feels alone and abandoned and separated by a wall from his Guru. He feels God has forgotten him. This dark night may last a short time or long years. He is unable to read spiritual things, or think about them. There is no desire for ordinary things either. He feels sad and disappointed and may even try suicide. In this unhappiness even those who love him cannot bring him comfort. In both hemispheres, Western and Eastern, there is a saying: the night is darkest just before dawn. He is on the lowest point. After that, the Short Path brings back the Joy—just like clouds moving away from the Sun.

The best advice is, first, that it will not last forever; he must have patience. Second, he must have hope. Then he reaches a better level than ever before. The Dark Night of the Soul does not come to every seeker. It is like a shadow thrown by the Sun. When the Sun appears in the subconscious, the shadows arise. But it is the beginning of a great inner change. It is not a wasted time; there is a great deal of work going on—but in the subconscious—to root out the ego. It is being done by the Overself. It is a sign of Grace, but the aspirant nevertheless feels unhappy.

In the Short Path there are usually much fewer exercises to practise. It is not necessary to sit down specially to meditate, but to try to be always in meditation. When you are busy outwardly, meditation naturally takes a different form than when you sit down for it. During the active part of the day, meditation takes the form of remembrance, always to try to remember the Overself: IT IS (that is enough). In the special meditation time our object is not to improve the character. During the meditation we have to empty our mind of thoughts as quickly as possible, let the mind become still. Ordinarily we live in our thoughts, in our little selves, even if the thoughts are spiritual. Therefore we have to keep away from all thoughts. If you want to think of the Overself, which is without any form, it is not possible. We try, but any idea, form, or shape is wrong. You cannot imagine it. So better not to try but to be still. You must not remain in the ego. "Be still [let go] and know that I AM GOD," says the Bible.

Wu-Wei, meaning inaction, not trying, is the highest teaching of Taoism and Zen and it means the same as what has just been explained. The Overself is already there. You as ego must get out of the way. Most people have to combine the Long Path with the Short Path—perhaps one day or one week (whatever the inner urge directs) on the Long Path and the other day on the Short Path. The attitude will be a passive one because all intellectual ideas have only a limited value. We must be now guided by our inner feeling of what we need, or by our intuition. If people ask whether they have to study, the answer is that the books deal with the thoughts. What they give is not the Truth, but only intellectual statements of it. It will only prepare them for a better understanding. When they study these books they will only get more thoughts. In the end they have to come to the point where they need no books. There are good books but we must always discriminate between wrong teachings and right teachings, which may get mixed together in the same book. This is the highest we can go with such studies.

When changing to contemplation, the thinking stops. This is the deepest point within oneself. This is why everybody has to search within himself and to find his own Path. It is not necessary to travel on the Long Path any longer time than that which prepares you for the Short Path. It is quite important to have living faith in the Overself and to become like a child and to have as much dependence on the Overself as a little child has on its parents. This faith should be in the power of the Spirit itself, not in any other human being. If the aspirant is constantly anxious about his faults or weaknesses, then he is on the wrong Path. He can try to remove them but cannot do this completely until he is able to give up the ego.

The basis of the Short Path is that we are always divine. It is with us already, it is no new thing, and we only have to try to recognize what is already there.

2

THE MEASURE OF PROGRESS

Attitudes that help or hinder

He will have to recognize that not only the universe outside but his own nature inside is governed by precise laws, and that his spiritual progression is subject to such laws, too.

2

If the request for enlightenment comes from the bottom of your heart, the answer will likewise be given there. It may come at once, or after a long time. If you are too impatient, if you don't find it worth waiting for, if you give up too soon, you do not deserve it.

3

So long as he is measuring every inch of his progress along the spiritual path, so long as he is constantly measuring and often admiring his own virtues, he is really so preoccupied with his own ego that his bondage to it becomes more dangerous as it becomes more deceptive.

4

To the extent that he opens himself out passively to the higher self, its guidance, instruction, and messages, to that extent he will make real and safe progress. But he must be careful not to try to impose his own ideas upon this guidance, not to seek to instruct the mystic Instructor, not to interfere with the process of transmission from the higher self to the egoic mind.

5

With the intelligence to perceive and the frankness to confess his faults and shortcomings, progress becomes possible. Without them it remains slow and halting.

6

The key to understanding Lao Tzu's book, *The Simple Way*, is to understand that it describes a goal and not a path to a goal. It does not give advice to aspirants as to what they should do, but it describes the actualized condition of an adept. Hence it would be foolish for aspirants to adopt its policy of *Wu-wei*, meaning inaction, doing nothing, to take one instance, and let everything be done for them—as it would be foolish for a sheep to dress itself up in the skin of a lion and then attempt the exploits of a lion. It would be foolish for a beginner to apply the technique, adopt the way of life, assume the power, and expect the results of an adept. He would begin with self-deception and end with confusion. He would fail because he has not yet himself attained contact with the ruling power.

7

Progress does not consist in picking up different scraps from a medley of cults and sects. It consists in hard work in meditation, in taking oneself well in hand, in reflective study.

8

The way to make these changes for most people is not the herculean sudden way. It is to make them gradually and progressively, as the direction to do so comes from within themselves. Until then they will wait; they will not heroically go over to the new regime prematurely, just because some book or some reformer or some lecturer urges them to do so. This may not be the most self-flattering way but it is the most prudent way. They will not be troubled by secret longings for the abandoned regime.

9

It would be wrong to expect that he must duplicate somebody else's mystical experiences and equally wrong to regard himself as a failure because he does not have these experiences.

10

In most cases the imagination is excited by the belief that great secrets will be unveiled as the aspirant passes from grade to grade with the years. But the difficulty of making this passage is usually underrated and the nature of these secrets overrated.

11

The aspirant should emulate the philosopher's patience and not sit down every day to feel his spiritual pulse, as it were, constantly worrying as to whether he is making progress, remaining stagnant, or going backwards. He needs to remember that enlightenment cannot be attained by a single act but only by slow degrees and constant toil. Yet unexpected cycles of quickened progress may come on him unaware. There may be times when his inner being will seem to burst open in sudden bloom. But generally there will be no smooth onward progress all the way for him. His spiritual situation will vary strikingly from time to time. The final accomplishment can be brought about only in stages.

12

If he seems to be standing still, or if he seems to have lapsed and regressed, he ought to enquire at what point in the road left behind him he took the wrong turn.

13

Men, filled with pardonable anxiety or natural eagerness, often ask: How long will it take me to accomplish this spiritual work? A definite period in years cannot be stated in the answer. Whoever thinks in this way will never be able to succeed in the task. For how can he enter the Eternal while he thinks only of time? All hurry must be abandoned. Let results take care of themselves, is the *Bhagavad Gita*'s advice in this matter.

14

Progress along this path is not merely a matter of chronology; nobody may measure it with accuracy for nobody knows what forces may suddenly arise out of an individual's past to hinder him or what forces may suddenly arise out of the Overself to help him.

15

He must not forget that he is only a short way from the start of his journey, and should not assume attitudes or prerogatives suitable only to one who is well advanced.

16

How few are the aspirants who look for mastery of themselves as a reward not less gratifying than experience of spirit, for triumph over temper as being just as satisfactory as a mystical phenomenon!

17

The man who is ready to desert his quest or his master because no *visible* grace comes his way, because no joyous mystical ecstasies visit him, because nothing seems to happen in his inner life, needs to become acquainted with three facts of that life. The first is that grace may come and not be recognized for what it is. The second is that his personal emotions are not necessarily a correct measure of his spiritual progress. The third is that the true quest leads for a time through the dark lonely forest of inner poverty, where the man has nothing to boast of, is nothing to be proud of, and experiences nothing to compensate for the worldly life which he has sacrificed. It is indeed a dark night of the soul.

18

The aspirant who prefers to see himself as much more advanced than he really is, is suffering from the inflation of a strong ego. The aspirant who prefers the opposite view and prefers to underrate his position is suffering from the inferiority of a feeble ego. Both attitudes are undesirable.

19

Too many beginners become discouraged because progress is slow, or even non-existent. But, really, much depends on the point of view. Without succumbing to the sugary over-optimism of an Emerson, which could make him write that "the soul's highest duty is to be of good cheer"—in such contrast to Buddha's oft-repeated insistence that its highest duty is to see life as suffering—they can at least admit that they have made a start on this conscious quest of truth, that they have discovered there *is* such a quest, and that there is a magnificent climax to the human adventure. They can be thankful for all this. I have known some men who took this view, who enjoyed being questers, who were even enthusiastic although they had had no inner experiences and made no dramatic progress. They were positive, not negative, thinkers.

20

During my travels, I have watched so many aspirants make so many unavailing attempts to gain this higher awareness that I would have been unobservant indeed if I had not drawn the lesson. This was that those who were most easily discouraged and disheartened, failing to try out new roads or to persevere in the old one, were too frequently those who sank into the apathy of accepted failure.

21

Their very eagerness to advance incapacitates them from advancing, for it merely swells the ego from which they want to run away.

22

Too many aspirants complain about their seeming lack of progress, their failure to get encouraging inner experiences in payment for their effort. If they were humble enough they would not complain, for then they would not be measuring how high they had grown. If they must look at all, it would be better to look for a finer character than for stranger phenomena.

23

It is a mistake to believe that something must happen inwardly to show that he is making progress, that some dramatic experience or stimulating revelation must come to him as a reward for his taking time out to meditate. It is wiser to be satisfied with settling down and being calm, with the patient surrender to the Overself's will. He must learn how to wait.

24

If his actions lag behind his aspiration, he need not be unduly depressed. He can be modest and even humble in accepting the fact that he has far to go, but this acceptance should be made quietly and calmly because it should always be supported behind by hope and faith.

25

Murmurings against the paucity of dramatic or phenomenal or ecstatic results, and lamentations over the hardships of a quester's lot, may be expected but must be rejected. Did he anticipate a special good fortune because he took to the quest? Was he to become exempt from the darker side of the human condition as a reward? Did he not see then, and does he not realize today, that the search for truth is long and difficult by its very nature?

26

Lest the complacent consciousness of progress should give rise to spiritual pride, let him remember that a change of circumstances may shatter it.

27

We may take Buddha's half-smile as an encouragement: both to set our footsteps on the Way and to set all desires aside, to be content even with a slight result from our spiritual efforts.

28

If people stop half-way or quarter-way on this path, who can blame them? The more they come to know what is really demanded of them, the more they come to see its difficulty, even its seeming impossibility.

29

There are those who draw back after some years, or desert altogether, complaining that the disciplines and regimes of the Quest are too much for them, and that even the few successes took too many years out of a lifetime to be worth waiting for. There is no adequate reply for such complaints. Nobody is asked, forced, or cajoled to go on this quest. Each must come to it of his own free choice. Those who remain do so because they consider the worldly alternative to be worse.

30

Those who do not find that they make the expected progress and throw up the Quest in disappointment, reveal not only their own impatience but also insufficient understanding of what it is that they undertook.

31

It is perhaps pardonable that he should feel frustrated as the fulfilment of his aspirations, the matching of his perfectionist dreams, seems to slip farther away with the vanishing years.

32

Those who repine pessimistically at the slowness of their growth, who talk in disenchanted tones about the futility of the Quest, need to feel the invigorating and blessing touch of Grace.

33

His self-reproach and self-disgust will grow to such a height that a fresh start in a fresh birth will sometimes seem the only way out.

34

By contemplating the inner sun, the Overself, he is inevitably drawn upward in increasing light, whereas by excessively preoccupying himself with the ego he becomes depressed into increasing darkness. When the latter happens the very quest which was supposed to diminish his sorrow and enlarge his peace, becomes a fresh source of sorrow and agitation.

35

If the Quester's hopes are not fulfilled nor his aspirations realized, it may be that he is demanding too much too soon from himself, his spiritual guide, or his spiritual technique. It may also be that he is undertaking what he is unprepared for and that he has not equipped himself for the journey.

36

The inability to feel this presence is not necessarily a sign of failure; it is one of their vicissitudes which aspirants often complain about. It is well to remember that these usually come to an end. There are times when a man must not accept his follies and weaknesses but discipline them instead. Intelligence must take their place, and he must support it by yielding to its rulership.

37

Let him be sincere with himself, neither overrating his stature nor underrating it, neither indulging false hopes nor exaggerating his discouragements.

38

If his first step on this path is wrong, all his later steps will necessarily be wrong. In the end he will either have to retrace his steps or else take to the Short Path.

39

The student should keep in mind that it is not needful to feel tension about the Quest. He must strive to be patient and not try to measure his progress every few weeks.

40

He who thinks only of the obstacles in his way will never attain the goal. It is necessary to meditate on, and work to develop, positive qualities which will make progress possible.

41

If past efforts for many years have been useless and ended in failure, this merely means that he has exhausted the possibilities of the road he has been travelling and that he has to start on a new road.

42

Aspirants should beware of mistaking an evanescent and emotional feeling that they are making spiritual progress for the real thing.

43

He may find a little light after much searching.

44

Blavatsky herself, at the height of Theosophy's power and influence, stated that hardly six of her followers understood the Goal and had any favourable prospect of reaching it. Does it follow that a reasonable man will be too disheartened to enter on the path to such an inaccessible goal? No—he need not be.

45

The aspirant who frequently measures how far he has advanced, or retrograded, upon this path, or how long he has stood still, is seeking something to be gained for himself, is looking all the time at himself. He is measuring the ego instead of trying to transcend it altogether. He is clinging to self, instead of obeying Jesus' injunction to deny it. Looking at the ego, he unwittingly stands with his back to the Overself. If he is ever to become enlightened, he must turn round, cease this endless self-measurement, stop fussing over little steps forward or backward, let all thoughts about his own backwardness or greatness cease, and look directly at the goal itself.

46

If, however, he dwells upon his spiritual development and changes of mood, his sins and faults all the time and with all his mind, he is likely to overbalance himself. An extravagant preoccupation with his own ego would then result. This would not be true progress. A wise spiritual director, if he has one, could do no better than thoroughly shake him and tell him to go out and get some social enjoyment or see some funny plays, where he can forget himself and lose this unhealthy obsession with his self-centered thoughts and morbid emotions.

47

Trapped as they are by their own limitations, looking in the wrong direction for fulfilment of aspiration, bound to their past and therefore going round in circles, it is understandable if they complain of the failure to make any substantial progress.

48

It is a fact that as he progresses on this quest methods, techniques, ideas, and practices which suited the elementary stages of development later obstruct him.

49

If you find progress to be slow and the promised rewards still out of sight, do not despair. Be patient as Nature herself is patient. Find, if you can, the friendship of those more advanced than yourself and receive from their presence the stimulus to become unhurried by time and unhurt by moods of impatience. The path may be a long one, but when success comes it comes unexpectedly and the final stages are short and rapid. It is the earlier and more elementary stages which are long drawn out. You are not in a position to judge exactly what progress you have made. This is why you must have great patience.

Sources, signs, and stages of growth

50

Whether one is hardened by overcoming unpleasant setbacks or encouraged by the sunshine of cheering successes, this is the strange paradox of the path: out of its multitude of defeats and disappointments, mistakes and disillusionments comes forth wisdom, and after wisdom, victory.

51

It is true that there are sacrifices to be made on the way, culminating one day perhaps in the biggest one—the ego's compulsive will to insert itself in every situation or activity—but there are also consolations and compensations to counterbalance them. If certain habits have to be given up and certain satisfactions dropped, new intuitions, signs of progress, inner supports, encouragements, and learnings appear.

52

He may know that he is beginning to progress when he becomes his own strictest judge, his own severest critic.

53

His degree of advancement will not only be shown by the deepest point touched in meditation but also by the way of handling everyday situations.

54

Even if he did no more than study the teaching, even if he felt that inward weakness and outward circumstance placed its practice beyond his reach, his time would not be wasted and the study would still be beneficial. For whilst he imbibed these ideas and dwelt upon them from time to time, they would have a long-range effect. Slowly, perhaps imperceptibly, his passions would abate, his faults would be tempered, and his virtues would be reinforced.

55

The fact that he has faithfully and perseveringly kept going on the course that leads to the higher self will count for something even if he fails to reach it. For it will satisfy conscience, attract occasional inspirations or enlightenments, and prepare the way for eventual success in another birth. The constant effort to follow the spiritual quest produces in time all the qualifications needed to achieve its goal.

56

The very changes which he makes in habits, regimes of living, and inherited customs, are often signs that the Overself is being allowed to do its cleansing work in him.

57

Quite apart from the spiritual rewards, there are additional and tangible ones also—better health, greater achievement, and less avoidable self-earned trouble.

58

Not only when his associates find his outer behaviour, which they can observe, unobjectionable but also when he finds his inner reactions to them, which they cannot observe, unobjectionable, should he be satisfied that his faults are amended.

59

The seeker passes through different moods, phases, and states during the years. Equanimity is still only an ideal but its attainment is more likely to be nearer than not as the years pass. But he may not think so until he measures his attitudes of an earlier date with those of today.

60

When a man turns his back on erroneous thought and sinful conduct and penitently seeks to cultivate wisdom and virtue, he enters on a path whose rate of progression and particular course are alike incalculable. For they are in God's hands and only partly in his own.

61

Study, prayer, meditation, and discipline of motive, mind, and body will yield their results according to the intensity with which they are undertaken and the wisdom with which they are combined. The best results naturally come from the greatest intensity and the fittest balance.

62

He has gone far on this path when his last thought on falling asleep at night is the Overself and his first thought on waking up in the morning is again the Overself.

63

You may certainly hope for success when the whole trend of your thinking and the whole trend of your action is strongly directed to this single purpose only, when you have resolutely subordinated personal feelings and temperamental predilections to the solution of the problem of truth.

64

If the discovery of Overself is still absent, then the search has not been deep enough or long enough or valued enough.

65

When the sense of his own imperfections, his own failings, so overwhelms him at times that he falls into deep depression, into gloomy despondency, it will help to weaken the ego's pride and conceit.

66

There are definite stages wherein the feelings become purer, nobler and calmer, the desires thinner, lesser, and more refined, the thoughts positive, larger, and more concentrated.

67

He who has nurtured the thoughts and cultivated the stillness and behaved by the injunctions which philosophy has offered him will, when the late evening of his life comes, not only never regret it but be glad for it.

68

Let him look to the condition of his consciousness: Is it steady or fluctuating? Is it permeated with egoism to the point of being shrivelled up? Is it widely impersonal? These and several other signs may give the measure of his progress.

69

The kind of question he asks and even the way in which he puts it helps to show where he stands on the path to Truth and how much he has understood.

70

The quester moves from beginning to end—if it could be said that there really is an end—under a higher will. It is not only the point that he sets out to reach that matters but also the point that he will be permitted to reach. But this is not arbitrarily and capriciously predetermined. His own karma comes into play here.

71

If anyone really wants to progress, let alone succeed, I do not know any way of escaping these two indispensable conditions: exercise and perseverance.

72

Two trustworthy evidences of real progress are attainment of balance and attenuation of ego.

73

When the student on this path assumes failure will be the only outcome of his efforts to progress spiritually, this pessimistic attitude overlooks the fact of grace. Admittedly the actuality of forgiveness for past errors does depend on sincere, humble repentance in prayer and to a certain extent on self-denying amendment and self-disciplining reform. If this is done, a basis for hope does exist and can be sought.

Even if for any reason immediate achievements are not possible, there yet exist other motives for striving to do what he can in self-improvement. By that, the remaining years of his lifetime would be assisted and protected in different ways and, at the last, the next reincarnation would be made so much better and probably easier. If he really accepts the principle of rebirth, then both the long view and the immediate possibility counsel a continuance of aspiration and endeavour. Hope is dead only when faith is dead.

74

That few persons out of many seekers succeed in finding this spiritual fulfilment to more than a relative extent is undeniable. Why this should be so is not only due to the difficulty of complying with all the requirements of the Quest but also to the kind of nervous system inherited from parents; to the character of the destiny allotted by the Law of Recompense; to the environmental and educational conditioning of the earlier years of child-hood, adolescence, and young adulthood; and finally to the rarity of competent teachers or guides.

75

They can measure progress less by these things than by how much they have mastered the lower nature, how often they deny the ego its desire to preponderate, and how willing they are to detach themselves from emotional reactions.

76

The quester who stops somewhere on the way, either dismayed by his own transgressions or exhausted by the paucity of results, is excusably human. The sooner he gets back to the herd the better for his comfort. The fact is that no results can be promised: all results are only probable. If he expects to obtain a mystical experience, he must not forget that Grace is the giver of it, not his own efforts.

77

He may measure progress partly by the signs of strengthened intuition and partly by the signs of strengthened will.

78

It is a sign of inner growth when a man lets go of anxieties in his mind while doing what he can in his body.

79

Although he will feel greater humility as he advances, it is also true that he will feel greater certainty.

80

There is the ever growing awareness of transmaterial existence, the deepening peace of it, and the increasing accumulation of inspiring knowledge.

81

Growth is to be measured in terms of consciousness and understanding, character and intelligence, intuition and balance in their totality, and not in terms of any single one of these alone.

82

If it be asked why cases of illumination are so rare and so isolated, we must point to the steep, rugged character of the way leading to it.

83

In the end, it is individual endeavour helped by grace that wins. The one is not without the other.

84

If these statements quoted—one from the *Bhagavad Gita* declaring that of thousands who seek the Atman only one finds it, and the other from the New Testament declaring that many are called but few are chosen—if these statements are to be taken literally, then the efforts of the vast majority of aspirants are doomed to tragic failure and it then becomes a question why anyone should engage in such a hopeless lottery with the odds against him so formidable as to make the game not worthwhile. Why too did those great seers who made these statements nevertheless go on to encourage their followers to engage in the task? Why if they really wanted their followers to engage in it did they not keep secret the hopelessness of the task? These are serious questions.

85

He must remember that he is subject to trials of faith and character which he might not otherwise have had. He simply must believe that if he does his share towards the fulfilment of his duties the results pass out of his hands and become God's concern. He must therefore leave it to God to arrange the ways and means whereby he will be able to discharge his responsibilities. He must have enough faith to believe that he will not be let down. It often happens to one on this path that what he greatly needs does not come to him when he prematurely asks for it but only comes when the need is actually ripe. This combination of doing his bit and then trusting in God will carry him through all his difficulties.

86

Slowly, imperceptibly, hectic impatience, unnecessary haste, often even flaming anger, fade out of his being as peace comes into it.

87

It is true that no spiritual effort is ever made in vain either in the individual struggle for progress or in the way individual progress influences others.

88

The Quest is a long drawn-out affair and self-improvement is a slow, unsatisfying process. Nevertheless, from a long-range point-of-view, a great deal of progress can be made in a single lifetime, and he who seeks to traverse this path is not walking alone.

89

The time may suddenly arise when Grace will take a hand in the matter, and the student's outward life will begin to conform to the mental ideal which he has so long—and, seemingly, so vainly—held for it.

90

Even if an aspirant does not attain his goals, if he is patient and persevering, studious and reflective, he should be able to get from the years a modicum of settled peace. It may not be much, but at least it is something which most others do not have.

91

Eventually, one will tend to dislodge oneself from less worthwhile pursuits. Ordinary automatic responses to these and other worldly affairs will cease as one feels the deepening need for thought-stilling and inner peace.

92

The mind must go on gradually parting with its ancient illusions, its time-fed prejudices, hardly aware of any progress, until one fateful day truth triumphs abruptly in a vivid flash of supreme illumination.

93

The longing for personal affection to come from another person will fall away just as, at an earlier stage, the craving for the physical gratification fell away.

94

The errors and superstitions of the earlier stages have to be discarded as he advances, but the truths and achievements retained.

95

When this feverish desire for wonderful or emotional mystic experiences comes to an end, being replaced by recognition of the great fundamental truths about God and Overself, or by a quiet trust which turns his spiritual future over to the higher power's care, he will have made a real advance.

96

Ever mindful of the presence of the World-Idea in all events and all history, of the working of the World-Mind through cosmic change, development, and decay, his conviction becomes ever stronger as proof accumulates.

97

It takes much inner experience, much reflection on the immutable laws, and much outer experience that confirms those laws before his confidence in the divine wisdom becomes as unshakable as a rock, and before all negative moods become powerless to touch him.

98

His quest will begin to bear fruit when the sacrifice it entails and the discipline it enjoins are borne, not with unwilling emotions and hesitating thoughts, but with clear understanding and patient resignation.

99

It is quite possible to make progress on the Quest without the aid of a teacher. The aspirant's own higher self will give him the guidance and assistance he needs—provided he has sufficient faith in its existence.

100

The exhilarating phenomena and ecstatic experiences which often make the quest's beginning so colourful have no permanence in themselves but only in their effects. When they come to an end, a force is left behind which works upon the psyche both to integrate it with the departed inspiration and to prepare it for the next one.

101

All classifications and systemizations of the mystical ascent are in a certain sense artificial and arbitrary. They exist to satisfy the intellect's requirements but by themselves they cannot satisfy the Overself's requirements. Aspiration, faith, determination, sacrifice, or service may, if carried to extreme intensity, upset all such schemes and quickly win its Grace. The aspirant will pass through a succession of levels of spiritual awareness, each higher than the one before. But he will not pass through it mechanically and smoothly. Between the first step on the mystical path and the gaining of its glorious prize, an existence of ups and downs, of terrible darknesses and exhilarating enlightenments, of shameful weakness and satisfying endeavour, awaits him.

Owing to the presence of such unknown factors as Grace and emotional stability, a fixed period cannot be assigned for development and it is not possible to make correct, generalized statements about the time required for its various stages. That is entirely a matter of the individual's situation, character, and the development he has brought over from former births. Also it would be wrong to suppose that during the ascent, these stages always and necessarily follow each other in the prescribed order. This would have to be the case if we were climbing a physical mountain like the Matterhorn or if we were mastering an intellectual profession like law. But here there is, first, an X-factor involved—Grace—and, second, delayed-action tendencies or acquirements from former earth-lives. Therefore, the different stages may sometimes exist side by side.

Some who enter upon this Quest pass swiftly through its early stages but most do not. Most men are destined to pursue the Quest through a long discipleship. Alas! how long is the way, how slow the journey of self-unmasking. On this road one eventually learns that the notion of a quick, abrupt victory is often a deceptive one. Rather will it be found that nature's usual way of slow growth with occasional spurts must be followed.

If this quest is pursued, then the advance of age should bring advance of wisdom to the philosophical student who should grow morally stronger and mentally taller with the years. With continuous perseverance on the quest, his life becomes stabilized and his energies concentrated. His advance will be marked no less by deeper thoughts and steadier emotions, by kindlier words and nobler emotions in the ordinary round of daily life, as by subtler intuitions and serener meditations in the hidden life. He will advance inwardly beyond the common intellectual limitations and find that no book can give him the feeling of rich living presence, the sense of real glorious being, that these intuitions evoke within him. Out of these long years of spiritual travail, he will emerge with chastened mood and deepened conscience; indeed, the measure of his advancement will be tokened by the gradual alteration of his reaction to events, by the serenity which replaces sorrow and the indifference which replaces joy.

How he is to apply this philosophy to particular situations in everyday living—for we live in practical times and a teaching is judged and tested not only by what it claims to do but also by what it actually does—is quite rightly a man's own business and responsibility. He has taken to philosophy not only for the truth it contains but also for the happiness it yields. He desires its intellectual doctrines and delights in its practical results. The philosophic mentality is sufficiently realistic not to waste time on impossible goals. It is sufficiently idealist not to leave out the nobler possibilities of regulating and governing itself for both its spiritual and physical benefit. It is neither foolishly sentimental nor brutally calculating. It understands both what can immediately be done to better its life and what will eventually have to be done. Anyone can sit down and draw up a program for self-reform which will fall to pieces when put to the test of practical experiment, but only a philosopher can sit down and draw up a program based on hard facts yet illumined by the lantern of a true desire to improve his spiritual situation and infused with the imagination to understand and the understanding to imagine the better man that he ought to be. If the philosopher has no time to indulge in impracticable mirage-like plans, he has the capacity to perceive practical possibilities not beyond actual human scope although they may be beyond conventional human vision.

So, the natural question which arises, "What is the meaning, what is the value of philosophy for *my* life?" may be answered.

102

When the picture of himself is no longer pleasing to him but on the contrary, painful, he is beginning to see truly. When he passes from the stage of self-pity to that of self-loathing he is beginning to progress effectively.

103

During this first period of his development he learns to shed tensions and to achieve poise.

104

In the earlier stages of his development the aspirant is helped by being told exactly what to do. But in the later stages the less this is done the better for him.

105

To say, as some mystics do, that no method can be formulated for the progress of man toward spiritual self-realization, is to confess their own inadequacy. Did not the foremost of Spanish mystics, Saint John of the Cross, write out an almost mathematical chart of this progress?

106

There are remarkable experiences on the way, each of which may seem to signal the finding of God and lead him to tell others about it or to set out to advise and help them. But they are pseudo-enlightenments in the sense that the goal is still farther away.

107

Is it possible to take part in the world's pursuits and still make solid spiritual progress? The answer depends upon the particular phase of inner life through which a man is passing. The young tender plant could not endure what the older and more solidly established one could.

108

It is true that many may find the quest more difficult without personal freedom to meditate undisturbed and without privacy to study the inspired texts. This will be more pronounced in the beginning perhaps. But a time will come when the circumstances may change outwardly or inwardly by the benignant work of grace.

109

Most aspirants go through a period of disgust with the world and of scorn for the petty aims of their fellows. They feel, as in this scrap of verse by H.G. Hopkins, "Now, severed from my kind by my contempt, I live apart and beat my lonely drum."

110

A mere belief in the soul's existence is the first and shortest step. An intellectual study of its nature and a devotional discipline of the self is the next and longest step. A direct intuitive realization of the soul's presence is the third and last one.

111

At a certain stage, following a period of concentrated study or activity, it may become necessary to slow down for a while in order to achieve some measure of clarity and harmony—both in one's inward and in one's outward life. Further progress is not possible until this has been satisfactorily accomplished.

112

At a certain stage of development, it is more important to work hard at self-improvement and to detect hidden weaknesses and remedy them than to attempt anything else.

113

There is a definite spiritual pattern to be worked out in the quester's life. At some time, for instance, he will be urged from within or driven from without to care properly for the body through diet, cleansings, breathings, and exercise. These are important for his purification.

114

The quester who has reached a sufficiently advanced stage becomes keenly aware of the paradoxes and contrarieties of his life.

115

The Soul is always there but he has to use prayer, meditation, and moral self-discipline to become aware of it. He should pray for its Grace, meditate on its presence and reality, and purify his thoughts and emotions by disciplining them. To turn away from human desires is hard. So to speed the process, the Soul puts him through agonizing ordeals, tragic bereavements, or great losses. Only after a deep melancholy falls on the mind and a thorough disgust for the unsatisfactoriness of earthly life settles on the heart, does he really yearn for the Soul. This is the mystic death. Only after it comes the second birth.

116

His spiritual progress comes to a standstill because the motive of using it for healing disease or changing material conditions has served its purpose. It took him from a limited orthodoxy or a barren scepticism to a higher level of truth. Now he is called upon to relinquish this motive if he is to climb to a still higher level and thus fulfil the purpose of living.

117

At first he will find nothing more on the path than what his efforts can secure for him. This is why the earlier years often seem so long, so sterile, and so monotonous. But during the next period grace mingles with his efforts and encouraging results then appear. The third and last stage witnesses the gifts of the Overself falling like ripe plums into his lap without any further efforts on his part. Here all is done by the simple working of grace. Then the major virtues of life will come into his possession, not as arbitrary compulsions of an unwilling ego, but as ripe fruit falling into his hands from a sap-filled tree. For although it is often said that the spiritually evolved man undergoes a profound self-loss, which penetrates his whole nature and affects his whole expression, the truth is that he does not really lose himself in the new consciousness which has taken possession of him. He loses only his frailty and ignorance, his egoistic pettiness and mental distractedness, his body-based materialism and useless sorrow.

3

UNCERTAINTIES OF PROGRESS

Understanding the pace of development

If the purpose of life on earth be a wide and deep spiritual growth, and if one attends above all else to that purpose, then whatever the future may bring it could only bring fresh material for such growth. Its own uncertainty cannot dissipate this certainty. One's growth is guaranteed, whether the future be pleasant or unpleasant, so long as one lives in the present strictly according to his dedicated ideal.

2

Life is a struggle and man is frail. Hindrances are around him on every side and limitations are within him on every occasion. Therefore, what is essential is that right direction should always be present, and what is important is that the *ideal* of the quest should never be abandoned.

3

The direction in which we are to move and the purpose which is to engage our striving are more valuable, more important, than program and plan. They are more flexible, leave one freer.

4

Such aims are not going to be achieved in a single day. They will take years, nay an entire lifetime, even to approach. The defects inside himself and the hindrances outside himself may in the end prove too much for a man. What then is he to do? Shall he show his humility and realism by renouncing these lofty aspirations altogether and give up trying to improve himself? Or shall he carry on with a hopeless fight, one foredoomed to unbroken defeat? He should do neither. He should inwardly hold to his aspirations as firmly as ever but he should outwardly defer his attempts to promote them until the next birth. He must fix them before his eyes as something to work for one day or he will not get nearer them at all. A sound aim, a right intention, is of the first importance. Let personal limitations and external circumstances create what delays they will, he will know at least that his feet are planted on the right path, his movement headed in the right direction.

5

In most cases this quest requires a change in the way of life, both mental and physical. But the aspirant may set his own pace if he is unwilling or unable to make the change more drastically or more rapidly. The essential point is that he knows and accepts the direction and the ideal—both.

6

The aspirant who gets discouraged because no light falls upon his path, no Glimpse flashes into his mind, no mystical experience comes to delight his heart, no revelation opens secret doors, may make a last attempt to secure one by threatening to leave the quest altogether unless it is received quickly! A neophyte I knew practised a certain exercise for about a year, then gave it up, folded his tent, and left; another delivered a challenge to the higher power, giving It two months in which to appear. Otherwise he, too, would abandon the quest, which he did when the time passed. What was this second man doing but dictating to the Overself and demanding that It conform to his little ego's requirements? The correct attitude would have been to declare that even if he died before any encouraging experience occurred, he would still be faithful to the quest. It is still worthwhile for its own sake, quite apart from its rewards. If these impatient aspirants really understood its preciousness, they would then understand that it is not the distance travelled but the direction taken which really matters!

7

He may believe that, with the material he is born with, his quest is unlikely to come anywhere near success. But that is not the point. That is where grace enters the picture. What he is concerned with is the attempt itself.

8

Why become miserable because you have not realized any or all of the hopes for your inner life, or experienced the joys of its successful fruition? Is it nothing that you have learnt the truths, found the direction, and taken the first steps on the road to such realization?

9

The intuition cannot be completely cultivated in a few weeks, the passions cannot be overcome successfully in a few months, the thoughts cannot be brought to a standstill finally in a few years, the ego's deeply rooted point of view cannot be changed permanently in many years. The disciple's growth needs time and therefore needs patience. If he cannot shake the old Adam forever out of his mind and heart as quickly as he would like to, there will be other births in which he can take up the work again and continue it.

10

What is important is to move in the right direction, for then two things are happening. First, one is moving and, secondly, one is moving near to the correct goal. But those who are stuck fast in the worship of material values are doing neither one nor the other.

11

This Quest requires him to set up certain standards. They are ideal ones, of course, but at least they give him right direction. If at times looking at them and at his actual state he gets a sense of failure, let him use this sense as a reminder that the standards are ideal, are at the peak of the mountain, and that he has yet to climb.

12

To the man tied to a variety of desires, aware of his personal shortcomings and ignorance, hindered by circumstance, environment, society, and despondency, this may seem an unachievable goal. All the same it is there and some—admittedly only a small number—have achieved it. But I have said it often before, that even if it were true that the feat is not possible for us, that complete peace of mind is not within our personal reach, either a partial or intermittent peace *is*. This is why direction is important, be the starting-point however unpromising.

13

The image of the sought-after goal which the aspirant is taught to strive for may, after a certain effort of trying to attain it, require revision downward. It may need adjustment to become more in alignment with the reality of his present state of development. The most important point is to get the right direction towards a noble goal, his higher self.

14

To ask a man to act with complete disinterestedness, think with utter impersonality, and feel with perfect selflessness is to ask what is close to the impossible. But to ask him to polarize himself towards these goals so that he has *direction*, is to ask what is both reasonable and desirable.

15

The way to spiritual attainment is admittedly difficult and lonely but there are compensations; inner blessings and glimpses of the goal will be given one from time to time. And one should never forget the all-important fact that he is progressing in the *right* direction.

16

With all humanity's limitations, it is enough for him to know that he is moving in the right direction regardless of the rises and falls and of the periods of inner storm and stress. The path is tremendously difficult and the *Gita* reminds us that few succeed in finishing it successfully. It is enough to know that we have found it and that we are making valiant efforts to overcome the adverse influences which surround mankind and seem so determined to keep us from the goal. However, philosophy teaches that every sincere seeker finds a certain compensation—in a beautiful and ethereal world after death—for the failures, disappointments, and miseries which make up so much of the stuff of the human story.

17

What is more important than progress in meditation is one's fundamental attitude toward life itself. If one can develop a sense of right direction, plus some amount of aspiration towards a better and Higher Self, one need not be concerned about the speed with which he travels in that direction.

18

Let us not say that the aspirant has set himself an impossible task. Let us say rather that he has set himself a task whose accomplishment is so distant that it must be looked for in a later incarnation.

19

The aspiration is a praiseworthy one but the attempt to realize it is a premature one. The timing is wrong.

20

Many are the aspirants who complain that they have had no mystical experiences, no rapt ecstatic exaltations, no great awe-inspiring enlightenments. "Give me just a single Glimpse," they cry disheartened, "and I will then be sure that your path is correct, your way is the one for me. Otherwise . . ." Some of them drift away to join sects, teachers, cults, or to embrace new doctrines, techniques, systems. Some remain but are half-hearted, apathetic, and often critical. A few concern themselves with fundamental issues and work patiently on, holding the view that this quest must be followed to the end *for its own sake*, whether Glimpses do or do not come.

21

Always at the beginning, at intervals on the road, glimpses are given us of this far-off state. Thus we are guided as to the direction we are to pursue: "He gives us some token of His immediate presence, as if to assure the soul for a moment, that He was with it in its tribulation. I say for a moment, for it is of no service subsequently as a support, but is rather *intended to point out the way and invite the soul to further loss of self,*" writes Madame Guyon, the French mystic.

22

There will always be opportunities for the follower of this path to put his philosophy into practice. Whether pleasant or unpleasant, they should be welcomed! The more he tries, the more he is likely to accomplish. He should take care not to depend upon his personal judgement alone. If he makes the beginnings of a right (that is, impersonal and egoless) response to each problem, help may mysteriously appear to guide him to a right solution. Even tests and trials will provide him with the chance to grow spiritually, and to bring him closer to his goal.

23

He will be delighted when he feels that he is starting to make inner progress and that spiritual currents are beginning to stir within his consciousness. But this is only a beginning. The road before him has its ups and downs, its shine and shadow, and there is no such thing as a mechanical, straight-line progress.

24

Whilst we are walking by the broken lamp of personal thought and sensuous intelligence, it is inevitable that our journey shall be troubled by slips and falls, by mistakes and even disasters. Impulses from below will masquerade as intuitions from above. Desire will even meddle with the authentic promptings of the Overself and thus lead us into mixed deeds and tainted results. At best we shall only half-know whither we are going and only when pain comes shall we understand how we have gone astray. Hence when we are uncertain we must learn to wait. Perhaps intuition is trying to tell us what we have to do, but other voices, like blind self-interest or reason's inability to understand, are interfering with the transmission. We have then to wait a day or two, a week or two, sometimes a month or two, until the situation becomes somewhat clearer, as it usually does.

25

The path may be long and hard, and he may lose much time in negotiating its boulders, pitfalls, snares, and obstacles. The chances for a quick sprint forward will be few and rare. Nevertheless, he must continue to travel it. He should let no person and no event involving another person turn him from the quest's straight course. Is he to abandon hope and discard an ideal because its realization seems too remote? Is the finest element of human character doomed to acknowledge defeat? For what does it really matter if the ideal is not realizable during his own lifetime? Is not the struggle merely to approach such realization part of a worthwhile way of living? Were these the only considerations, they would be enough to justify his continuance, but they are not. Man's story is a serial one. It proceeds through body after body, birth after birth. But the fact is that once he really absorbs the spirit of this quest he will be unable to desert it for more than an interval, even should he wish to. He will be inexorably driven back to it by mysterious forces within his own psyche, made to re-engage himself in it—however unwillingly—by a deep, silent, recurrent, inner void.

26

The good in him may bring him to the mount of wisdom, but the evil in him may take him away from it. Man is a complex creature: this is why his inner life is marked by different phases of rise and fall.

27

They will then find, as Himalayan climbers often find, that after they have mounted what seemed the steepest cliff and reached what seemed to be its peak, the real summit suddenly appears before them. It was hidden because it was set back by an ice-covered ridge. Once again they must bestir themselves to arduous climbing and of a somewhat different kind. For theirs was an inconclusive achievement, a partial and transitional result. This need not disappoint them, for if their further climb brings them a new and wider view, the pseudo-summit can still be seen because it still exists, even though it will now appear smaller and less important.

28

The notion that there will be a steady advance is not correct or at least is not reflected by the cases exhibited in life itself. Development is often slow and always uncertain, enlivened at long intervals by brief spurts of growth in knowledge and mastery in power but retarded by retreats, setbacks, failures, frailties, and shortcomings.

29

Progressive Stages of the Quest.

1. *Glimpses and flashes of insight.*

Consciousness is the unique element in every experience.

Once we learn the secret of our true nature we begin to perceive.

A ray from the Overself will shine upon our normal mind and transform and transfigure it. But moments of spiritual ecstasy are heralds of the high state which is yet to come when the Overself is taken fully into our councils and we have let go of the terrestrial ego with its dwarfed personal viewpoint.

2. *Surrender of the ego.*

To give up the "I" is very hard, yet that is our one and only task. The right attitude eclipses the ego and brings peace, whereas the wrong attitude enhances the ego and brings pain.

Habitually if unconsciously we split all experience into the world that is known and the I that knows it, into the "not I" and the "I."

Consider what happens when we become intensely interested in a story unfolding itself on a cinema screen. What happens during the deepest points of such concentration? For the time being we actually forget ourselves, and we drop the whole burden of personal memories, relations, desires, anxieties, and pettinesses which constitute the ego. Temporarily the "I" is transcended. The attainment of the Overself is nothing more than the ability to detach, not destroy, the ego at will.

Our sufferings arise out of our own failings, out of our inability to pass tests unconsciously invoked by our entry into the orbit of this quest. But even those sufferings, like all which come out of such contacts, carry tremendous spiritual lessons, and we can, if we will, turn them to great profit and inner progress. For what is progress after all? It is movement from the standpoint of the ego to that of the non-ego, the Overself.

The personality is but a transient shadow; a shadow presupposes a light; the light of the real self exists; renounce living in the shadow and move over to the light.

Personal bias is often quite unconscious and constitutes a hindrance on the path to truth.

Jesus said, "Except ye become as little children ye cannot enter the kingdom of Heaven." What did he mean? Consider the minds of children in whom the ego is but little developed. How egoless they are. How spontaneous and immediate is their knowledge of the world around them.

The giving up of thoughts leads to the giving up of the personal self.

In his quietest moments a man hears in the depths of his being a voice which tells him that he comes from a country to which one day he must return.

3. *The lonely nature of the path.*

Some complain that this quest makes them feel inwardly lonely and isolated. That is true. In one sense the study of philosophy will condemn the student to a forlorn solitude, for he will find few that care for it and many who despise it. But the loneliness is to help him to find and feel the presence of the best companion, the Overself. This brings him into sympathetic touch with all mankind through its revelation of unity. The feeling of isolation is only the inevitable differentiation from the self-deceived, the superficial, and the intuitionally backward.

4. *Preparation and tests.*

Preparation must precede enquiry. No student can profitably undertake Vedantic enquiry who skips through this earlier stage. His enquiries will always be limited in depth and scope as well as ineffective in final result if he lacks the sound training of intelligence which should come first.

Do not be impatient. For you are learning the alphabet of a higher life. When you have mastered that you will begin to form words, and later sentences, and in time whole paragraphs. You must prolong through years, if needs be, this disciplining of mind and mood.

Teak, which is among the hardest woods in the world, is cut from what is one of the slowest growing trees in the world. Perhaps the teak tree which we have seen growing in the Far East and nowhere else has picked up something of the Buddhistic atmosphere of those lands, with their wonderful patience, as befits a faith which perceives life to be beginning-less and endless; we do not know. Anyway, the moral is that the higher the goal the longer it takes to reach, and that the better the goal the more patient the aspirant must be in his struggles to reach it.

An authoritative Tibetan text says, "The best sign of spiritual progress is the gradual lessening of passions and selfishness." But the emphasis should be laid on the word "gradual." The student, like most earthborn mortals, may suffer from sporadic outbursts of sudden passion or shameful anger. But this is insufficient reason for abandoning the quest. The sincere student will always be conscious that the path *must* be followed despite the grey hours of despondency and failure. It will always call him back with such insistency that he will now know life will grant him rest only when the goal is attained.

We may well feel that we fall far short of that standard which should be attained by enlightened people, but this does not mean that the quest is too difficult for us. It means rather that we must patiently pursue our way undeterred by failures, knowing that what is not achieved during the present incarnation will surely if gradually be achieved during coming incarnations. It means that we are never to permit hope to desert us but only to temper it with understanding.

Most of us cannot help being mistaken at times, but all of us can help being stubborn after our mistakes have been pointed out to us, either by our own experiences or by another human being.

We start with psychology, proceed to epistemology, and end with ontology. In other words, we start with what is given to consciousness, we proceed to what is really known, and we discover that knowing must end in being.

Realization is not a mere feeling because feeling is sub-rational. It is not a mere concept because concepts are finite. Yet it fulfils the demands of both feeling and reason inasmuch as it contains both categories. Paradox-ically, however, it also transcends them. The flux of life is transformed into diviner shapes.

30

If he remains loyal to these ideals, then, through both dreary lapses and bright spurts alike, his spiritual life will grow in strong intensity and quality.

31

The man who announces his readiness to go upon this quest usually looks forward to its exhilarations and illuminations. Does he understand that he must be ready also for its vicissitudes, must expect its depressions and darknesses?

32

Since the whole of the human entity has to be developed and not merely a part of it, there is no possible way of skipping the unfinished development and leaping to the goal at a single bound. Those who offer shortcuts deceive themselves.

33

The expectation that progress will be constant and steady fills many beginners until time and experience teach otherwise. They have failed to allow for the possibility that there may be steps back and aside as well as interminably long pauses. Some go still farther and expect Grace, whether direct or through a master, to come prematurely or to work some spiritual conjuring-trick and change their nature almost overnight. The error of these egoistic expectations should be replaced by the correct attitude, which is hope. This is inspired by nothing less than the Overself. It is a genuinely intuitive leading. But it must be followed in patience and without imposing the ego's false emotions upon it.

34

It would be welcome indeed to learn that an aspirant could accomplish this at a single and sudden bound. But neither life nor the quest is so easy as that. There must be a linked continuity between the goal and his preliminary efforts. The talk of Satori or sudden enlightenment in Zen Buddhism often leads to misunderstanding of this point.

35

It is true that the inner life of most aspirants usually proceeds after the first stirring awakening on a somewhat monotonous flat ground. The advance, if any, is slow. But it is also true that certain times come at the end of these long intervals when it is possible to make a definite spurt forward, rapidly and decisively. The aspirant has to watch vigilantly for such opportunity and make the most of it when it does come. The most noteworthy sign of its presence is a sudden, unexpected surge of determination and resolution to bring about certain changes in the inner life. With this emotional arousing there comes some or all of the strength to effect the changes. The utmost advantage should be taken of these feelings while they temporarily manifest themselves. For the extent of the advance will depend upon the jolting force, the spiritual violence, and the positive and affirmative character of the thoughts held at the time, which are used to implement the new resolve. Quite often it may involve making a revolutionary decision requiring some courage or at least enough to desert an old standpoint for a new one. Naturally the emotions which enter into such a change will be the higher ones. These energetic spurts arise from a brief arousal of the force called Spirit-Fire by the Orientals and are induced by the accumulation and release of favourable karma or by the gracious contact with an adept. They stimulate effort and energize the will beyond the ordinary. Every advantage should be taken of these stimulations while they last for they usually pass away after a time.

36

If a man has been following the Quest, but subsequently deserts it, he will lose whatever control he has over his personal welfare until he returns to the path again. The more he refuses to heed the sacred call, the more will he move to his own destruction. His only hope of mending his fortunes is to return to the path which he has deserted.

37

The sudden acceleration of progress which comes at certain times should be fully exploited by humble prayer, by further effort, and by resisting the tendency to rest complacently in it.

38

The highest spiritual opportunities come only one time in a man's life. Although other opportunities may come, they will not be of the same magnitude nor will the man be able to take advantage of them with the same force.

39

Progress is not constant from one year to another. Rather is it an erratic movement. This is because human feelings are the raw material being worked on, not wood or iron. It moves over long monotonous plateaus where, apparently, no upward ascent is happening, as well as over steep hills where height is gained with every step.

40

No philosopher has ever turned away from these teachings. No student of philosophy has ever done so without returning again after, with time and experience, he had more thoroughly tested its comparative worth or truth against whatever else he had tried.

41

There are long stretched-out intervals of spiritually impotent, inspirationally lifeless existence.

42

It is important to let everything happen naturally, not to try to force an inner mystical experience, not to be anxious about its non-arisal.

43

He may walk haltingly on this path and come into view of its more meaningful phases only belatedly.

44

If blunders and falls appear in his own spiritual career, he may remember that they do so in the career of many other aspirants.

45

There is no universal experience which makes the spiritual progress of all aspirants exactly the same. With some it is slow and steady; with others nearly imperceptible or apparently absent; with a third group it is quicker but followed by lapses and losses; with a fourth group it is slight for long periods and then dramatically advances by a series of forward leaps and abrupt awakenings; with a fifth it shows haphazardly and erratically; with a sixth it is a powerful climax to aspiration and discipline, releasing new and added energies for achievement in a particular desired direction.

46

We make growth only by degrees because we separate ourselves from the ego only by degrees. The notion that any man can annihilate the ego overnight is an illusory one. He only seems to do so. What actually happens in such a case is that the annihilation is the final culminating event of a long, hidden process—hidden, that is to say, in former incarnations and abruptly pushing its way into the surface consciousness of the present reincarnation. No man flies to such Himalayan altitudes; he can only climb to them.

47

We do not ordinarily develop at an even, steady pace. Most of us, alas! do not even feel for long stretches that we are developing at all.

48

Once the quest throws its spell over him, he is its prisoner for life. He may escape from time to time. He may shun its disciplines and deny its self-denials when fatigue or circumstance prompts him to do so. But always its mysterious fascination will force him to return eventually. The length of the period of his desertion may be a month or a dozen years; that is irrelevant.

49

The aspirant should not expect that the enthusiasm which he feels in the beginning will stay with him all the time. There will be moods when a cooler attitude will prevail and when even the whole jargon used in mystical and religious thought and discussion seems meaningless.

50

Progress on this path ought not to be imagined as moving in a direct, uninterrupted line. In practice it follows a wavelike course. The mind rises vigorously to the crest of its powers for a time and then, tired, sinks into the trough. Here it remains for a while resting and then begins the same alternation.

51

The path is punctuated by both setbacks and advances. It is human to feel an upsurge of alarm when reverses occur, but it is philosophic not to let this become panic. It is natural to feel depressed when bad news comes, but it is philosophic not to let this develop into despair. The student must not permit himself to be bowled over by first reactions. The personal self must lay its tribute at the feet of the Universal Being, and it must do this no less during times of misfortune as during times of happiness.

52

The process which leads to this attainment is a long one. Those who teach or believe otherwise, who see it as a sudden and magical one, dependent on the arbitrary grant of some master's grace or involving only a single stroke of effort, are refuted by the facts of experience and observation.

53

It is possible by a single day's sudden and excessive reversal of the way of life to lose part of the good results so far obtained.

54

Yes, the Quest is a lengthy affair, and its slowness sometimes dries up the sap of enthusiasm.

55

We all have karmic debts to meet, self-earned penalties for sins and errors committed in former lifetimes if not in this one. Therefore, the philosophic student should not be surprised if a cycle of pleasant karma is followed by a difficult cycle. This doesn't mean the student should resign himself and do nothing about his troubles. On the contrary, he must seek every practical means of overcoming them. By so doing, and if he does the best he can, then there is a possibility that the debt may be modified— sometimes even cancelled. He may always cling to hope.

56

He will find in the course of time that amid all the advances and relapses, the progressions and regressions, there will be a permanent remainder of real growth.

57

He must learn patience in the greatest of all quests. However, he must remember that there are compensations for protracted periods of wearisome waiting, that periods of progress into which he will enter will be quite rapid by comparison. Above all, he should know that a sound basis for mystical development must be built in the character. It must be stable, sound, moral, determined, enduring, balanced, and reliable.

58

A person may be unconsciously if intermittently aware of a sharp fall, a terrible contrast between what he once was and now is. There may be a resultant feeling of unused potentiality, of not being in his original status, of not having found himself. These moods of thought and fits of feeling are most potent after he lets himself sink too deeply and too vehemently into personal life, personal emotions, and the dynamism which may be a part of his natural temperament. What may such a one do about his trouble? He is a sick soul and needs a soul physician. However, it is most advisable that during the periods of productive effort, of electrifying energy, he should try to moderate his actions, deliberately tone down his feelings, and calm his thoughts. This stormy intensity should be displaced by abruptly remembering its existence and breaking off into momentary self-recollection, standing back suddenly from his tremendous immersion in the egoic life and holding in his thought its transience and evanescence. Such concentrated power is a tremendous asset when directed rightly, but he has to pay the price of its possession when the personality is unintegrated. He should not work too hard, neither in quantity nor so intensely in quality. He should practise habitual relaxation in the very midst of his productive periods.

59

The ups and downs through which some must pass are partly in the emotional sphere and partly in the sphere of reality. The emotional upheavals and melancholy moods are the natural reactions on the lower levels to what has happened on the higher ones.

60

It is not only that every thing, every activity, should be put in its proper place, graded to its proper level, but also not done prematurely or belatedly, but with proper regard to the time-scale.

61

The theory of perpetual infinite and automatic progress is found to contradict itself.

62

He can always begin anew, clear of the negative thoughts and disturbed emotions which beset his past. But he cannot always sustain the endeavour.

63

The quest follows both a zigzag course as well as an up-and-down one.

64

It has been said that too many of the younger questers, in their early enthusiasm, undertake too much too fast, and later end in disappointment and discouragement, so that they abandon the Quest or else suffer deeply. There is some truth in this criticism.

65

Stagnation may be mistaken for contentment or resignation.

66

Although he must travel this path at his own pace and under his own initiative, there will be special periods when the movement forward must be quickened, when the effort made can be intensified. Destiny may provide these periods through terrible hurt or tremendous good fortune or through a guru.

Facing the problems of development

67

From the first moment that he sets foot on this inner path until the last one when he has finished it, he will at intervals be assailed by tests which will try the stuff he is made of. Such trials are sent to the student to examine his mettle, to show how much he is really worth, and to reveal the strength and weakness that are really his, not what he believes are his. The hardships he encounters try the quality of his attainment and demonstrate whether his inner strength can survive them or will break down; the sufferings he experiences may engrave lessons on his heart, and the ordeals he undergoes may purify it. Life is the teacher as well as the judge.(P)

68

The tests show whether he has become sufficiently strong to translate his ideals into action, whether he has conquered his passions and ruled his emotions at the bidding of those ideals, whether he will be willing to take the path of self-denial when the lower nature seeks to lure him away from the path.

69

Those who have much faith in the benevolent intentions of the Mind behind the universe, sooner or later find that faith severely tested. For the calamities of human life come to all of us.

70

Life itself is today the hierophant who tests his character and mentality, his power and endurance and responsiveness to intuitions. Life itself will sooner or later provide its square and compasses whereby his character may be measured, his earnestness proved, and his aims known. It does this for all men in a general sense, but it does this for disciples in a special sense. Whoever engages himself to tread this path, in our own times, will find that every important event becomes a sign of the activity of either good or evil forces. He must be forewarned that, at certain stages, he will be examined by his higher self and tested by the beneficent forces or tempted by the adverse ones. From this epoch-making date, the major episodes of an aspirant's life are purposely sent into it. Both good and evil powers pay special attention, within his personal karma, to his affairs. Once he has committed himself to this quest, he will find that events so arrange themselves as to indicate his sincerity, examine his motives, display his weaknesses, and find out his virtues. His devotion to the philosophic ideal will be tested, his loyalty to the goal will be tried.

71

Another danger of going astray at an early stage does not come from the obviously evil things. This mystical journey passes through a region where charlatans enter in pursuit of dupes, where quacks seek whom they may deceive, and where mental hallucination is often mistaken for divine vision. Hence, danger emanates from those men who take the name of God in vain, who seek to exploit or enslave inexperienced neophytes on the claim of Divine attainment. The quest should lead to greater freedom and not less, freedom to obey the voice of the soul inside rather than the voice of man outside. Yet few beginners realize this and false guides sedulously sap them of what little realization of it they may instinctively possess. The seeker must learn to beware of this type, especially of those occultists who, unburdened by ethical principles, try to conquer weaker minds by the perverted power of hypnotism. They are in ugly contrast to true sages, who try to liberate people by compassionate and competent service. Christ's warning against false prophets and unauthentic pretenders is apposite here. Thus, if the quest calls for keen discernment, metaphysical profundity, and moral earnestness to conquer the opposing force, it also calls for much prudence and more vigilance.

72

It is not only that new circumstances or new surroundings may draw out latent desires but even familiar ones may change sufficiently to do so.

73

Conflict not only tests the quality of our inner life, it also enables it to assert the higher will and develop its latent possibilities.

74

Tests. The manner in which he will approach trying, painful, or hostile situations will also betray the true measure of his spirituality, his devotion to higher values, and his comprehension of what he has undertaken. He has to show, by the way he meets these events and faces such conditions, what he really is and wants to be. He will adjust himself to such problems only according to the degree of maturity attained.

At certain times, during his exterior life, a crisis may occur which, though it may cause agony, will also provide opportunity. The challenge of opposition and adversity, of difficulty and suffering, provides opportunities to make progress through the struggle of overcoming them. But the art of rightly using these opportunities, instead of bungling them, is not easy to acquire.

The calamity, the bitterness, the despair, and the fatigue, which he may have to endure during these probationary years can all be turned to spiritual account, can all be made profitable in terms of better self-control, ennobled character, and truer values. Experience can be turned into a source of strength, wisdom, and growth; or it can remain a source of weakness, foolishness, and degeneration. It all depends upon the attitude he adopts toward it and the way he thinks and feels about it. Men have their faults in temperament and their defects in intelligence. Mistakes in action and errors in judgement, although never acceptable, are originally excusable. But continuance of the same mistakes and the same errors, despite repeated warnings in the shape of their results, is always inexcusable.

It is a painful process, this disentanglement from the lower human and merely animal natures, but it is a necessary one if inner peace is ever to be attained. Observation of other students' lives will be helpful in lessening its painfulness. The lessons he learns from the analytic contemplation of his own errors are excellent but costly, whereas those he learns from the contemplation of other men's errors are excellent and free. The chance to overcome difficulties and fight temptations is the chance both to test character and promote growth. The hours of trouble or distress shake up his psyche and, by enabling him to detect his weaknesses, by drawing attention to his faults, by forcing him to practise a stark self-examination, afford him the chance to get rid of them. All through this quest, but especially at certain critical periods, events will so happen and situations will so arrange themselves that the aspirant's weaknesses of character will be brought out into the open. The experience may be painful and its results may be saddening, but only by thus learning to know and discriminate against his bad qualities can he set out to submit them to the formative discipline of philosophy. Only so can he realize vividly what are the weak places in his character and strengthen them. If these incidents make him aware how pitifully slender are his own resources, if they bring him to realize how weak and faulty his character really is, then there is compensation for their painfulness. It is easy for him to believe he is virtuous or perceptive, but it is for life itself to reveal how far he is above temptation or error. Therefore, those experiences and events, contacts and persons, who afford the opportunity for this to be done, are indispensable. He may be strong in moral sincerity, but weak in critical judgement. It is his business now to become aware of this deficiency, to set about remedying it by attending to a co-equal cultivation of the different sides of personality.

If he succeeds in passing this probation, he will emerge stronger in the particular quality at stake than before. For it will have found fuller expression—it will have affected his practical will, his emotional feelings, his logical thinking, and even his capacity to receive and respond to intuitional guidance. Thus, to the extent that he is successful, to that extent will he bring the quality to a higher pitch of development. He may even learn to be grateful to time which brings healing, to afflictions which bring wisdom, and to opposition which elicits strength. If he is properly oriented, every external experience and every emotional and intellectual adventure will then help him towards a fuller and truer attitude towards life. If he obeys the injunctions of philosophy, in spirit as well as in letter, those very situations which before aroused his lower nature will now awaken his higher one. Each trouble can become a challenge to provoke the response of that serene detachment which can handle it more wisely. Each temptation can sound a call to be active in that penetrative analysis which can master it more effectually. If this inner life can sufficiently possess him, he will gain an independence of external things and events which can carry him unaffected and undisturbed through the severest ordeals. But this inward detachment will not be the correct kind if it weakens his sense of responsibility or causes failure in the carrying out of duties.

If a man cannot be wise, let him not therefore be foolish. No statement in the foregoing pages should be misconstrued as an injunction to go seeking either temptations on the one hand or tribulations on the other. No one is called upon to become either an experimental hedonist or a sentimental martyr. It is enough to ask anyone who thinks otherwise: What guarantee is there that he will be able to stop at the point where he proposes to stop?

He who has once embarked on this quest, may be diverted from it for a while, but he can never be driven from it forever. His eventual return is certain. Every fresh manifestation of human wrong-doing and human wickedness of which he is the sufferer, every new reverse of fortune and loss of possession, should only strengthen his determination to follow this quest and cultivate its calm detachment because it should strengthen his realization of the futility of basing his happiness on earthly things alone. He needs always to remember that the ordeal is transient but its prize is permanent, that if he succeeds in emerging from its tests still loyal to the ideal, he will also emerge with ennobled character, greater power, and increased faculty. When he wins through, in the end, then the long sufferings of past failures will bloom into pity for others and into strength for himself.

Hitherto, he has always been liable to miss his steps or fall by the wayside. But when he is established in the final stage, he is established in security. The roots of evil have been totally destroyed within him. Never again will they have the chance to grow and yield bitter fruit. When memories of his past life recur, he will find it hard to believe that they did not happen to someone else rather than to himself. He will look back with astonishment at the man he formerly was, at the ignorance and weakness which held him in bonds.

Reaching this final paragraph and casting about in mind for a valedictory thought, it is a fact, and a most extraordinary one, that after this beautiful entry into the higher level of his being, the past loses its capacity to hurt him, memory can no longer depress him, and the host of old blunders, sins, or tragedies are blotted out as though they had never been. Thus, at long last, those trying years of toilsome exercises and studies, hard sacrifices and disappointments, show their pleasant, satisfying result. By his success in passing these recurring tests, he has thereby shown that he fully deserves the higher and holier consciousness which now follows them.

75

From these reasons alone, we may see why philosophy declares that the mystical achievement of peace is not enough and why we have to go much farther than that and unfold wisdom also. The mystic's peace does not protect him from the path's pitfalls, which are set at intervals along its sides.

The glamour which surrounds occultism continues, even as in remote antiquity and in medieval Europe, to draw numerous human moths. They flutter agitatedly around its cheap sensationalism and want to become twentieth-century wizards or wonder-working Oriental fakirs—only to live for years self-hypnotized in vain hope rather than in actual satisfaction.

Would-be mystics have thus been sidetracked from their original purpose, have gradually lost sight of the diviner destination which once formed their goal, and have bestowed the time and energy of half a lifetime, perhaps, in dangerous dabbling and futile striving to attain (for them) unattainable powers—an effort which, if put forth towards loftier aims, might have brought worthwhile mental possessions such as inward serenity. There are even cases where people have spent twenty years trying to find out pseudo-secrets that are not worth the trouble of learning or which are even utterly non-existent, when they might have gathered imperishable life-giving truths into the nets of their minds within as many months. The wise seeker will leave this tempting but dubious pursuit alone—not all are fit to pry into dark occult corners or to grapple with shadowy, eerie forces, which Nature has wisely veiled from the unready.

Many waste their time and energies seeking extraordinary states of consciousness when they have not done the requisite preparatory work upon their ordinary state of consciousness. Without such preparation, it is either impossible to achieve their goal or, if partly achieved, it will be in so unbalanced a form that they will harm themselves and spread error amongst others. Instead, therefore, of meditating upon the higher consciousness, let them look to their lower faults of conduct, their undeveloped intelligence and unawakened intuition, their ungoverned passions and uncontrolled thoughts. Let them ruminate over the causes and consequences of these defects, meditate over the proper remedies, and cultivate the opposite qualities. They must improve self before they can really illumine self. They may not shirk this duty, which is nothing less than a full-time job in human engineering. Just as some of the alluring temptations will try their sincerity of purpose to the uttermost, just so some of the inevitable tragedies of life will test the quality of their character to the limit. Just as they will have to learn how to overcome temptation, so will they have to learn how to endure tribulation.

76

He should not desert the quest in resentment because earthly sufferings have come upon him. For if he does so, then he is inviting still further sufferings to come as a consequence of infidelity. Let him rather look upon them as mostly of his own making, through which he may learn lessons for the ultimate perfecting of his character, and always as tests of the sincerity with which he embarked on the quest. He must use these trials as opportunities to show forth endurance, steadfastness, and faithfulness, as well as to increase his wisdom. They do not come by chance. Earthly sufferings are as useful to him if not more so than the earthly joys which he so readily welcomes.

77

Compulsory association with a disliked or irritating person can be met in the ordinary way with negative emotions or in the philosophic way with constructive ones. It is to be regarded as a provocation to deny the former ones at the very moment of their rising and show forth later those of opposite character. The instant practice of a Spiritual Declaration is a useful help for some persons and the immediate concentration of attention on the needed virtues is a help for others. The longer the trial has to be suffered (and it is there under the law of destiny), the more deeply and firmly rooted will be the qualities and controls developed by the correct attitude. The test itself will pass away into a fading memory but those benefits will remain permanent.

78

In many situations you may put Truth to the test, but in others Truth may put you to the test.

79

This quest holds situations hidden in its eventual course which will stun him with their paradox and amaze him with their contradictions.

80

There is a period in the lives of some aspirants, but not all, when they look back at the results of entering the Quest and become dissatisfied with them. They still have no satisfying mystical experience to record, or if they have it is too far back in time and too transient in nature. They are definitely unhappy about their present situation, afflicted by morbid discouragement and tormented by intruding doubts. It is a testing period, a dark night not of the soul but of the emotions and thoughts.

81

If a man is seriously embarked on this quest, he will understand that when a desirable object is being put into his possession, or torn away from it, his sincerity will be tested by the impersonality with which he regards the event and deduces its meaning.

82

Why not apply creative imagination to these testing periods? When you know that you are about to enter one of them, imagine that you will pass through it quite successfully, see yourself in your mind's eye measuring up to ideal conduct.

83

If he wants to keep his earthly outlook and his animal desires, all society will come to his side, to support and even strengthen them. It has plenty to offer that will help him do so. But if he wants to make them subordinate to his higher quest, then it moves into opposition. Every kind of stimulus will be provided to get hold of his heart and mind; attention will be drawn outwards.

84

He finds himself confronted with a critical choice: either imposing control to eliminate wayward thoughts or confining himself to theoretical interest only.

85

Whenever he comes to a crucial turn in the road, where a personal choice must be made with serious consequences, he finds a warning waiting for him.

86

From the day when the resolution forms itself to live up, however partially, to the philosophic ideal, until the day when he is near the threshold of its full realization, the aspirant will have to face and overcome the opposition which this very attitude has aroused not only in himself but also in those outside, not only through weaknesses in his character and promptings in his heart, but also through troubles or temptations in his environment.

87

It is easy to stray from the path, hard to keep faithfully on it. Sometimes a thread's width alone separates the straightway from the deviation.

88

In each test there exists the chance, through success, to gain strength and pass up in Initiation to a higher level or, through failure, to display weakness and fall in conduct to a lower one.

89

The tests will come, inevitably. Can he keep his serenity amid crushing trouble, in destructive loss, under sore bereavement?

90

Sometimes he will be warned in some way, and thus prepared for it, that a test is impending. At other times he will not, and then his danger of being unsuspectingly led astray from the path will be greater.

91

In the Egyptian Mysteries, his capacity to resist a sexual temptation was deliberately tested. If he failed, the initiator would dismiss him, after addressing him thus: "You have yielded to the attraction of the senses. Whoever lives in the senses remains in darkness." If he succeeded, he would be granted leave to attend the temple college and receive instruction for some years in the mysteries of man and the universe.

92

Every test successfully met is rewarded by some growth in intuitive knowledge, strengthening of character, or initiation into a higher consciousness.

93

What are the different kinds of tests which the disciple may reasonably expect to undergo at different times of his spiritual career? There will be the test of his faith. This will take different forms, some of which will be easy to detect but others harder; some will be very obvious but others extremely subtle. Through the spoken voice or the printed word, esteemed authorities will tell him that the objects of his faith are mere chimeras, utter delusions, or worse. During periods of distress and suffering he will tell himself, through the emotions of discouragement and misgiving, the same thing. If the criticism of these enemies cannot dislodge him from his beliefs, the ridicule of his friends may do so. His trust in the truth of philosophic teaching, in the wisdom and virtues of the spiritual guide, in the necessity of following moral ideals, and in the likelihood of advancement on the spiritual Quest, will be tried in a crucible of fire.

94

It will depend largely upon the disciple how long his term of probation lasts. It is true that periods of one, three, five, or seven years have been mentioned in this connection historically, but it would be quite arbitrary to hold a man to any such period, irrespective of his character, circumstances, and karma. When he is able to pass the basic requirements of the Quest in morality and loyalty, in intuition and comprehension, his term will come to an end. The ego will not hesitate to use even a pretense of spirituality in order to keep its hold over him. It will persuade him flatteringly to believe that he is better than he really is. If he falls into this trap, he will not only become ensnared in spiritual pride, but also fall into various mistakes of judgement and conduct because he will be blissfully unaware of serious defects in himself.

95

These issues must be faced and mastered. If he evades their recognition he merely confesses his complete failure, and if he delays dealing with them, he only aggravates the consequent danger. The karmic forces which are at work in such a test are like an irresistible tide. He must make up his mind to adjust himself prudently to them or else submit to the certain fate of being injured by them.

96

Every test is a teacher to guide us to a higher level, a providential friend to give us the quality we most need.

97

The test will come with every major crisis, every minor ordeal. If his inner work has been well done he will be surprised at the calmness with which he meets and passes the event, astonished at his strength.

98

Both wisdom and prudence call for an exact appraisal of such situations; he cannot afford either to under-assess the forces to be dealt with or to over-assess them.

99

Before passing into a higher phase of his development, the disciple is usually confronted by life with a situation which will test his fitness for it. His success in meeting this test will open a gate leading to the next degree.

100

In most cases ill-health troubles are traceable to ordinary causes, but in other cases their origin must be largely sought for in the tests and ordeals to which advanced students are subjected at some time or other. This does not mean that every advanced student has to experience ill-health but that he has to experience great ordeals as well as great temptations towards the end of a phase of his development or after the beginning of a new one. The former may and do come in the shape of ill-health, but they may also come in quite different shapes.

101

If he is to become a philosopher in the real sense, he must look upon the trials and tests of these years as a means of helping him to do this. There are of course other and pleasanter means too. But, as *Light on the Path* says, all steps are necessary to reach the goal.

102

He who has given his allegiance to this quest, must be prepared for the sudden shocks of revelation which may come to him before, during, or after these tests. He will find that, spiritually viewed by his own true self, his inner life is not as he has thought it to be. He will find that the ego has tricked him in the most important things, whilst giving him the deceitful satisfaction of victory in the trivial ones.

103

The most important ones come mostly as soon as an important development or change happens in his life, his worldly fortunes, or his inner quest.

104

Quite often, the aspirant will not be aware how far he has grown in virtue until some crucial test arises in the sphere of everyday living. Then, to his surprise and pleasure, he may note the ease with which he passes it.

105

A test need not necessarily come on the physical plane of event only. It may also come on the mental one through imagination or memory or even in dreams.

106

We may take refuge in escapism from a situation that is a sharp test of character. The ego may even lead us into failure to recognize it properly or to overcome it rightly. But if we are on the Quest we may be sure that one day it will return and trouble us later, even if in another form.

107

The tests will necessarily have to come in various ways. One situation will have all the circumstances which provoke a passion like anger while another will have all those which provoke an emotion that is equally undesirable.

108

In every test he has the possible chance to reveal himself as he would like to be, as well as the certain chance to reveal what he already is.

109

Each test not only gives him the chance to distinguish between truth and error, to discern reality from illusion, but also the chance to move beyond his present moral vacillation into moral firmness.

110

He accepts this welcome penitence but he does not trust this new-found allegiance. That will need time to prove itself.

111

The test represents the vanities, the passions, the greeds, the delusions, and the hatreds of those to whom it comes. It can be looked upon as a test only by people in whom these things are themselves lying latent or half-present. Hence it would be wrong to consider it as an utterly isolated phenomenon in connection with their personal history. It is the logical culmination of the demand to enter the quest. If it be argued that they are innocent people led astray, then it should be answered that there must have been some weakness in their character which itself tended to take the direction of the path down which they went astray. If not then, it would have shown itself at some later time.

112

Those who take to this spiritual road have to endure its tests. It is not enough to have faith or feel spiritual when life's course is smooth and fortunate. They must learn to hold their faith and feeling when its course runs through difficulties and sickness also. If the test reveals that they lose their hold at such times, then it shows their need of doing further work on themselves. For this failure shows that they want good fortune and good health even more than they want to fulfil the higher spiritual purpose of their incarnation.

113

It is a curious fact and at first an incredible one that whenever an aspirant makes some effort and gets a little gain in consequence, and certainly whenever he makes a great effort and seems near a great gain, something happens in his outer life to defeat his purpose and deprive him of his gains unless he displays much discriminative prudence and more impersonal strength. In this way the evil forces and adverse destinies are permitted to test him. If they succeed in hindering him he fails. If they fail to turn him aside from the immediate objective of his quest, he succeeds in it.

114

At the very gate of this higher quest, you will find certain obstacles obstructing your entry. They are not alien to you, they are in your mind. Your primary duty, therefore, is to overcome them.

115

If a beginner is conscious of his weakness, then it would be prudent for him to avoid those things and those people who emphasize it.

116

The twelve trials of Hercules correspond with the twelve stages through which the Egyptian candidate had to pass. The fable openly admits that before the last and most difficult trial Hercules was initiated into the Eleusis Mysteries.

117

If after some years of constant yearning but fitful striving, he believes that no concrete results have been obtained he may easily get tired and admit defeat. Much courage and more patience must be exercised during such a rehabilitation period, and most of the time without any concrete help appearing. But this is part of his test.

118

The forces set in operation by his determined attempt to approach the Overself in every phase of his living habits eventually produce a vigorous effort on the part of his subconscious mind to cleanse itself of ancient accumulations of negative animalistic and egoistic tendencies. Although the process produces disagreeable and evil symptoms, it is not to be regarded as other than a self-purifying one, a natural way of vomiting debris from the depths, removing and expelling it. The more earnestly he takes to this quest, the more will his latent evil qualities be stirred up and then make their appearance in his character or conduct. He, as well as others, may be surprised and perturbed at this result. Yet it is only an effort on the part of the inner forces to throw up the good for further development and throw out the morbid qualities for ultimate expulsion. It may be an unpleasant method, its symptoms an unpleasant surprise, but it is essential if these tendencies are to be eradicated at all. Otherwise they will appear one by one in their own time and periodically block his path to the goal. Ordinarily they are suppressed in self-defense by the conscious mind, and their existence hidden because it has quite enough to deal with. But the candidate for illumination has flung out a challenge to vigorous war.

119

The Overself will take him at his word and will let his destiny bring him not only those experiences which he earns but especially those which he needs. If he comprehends this situation impersonally he will realize that he must welcome them all, and not single out the pleasant ones alone for his favour. All can become his teachers if he will let them, so all should be received rightly and attentively. Rebellion and resentment merely shut out the lesson they have to teach him: if he misses this lesson he will have to go through the same experience again at some future time and repeat the same suffering so needlessly.

120

Those who have previously made satisfying spiritual advance often find themselves pulled up and unable to go farther, sometimes for years. This is because the undeveloped and imperfect parts of their natures offer obstruction to further progress. If the higher forces were to descend on them while they are purified only in parts and developed only in some faculties, these forces would prove harmful instead of helpful. Consequently, these parts are brought up by events to the surface of his life in order that they may be dealt with.

121

There are those who possess a cozy feeling of what they take to be spiritual peace. They may have arrived at this through various means, but life will put them to the test whereby they can discover for themselves whether this peace is the genuine article or whether it is pseudo-peace which breaks down when the blows of fate hammer the person.

122

In one sense troubles are our teachers and the greater the trouble the greater the teaching impressioned upon us.

123

The test must be whether he can withdraw at will from his external activities, and especially from those to which he is most attached, or those which yield him the most pleasure or the most success. It is for him to decide how much that he is in the habit of doing every day should really be allowed to take up time that could be given to higher things. He should pick a time of the day when he can go into retreat, putting aside all earthly interests, no matter how busy, how filled, the remainder of that day is. If he fails to devote to meditation the time allotted to it, only because he submits to the pressure and haste which tend to kill finer qualities in modern life, he fails, to that extent, in his quest.

124

He may have to pass through a period when the idols in his mind have to be broken up, or when the image he carries of God or guru has to be given up.

125

Any inner excellence which is used to glorify the man's ambition and self-flattery may become his test.

126

There is protection, there is guidance for the sincere, earnest, and sensible quester; but it is not always apparent. Or, if perceived, it is so only long after the event. Both these statements are true of some questers, but not true of those others who recognize the warning for what it is, and who heed it in their subsequent actions.

127

The changes within and without through which one is often called upon to pass usually are not unexpected. The aspirant, himself, involuntarily calls them into being as a result of his work and study. They are useful as they test the spiritual growth so far attained, revealing how much of it is firmly established, and in what directions one should apply deeper effort toward building a steadier foundation.

128

It is unfortunate but true that the spiritual path is beset with dangers, pitfalls, tests, and oppositions. They never bear any placard to announce their real nature, but, on the contrary, bear a deceptive appearance. The average seeker is usually unaware of them and quite often becomes their victim.

129

The aspirant must never give way to excessive grief. Any period of grave difficulty may be regarded, perhaps, as a test of his faith. At such a time, he should constantly practise his philosophy, while also praying for greater strength and understanding. In the Overself there is no agony or pain; these belong to the sphere of illusion.

130

When one is up against an especially difficult situation for which no immediate solution can be found, it will help him if he will use the time while waiting for the change—which will come—in order to deliberately cultivate greater patience and forebearance, as well as a more objective attitude.

131

A difficult or frightening situation must be considered a challenge. At such a time, the student should seek even more intensely through prayer, meditation, and faith—while also practising self-control to the best degree he is able—to achieve the needed spiritual strength and understanding in order to endure and overcome his troubles. In times of actual danger, the calm remembrance of the Overself will help to protect him.

132

He challenges the gods who takes the Quest so seriously and, let him be warned, it will ferret out his weakest spot and expose it for his ultimate benefit. However, all the anguish through which he must pass can be converted into peace and strength if only he will learn from it and not allow himself to be bitter towards the man who caused it.

133

There are serious and even tragic tests on this path, the results of which are sometimes different in the end from what they were in the beginning. We all need Grace. The way is so hard, the gloom so thick, and the adverse force so strong.

134

When a great crisis comes, he should always try to remember the spiritual teachings which the teacher has tried to impart to him, together with the indissoluble character of the inner tie that binds student and teacher together. Amidst all the dangers and hardships of the coming crisis, let him strive to keep open the inner channels of inspiration, protection, and guidance with the Divine Power. It will be very hard to do so under great outer pressures, but even two or three minutes of thought of it each day will be a help in this direction. The importance cannot be overestimated of simple recurring remembrance of (a) the Overself and (b) the teacher, and of trying to carry on in the atmosphere of such remembrance. It is a yoga path of its own and is as good in its way as any other. But if he cannot do more, even mere recollection for a minute of the mental image of the teacher will be a help.

135

His troubles may at times leave him with a sense of frustration and defeat. This is natural. It simply means that a difficult hand is being dealt out to him by fate. He should appraise it philosophically as a general indication of the unsatisfactoriness of earthly life in the Buddhistic sense. On this path he gets all kinds of vicissitudes and ups and downs, partly to demonstrate vividly that the inner reality is the only unchanging value and thus compel a resort to its quest, and partly to bring out latent qualities. But he will not be tried beyond what he can bear.

136

There is no need for pessimism when his career seems to meet with insuperable obstacles and when he seems to come to an impasse which brings out nothing but a feeling of great frustration. At such times, he must remember that karma may begin to work out her own plans and that a reorientation of activities may be indicated. He should do all he can to *create* his specific opportunities and thus shorten the waiting time. The developed aspirant does not fall into conventional categories and that is why he has to strike out on a new path for himself. It needs courage, faith, imagination, intuition, and the ability to recognize karmic opportunities and make the most of them.

137

Having found his spiritual path he should stick to it and not be tempted aside by paths which may suit other people but which are not for him. For snares, pitfalls, illusions and betrayals, tests and temptations are set at important or critical periods and he needs his intelligence, intuition, and loyalty to overcome them. It is easy to stray onto sidetracks and then waste years before finding the way back again.

138

Now and then karma unloads trials and troubles which are not pleasant to endure. All the same they have something to teach us—if only the ancient lesson of the need to find a more satisfactory inner life to compensate for the transiency and the vicissitudes of the outer life. He cannot escape from these so long as he lives upon this earth but he can hope to understand them and eventually to master his mental reactions to them. Therein lies peace and wisdom.

139

Although worldly desires are all right in their place and may be legit-imately satisfied, they must remain subordinate to the spiritual aspiration for self-realization. To help the individual to agree voluntarily to such subordination, the Overself, which has been invoked, deliberately arranges experience (under karma) in such a way as to underline spiritual values. Once he is able to bring feelings into accord with such values, he will find that the very things which eluded his grasp when he sought them, now come to him of their own accord. Thus sacrifices demanded turn out to be merely temporary, whereas the happiness obtained is double—both earthly and spiritual. This is why Jesus said: "Seek ye first the kingdom of heaven and all these things shall be added unto you."

140

In terrible times of suffering and anxiety it is more necessary than ever to cultivate receptivity to the divine forces within ourselves through spiritual studies and meditation.

141

The path is veritably a "razor's edge." One with limited awareness cannot know how grave his situation may be nor how narrow an escape he may, at some time, have had. If, at such a time, great efforts are put forth for him by someone highly advanced, satisfactory results may still be achieved, notwithstanding the student's mistakes. When his weaknesses are counterbalanced by earnest aspiration and faith, if he never deserts his Ideal no matter what happens, if he clings to his desire for conscious attainment of unity with the Overself as the highest goal life offers and measures all other rewards accordingly, then the student may always count on the assistance which brought him safely through his time of crisis.

142

Enjoy your successes but study your failures.

143

The profit of errors comes in when, and if, they are used to redraw the pattern of living.

144

An experience which ended in disillusionment is not necessarily a wasted one. It may have its positive side: it may have contributed certain ideas.

145

It is the belief, indignantly repeated in complaint, of some disappointed persons who have lost money and years or failed to regain health by following such leaders or teachings, that their aspiration and faith should have protected them. But they do not see that behind the deception or incompetence of the leader, or error of his teaching, was the fault of wrong judgement in their own mentality which led them to him. Merely to have prevented them from giving their allegiance would not have removed this fault from them, and would have hidden its existence from them. One day it would have led them into the same mistake again. If their aspiration for self-improvement was quite earnest and their faith in the higher power quite sincere, then a warning against the attachment they were about to make must have come to them through some person, book, happening, or inner feeling of doubt and unease, but they disregarded it.

146

If their delusion collapses, their chance to win mental profit from their shattered hopes and disappointed ideals is good—but only if they examine into the causes within themselves which led them into the situation. If they fail or refuse to do this, then the same causes will operate and still another delusion will rise up, first to capture, and later, to punish them.

147

He will be tested by experiences which will show how far, or how little, he has travelled above emotion and beyond ambition.

148

Nothing but a great and unexpected upheaval will precipitate a change in their mental habits or impel a deviation from their physical habits. If it does come, they look upon it as a disaster, although when time gives them a longer perspective they look upon it as an enlightenment.

149

The particular problems which life has presented him with are exactly the ones suited to his own personal development. In their solution by his own efforts and his own thinking, lies his own advantage and growth. To turn them over to someone else is an evasive and undignified action, harmful in the end.

150

Some are not deterred by opposition or obstacles, but actually stimulated by them.

151

He may be sure of one thing, that his fidelity to ideas and ideals, to teacher and teachings, will be tested. This is inescapable if his will is to be surrendered to the higher will, if his character is to be purified and his attitude cleansed of its egoism.

152

Meet your trials and temptations in the name and strength of your master, if you have one, or of the Overself, if you have not. Do not depend on the little ego alone.

153

The aspirant may expect all kinds of tests and trials on his path, no less than temptations at unpredictable times, but invariably when he is successful enough so as to near the gate of illumination he will be subject to severe attacks by the adverse elements in nature which seek to prevent his attainment. In the old Indian books it is said that divine knowledge-consciousness is very difficult to attain because even when one has got near to it, adverse spirits make it their work to prevent one's entry into that state.

154

It is during the periods of test that he must hold on to balance more than at other times.

155

A missed chance or a failed test in one year may lead directly, if the lesson be heeded, to a used chance or a successful test in a later year.

156

Defeat is only an alarm clock calling you to get up and get going once more.

157

At every important turn on his path the aspirant will find a choice awaiting him. He will find himself facing a set of circumstances which test his motive, strength, and attainment. These periodical tests can be neither evaded nor avoided, and often they are not recognized for what they are. Temptation may camouflage them under attractive colours. Nevertheless the student's conduct in regard to them will decide whether he passes onward and upward, or falls back into pain and purification.

158

Long after the naïveté of the novice has left him, he may yet fall victim to teachings or teachers of an undesirable sort.

159

He who has had to bear a great trial in the course of conducting his worldly business must, at such a time, look more than ever before to the higher power for sustenance and comfort. The more he is tried the greater the inner reward will be if he holds to the faith that is in him.

160

When one hits upon tragic times and difficult circumstances, the essential thing is to try within his power, however humbly that may be, to *live* the spiritual Quest. This is harder to do than ever before, yet it is almost more necessary than ever before. He must keep up his endeavours to understand and to practise what is right. Although great patience is called for during such times, great benefits will also show themselves in the end.

161

He is sometimes taken at his word and made to undergo what *Light on the Path* refers to as the keenest anguish, which is brought to bear upon the disciple in order to lift him or her finally above the oscillations of experience. The path is no joke. It is as terrible as it is beautiful at other times.

162

There are times when a man is thrown back on his own inner resources. If they are few and weak, fear spreads itself in him. But if he has taken the trouble to cultivate them, he will show a hard front to whatever the trouble is and meet it with more calm and less distress than others would.

163

In painful or trying hours he should make it a serious point to remember that glorious moment when the skies parted, the veil was rent, and the Soul showed its lovely face to him. He should recall it in worldly distress or emotional darkness and it will sustain, comfort, and guide him. From this secret source he will derive a strength to bear whatever may happen to him, an understanding to lead him aright throughout life.

164

Learn to penetrate within yourself, your deeper, almost unknown self. It will need patience to return day after day, not stopping until the truth is reached, the peace is felt, the blessing descends. It will need perseverance until the source of strength is found. Thereafter it will take you over: this is grace. But remember—with each return from the day's efforts you will be confronted by the world again, by its harsh reality yet glorious beauty, its stark conflicts yet benign interludes. So—know this world in which you have to live, its petty minds and noble souls. Learn from both. And when you have seen enough of the world's surface ask for its tremendous secret.

165

To produce a great result, a great effort is needed.

166

It is a truth which can uphold the heart of a man through the bitterest adversity or the direst affliction. There is no situation, however bad, in which it cannot give help.

167

As the aspirant progressively follows the pattern of this teaching two, three, and four times over, he will find the answers to many questions which arose in his mind at the first study. Those philosophical statements which were meaningless at the first reading, may now seem meaningful at the tenth. Time and trial and familiarity will help solve this abstruse doctrine.

168

When Jesus declared, "Knock, and it shall be opened unto you," he did not declare that this would happen after a single knock, nor even after a hundred knocks. If he meant anything at all, he meant ceaselessly repeated knocking.

169

The more successful type of Quester is the one who can keep his interest, enthusiasm, and practices in a stable, unwaning condition.

170

Let him persevere in efforts along the spiritual path, continue endeavours towards self-improvement and character building, and keep up the regular practice of meditation and prayer—all these are essential to development. Every effort he puts forward calls forth a corresponding aid on the part of the Divine Grace.

171

He may have his doubts, hesitations, criticisms, and even rebellions later—they may stretch out far in time—but in the end they cannot alter his course. For the quest he was born; to the quest he must surrender. The obligation is a lifelong one.

172

If the aspirant discovers after several years that Nature is still resistant, that the leopard spots are too deeply dyed to change easily, and that his character keeps its weaknesses despite all his efforts to dislodge them, then the hopes with which he began the quest may begin to fade in this grey dawn. He realizes that they were over-exultant and over-optimistic. He despairs of ever remaking himself successfully. He even has thoughts of abandoning the quest entirely. But does this discovery really call for such defeatism and such despondency? No, it calls for a resigned acceptance of the situation as it is, for a realistic measurement of what can be done within the limits of a single lifetime, for a recognition of the wisdom of Nature in providing him with numerous future reincarnations in which to achieve his purpose. He must refuse to follow the common error and identify himself with this one physical body of the present incarnation.

Rather, he must identify himself with his mental being and feel this as something immortal, something reappearing on earth time after time and coming closer and closer, with each appearance, to the goal. He must believe in the truth of evolution, even while he perceives that it takes time, plenty of time, for such evolution to become a fact. He must admit that he is not left without signs by the way, nor without glimpses to inspire him, nor tokens to encourage him. Against the pessimistic moan that the leopard cannot change his spots, there is the optimistic teaching of Socrates that "virtue can be learned." Against the worldling's sneer that the quest sets itself an impossible task, there is the encouragement of every religious prophet and seer history has known. The last gift that lies waiting with cheerful patience in Pandora's box, the voice of hope, is for him. Admit that the discipline is hard, attainment is rare, *and few* are in a position to turn their minds away from the pressure of environment and circumstance in which they find themselves. However, glimpses, intuitions, uplifts do come at times, even if after long intervals. Most people can and should get a correct sense of general direction for the course of their inner life. This alone is a great gain.

173

What things oppose his quest? In the end they all lead back to himself. Habits of thought, directions taken by natural energies, turn him outward through the body's senses. Release from past tendencies, return inwards, needs tremendous sustained determination.

174

A man who sets out to wage war against his own thoughts and to constrain his own impulses may properly be called a warrior. Let him not look for peace until the enemy is defeated, and since the enemy will not yield for a long time, but will resist with the utmost desperation, the man will need all the patience he can gather and all the endurance he can muster.

175

If he is not willing to wait, this quest does not offer much for him. It is not only in meditation—although primarily in it—that patience is a requisite, but also in the work of purifying and ennobling character.

176

Pursue the quest, practise its exercises, and undergo its disciplines with a patience that does not halt for an instant. If you do this, the time will come when the Overself can hold out no longer. It will then no longer dwell in secret but in your heart.

177

If he will remain steadfast in his faith and unshakeable in his ideal, the quest will become easier than it seems and more rewarding than it appears to be.

178

You must never give up the quest; no matter how long drawn out or how painful or how many disappointments and deceivings, you must still keep up the search after God or after a Master; this determination will receive its reward ultimately. Even a man who has practised meditation all his life and apparently got no results, may very likely be given the reward at the moment of death.

179

Aspirations should not be put into cold storage. He need not stop trying because something-or-other that is either very pleasant or else very unpleasant has happened.

180

Even if you have to wade year after year through all the spheres of doctrinal illusion, through all the false ideas of men about Truth, only to find disappointment in the end, yet you must keep up that burning longing for it. You have to be unhappy about it, to grumble and rage and despair, and the next day go on with the Quest. If you can do this you are fit to find Truth in the end.

181

He must expect to err, as so many other human beings will err, in ideas and actions. But he will pick himself up and learn, will let himself be corrected, simply because he is on this Quest.

182

"Hitch your wagon to a star" was the advice of that smiling optimist, Emerson. It probably looked well on paper, and even better in print, but some of us grow impatient, and get a little tired of sighing for distant constellations. Ideals have an exasperating way of eluding us. We begin to pursue them with fiery enthusiasm; we end with empty hands and calloused feet. We rise rapidly to lofty purposes, but before long the parachute of inspiration makes a sad descent. The student must strive to keep his judgement unaffected by hectic enthusiasms, biased propaganda, axe-grinding advertisements.

183

If he perseveringly works at trying to understand the teaching of true sages, however difficult this may be in the beginning, time added to the perseverance must bring some positive result. Total success requires an inborn capacity but partial success does not.

184

You may feel and think that such glory is for others, not for you—that the common humdrum days remain unshining in your life. But try to quieten thoughts every now and then. Remember that patience is a necessity in this inner work, remember too that it is a moral work also. Do not abate hope because the Glimpse did not come so far. Find out what more is asked of you.

185

No matter how difficult the Quest may sometimes appear, nor how far down on its scale the student feels himself to be, he may draw hope and courage from the fact that his feet are on it. He must have faith and patience. The Divine Overself is well aware of his problems and takes into account his deficiencies.

186

If one sticks to the Quest, come what may, he can be certain that his perseverance will eventually bring results. Some of the metaphysical studies and mystical exercises seem hard at first, but if one persists with them, the time will surely come when much which was hitherto obscure will suddenly become brilliantly clear and meaningful in a single instant before his eyes.

187

An aspirant on this Quest must hold on to his determination to improve and discipline himself even amidst all the different temptations and difficulties which he comes up against from time to time. For this is the way he builds the foundation for his future. Students are often apt to forget that it is their present thoughts, feelings, and actions which are predetermining the favourable or unfavourable conditions of incarnations to come, as well as the remainder of this one.

188

The aspirant should not give way to feelings of despair about the long road ahead of him. He may go far in this incarnation, particularly after he begins to recognize his "failures" for the stepping-stones they are, and to use the knowledge and discrimination gained from these experiences to safeguard his future progress from similar mishaps. Besides, he is not alone in his efforts and help *is* available.

189

The aspirant must remember that even if he is deterred seventy times from achieving higher ground and is seventy times swept back by a flood of opposition, he must try again a seventy-first time and even again and still again, until at last he succeeds. At the same time, he must take care never to give way completely to feelings of despair or to thoughts of failure. By holding on in this way, the day *will* come when he will receive the miraculous Grace of the Overself.

190

The aspirant must remember that it is the constantly applied efforts to improve himself—seemingly so tedious and unending—which provide the prerequisite conditions for the later, more dramatic illuminations.

191

It is hard to get at the pure Truth—harder still to find a reliable teacher whose conduct is a worthy testament of it. Perseverance is necessary in both cases.

192

Mind puts great powers within our reach, but we have to work for them if we are to obtain them. They are not given free, nor provided arbitrarily by a capricious Creator or supernaturally by a holy man. I have quoted Emerson before and it is worth quoting him again on this point: "Take what thou wilt, but pay the price."

193

If he will do the exercises regularly and carefully, apply the mental and emotional disciplines honestly and perseveringly, his personal history will hardly be able to escape a change for the better.

194

It is inevitable that depressing failures and wearisome defeats should harass the pilgrim on this quest. He may grieve over them but he must not fall before them. He should accept their practical lessons but not their negative effects. An intelligent patience, a deep faith, and a quiet hope must fortify him.

195

Whoever wants quick results had better not begin this path. A man is willing to spend five years to prepare himself to master engineering, but he is frequently unwilling to spend more than five weeks to master mind itself.

196

He has to strive tediously and seek loyally for an end which he cannot exactly describe and for a goal which he can only believe does exist.

197

Philosophy asks the aspirant to *strive* earnestly and constantly to endow himself with these qualities, but it does not expect him to be perfectly equipped with them. If he were, he would himself be a full-fledged philosopher and not a novice seeking to master its wisdom. Almost every mystical aspirant at first falls far below the philosophical level, but he who *tries* to keep himself on it and who succeeds in doing so, even only partially, will find sufficient reward in the proportionate measure of wisdom, strength, calmness, and divine love that will accrue to him.

198

Patience is the twin of hope.

199

To keep to this inner work steadfastly and persistently, to make of its exercises and practices a regular routine, is to make the undertaking easier for oneself in the end, as well as more successful in its results.

200

If the aspirant deserts the quest in sheer fatigue or outer despair, he loses his way. For the world will satisfy him only for a limited time, and then discontent with it will erupt afresh. If, however, he continues to persevere, then holy visitations will come more frequently and remain longer. He will lose nothing in reality unless and until he loses heart. For that is in the realm of secret causes, while things are in the realm of visible effects. So long as failure does not get inside a man, so long is the road to victory still open before him. The patience which is required of the aspirant is often tremendous. He will be tempted again and again to give up in despair. Although conscious of his ignorance, sensitive to his inadequacy, and recognizing his incapacity, he will not escape falling into moods of despondency. He will need the rare quality of endurance where even repeated defeats will not make him give up the struggle. He will probably pass through various phases of enthusiasm for philosophy and antipathy for it, but despite these alternations he will know in his inmost heart that he can never forsake it. Eventually, he will get the philosophic outlook which, although it sees his own human limitations and knows his own human possibilities, will refuse to despair.

201

If he is patient enough in the end the truth will clear his mind. But patience is not to be coupled with idleness.

202

This search will not be given up so long as thought inquires into its own existence, so long as consciousness is continuously making itself known and felt, and so long as the queries remain unanswered to our satisfaction.

203

Whoever begins to seek in the mind for that divine Reality which supports the mind will have to feel his way very carefully, very prudently, and very patiently. At first he may get nothing back but his own thoughts and this may go on for quite a long time. This is one of the reasons why great patience is needed. He may be led astray by feelings or thoughts which are not true evidences of the divinity, and this is why prudence is needed.

4

PRACTISE MENTAL DISCIPLINE

Its nature

The aspirant must begin by examining himself, by enquiring into the honesty or dishonesty, the impartiality or partiality of his views, beliefs, and judgements, by questioning how much or how little his will is enslaved by passion, appetite, or instinct. For the average aspirant sets up inner resistance to that purification of his emotions, passions, egoisms, prejudices, intellectualizations, desires, and hatred which would permit him to reflect the undistorted truth. Emotional tensions and mental strains which cause inner suffering have first to be brought out into the open and resolved before he can approach truth in the atmosphere of tranquillity which she requires. The mental knots and passional complexes which exist within his personality, whether near the surface or deep out of sight, must be dealt with and dissolved before he can come at the truth. It is the conscious or unconscious forces, these obvious or unrecognized impulses that drive him into deeds hurtful to society and discouraging to himself. The complexes which dominate his mind and influence his beliefs must be brought into the open by the philosophic discipline. He must know where, psychologically, he stands. The desires and fears which operate in the subconscious can then be evaluated, developed, or discarded. He should seek to understand his own character, to perceive impartially its merits and demerits. On the basis of such self-understanding, he should root out persistently those faults which hinder progress.

2

To wade into the welter of modern materialistic metropolitan life and attempt to turn it to an inner purpose, is not so brave or beautiful as sitting down and cultivating one's soul despite the world's opinion.

3

There is no computerized program for this inner work. In a sense one has to feel his way, to try this procedure and that, to catch rare unexpected moments of sacred visitation and let them in, to think more deeply than ever before.

4

The machinery and the method, the technique and the process tend to become all-important in our eyes; but the truth is that the attitude and ideal, the spirit and heart behind them are even more important.

5

All quests involve some travelling, the periodical shift from one point to another. The spiritual quest involves constant intellectual travelling, but only a single important shift—that from the ego's standpoint to the Overself's.

6

What is the Overself waiting for, so long and so patiently? For our willingness to die in the ego that It may live in us. So soon as we make the signs of this willingness, by acceptance of each opportunity to achieve this destruction of egoism, the influx of new life begins to penetrate the vacated place.

7

Whatever helps to reduce the predominant influence of the ego helps his quest. Where the whole area of consciousness is taken up by it, attrition of the area is more important than the particular means used to secure it.

8

He should take the attitudes he has inherited by the accident of birth, the views he has acquired from the suggestions of environment, the beliefs he has accepted through tradition and instruction and deliberately and attentively submit them all to the searching light of these universal and eternal truths. It may be that social necessity will prevent him from applying some or even all the results of his enquiry, but for the sake of his own inner integrity this must be done.

9

On the battlefield of his heart where noble and ignoble emotions struggle repeatedly for dominion, he will find one part of his quest. In the self-absorbed thoughts of introspection, he will find another.

10

Let him face the fact that if he is seeking the Overself with one part of his being, he is also seeking his own ego with the other. He wants his desires satisfied and also wants That which is desireless at one and the same time. He is trying to walk in two different directions. One or the other must go.

11

It is from life and experience, events and books, nature and art, intuition and meditation that he is to gain incentive for ennobled thought and get inspiration for ennobled conduct.

12

The philosopher considers from time to time both the painful and pleasurable events which are likely to happen to him as a human being and imaginatively prepares in advance what his proper reaction to them should be. The profit of this practice lies not only in the better handling of these foreseen events, but also in the better attitude with which he is able to handle unforeseen ones.

13

He needs to become possessed by the feeling and magnetized by the belief that he has to get at least some brief glimpses of mystic light before the darkness descends.

14

In the effacement of his own egoism, brought about by a double discipline—first, the constant shaping of the character and second, learning to live in the deepest silence of meditation—he will allow the Overself to act within and through him.

15

You will make fate and free will find a fortunate conjunction if you are determined to do your utmost and yet to yield to the Overself.

16

Each time he attempts to deny the responsibility he bears for his own troubles and to shift it onto other people's shoulders, he makes the repeated appearance of those troubles in his life a certainty. For the inner causes still remain.

17

Nothing which will help him in his strivings toward illumination should be neglected.

18

Yes, the kingdom of heaven is certainly to be brought down and established on earth. But the meaning of Jesus was not social; it was individual. Each man is to establish it within his own sphere, within his own feelings, thoughts, and acts.

19

The vain man, the stupid man, or the lustful man cannot enter the kingdom of heaven. He must first be humble enough to silence the ego, intuitive enough to expose its deception, and strong enough to overcome its desires.

20

Although the intellectual study of metaphysical doctrine and mystical teaching is the least part of the fourfold path, still it is a valuable part.

21

What does getting rid of the ego's dominance mean? Until we see this clearly, we shall not see what effort we have to make to achieve it. First, it means constant training to regard ourself and our fortunes as coolly, disinterestedly, and impartially as we regard other men and their fortunes. Second, it means constant vigilance to keep out the distorting, befogging, and perverting interference of personal habits of thought and feeling. It is the blind following of these tendencies of our nature, accumulated since a far past, that makes up most of the ego's life. Third, it means constant practice in repressing thoughts and emotions while cultivating mental stillness.

22

You are yourself your biggest problem. You cannot hand it over to anyone else, be he saviour or master, and escape from it, except in delusive imagination or in erroneous belief.

23

Watching his daily conduct and reviewing it in retrospect is not less needful than practising meditation.

24

The place where you are, the people who surround you, the problems you encounter, and the happenings that take place just now—all have their special meaning for you. They come about under the law of recompense as well as under the particular needs of your spiritual growth. Study them well but impersonally, egolessly, and adjust your reactions accordingly. This will be hard and perhaps even unpalatable, yet it is the certain way to solving all your problems. This is what Jesus meant when he declared, "If any man will come after me, let him deny himself, and take up his cross daily, and follow me." This is that crucifixion of the ego which is true Christianity and which leads directly to the resurrection in the reality of the Overself. Regard your worst, most irritating trouble as the voice of your Overself. Try to hear what It says. Try to remove the obstructions It is pointing to within yourself. Look on this special ordeal, this particular trial, as having the most important significance in your own spiritual growth. The more crushing it is, the more effort is being made to draw you nearer to the Overself. At every point of your life, from one event, situation, contact to another, the Infinite Intelligence provides you with the means of growth, if only you will get out of the egoistic rut and take them.

25

He is always ready to revise his methods, habits, dogmas, because he is always ready to learn by experience.

26

Constant association with the wise, frequent hearing of discussions and statements about truth, gradually tend to the practice of philosophy, to the supersession of the personal and the passionate, and to the displacements of the old materialistic habits of thought.

27

Do not be so rigidly closed in by your practical affairs and personal relations. Open your soul to the admiration of Nature, the high flights of art, and above all, to stillness.

28

His work is to prepare the ground and sow the seed; Nature will do the rest. That is to say, he is to arrange the favourable physical circumstances and the proper psychological concentration in which inspiration can most easily be born.

29

To work diligently for a glimpse of the Overself is to put human energy to its best use.

30

We cannot live in the achievements of other men alone, however inspiring: our business is with ourselves. There is work to be done by ourselves for ourselves.

31

If he blames other men for his troubles, he thereby confesses his egoism. If he blames conditions as being their cause, he confesses his weakness. Every time he points outside himself in complaint he is unconsciously pointing to himself!

32

We must not become obsessed by technique but must learn to grow naturally like a plant, even while we use the technique.

33

Every technique of meditation, every system of metaphysical truth, is but a boat which one should use to cross the turbulent stream of earthly life, not a boat in which one is to sit forever.

34

Each man has to work on himself and leave others alone. To criticize and to condemn them is easy, but it is to fail to mind one's own business. And what is one's own business? It is to work on oneself until one is aware of the divine part of oneself.

35

His task is to discover the presence within himself of a deeper and diviner layer of the mind.

36

More and more man fell into illusion and ignorance as he fell more and more into identification with the body and with the ego. Mentalism tells us that they are really thought-complexes. All thought is derived from the mind. He can begin to undo these identifications if he will bring back his thoughts to their truth and reality and constantly let them stay there. By the activity of the Quest and by the non-activity of allowing truth to work upon him, the illusion will vanish and the real will take over.

37

Trying to develop the higher attributes of his being and the higher qualities of his character is certainly a part of the quest but just as certainly not the whole of it.

38

He is situated in measurable time and in massed form, yet is trying to understand, reach, and identify that which is timeless and formless. How can it be done unless the seeking self is transformed? But that merely removes obstructions: the further proviso is acceptance; let the self be dissolved into That: merger is finally the only way.

39

I have written at times that life was meant to be lived, that philosophy was not a hide-out for vague, shiftless dreamers or an escape for the timid into futility. But some who applauded the words of my protest narrowed their significance. I did not anywhere say that the implied action referred solely to physical living. For the life of man must include adequate attention to his inner mental, emotional, and intuitive self or it will remain incomplete.

40

Bring tomorrow into today by doing that which renders non-existent the unnecessary grief which would otherwise come tomorrow. This is related to, but not identical with, the idea that prevention is better than cure. For it is based on impersonal metaphysical truth which provides a higher philosophical motive, whereas the other is based on personal advantage which provides a lower, merely practical motive.

41

When one is working without a teacher, he must necessarily intensify his efforts. He should strive to develop a greater awareness of the meaning of all past and present experiences in the light of his new knowledge, to be more objective in his observance of himself, his thoughts and actions in every situation, and, finally, to recognize the fact that his own daily life is the material presented him to work on.

42

The aspirant need not feel troubled if he is unable to understand parts of the books written for those following this path. They are extremely hard to grasp and must necessarily take several years to comprehend. The most important task is that of spiritual self-improvement. Intellectual improvement is of secondary importance.

43

The student should continue to read what is within his understanding, realizing that each small advance in his own inner efforts will enable him to understand more that is in the books.

44

Humans ask for meaning, both in their own personal life and in the cosmic existence; but whatever they understand has to be ferreted out wholly by their own efforts. The universal itself remains deaf to their questionings.

45

Each individual has quite enough to do to carry out the higher purpose of life, which is clear and definite: to attain awareness of the Overself, to surrender the heart and will to it utterly, and to overcome the ego— which, in itself, calls for the whole nature of a man or a woman.

46

Everything that helps one to become more aware of the existence of something higher than his personal self, and every experience that induces him to aspire towards a more spiritual way of life should be cultivated. Here, religion, the arts, Nature, and contact with wiser, more experienced individuals than himself, are valuable aids.

47

It is necessary to point out that there is no escape from the price that has to be paid for the highest attainment. It is not by artificially avoiding sleep that the highest state will come. It is only by deliberately avoiding egoism. He has to let the universal life power which is already within him take full possession of his heart and mind. The thing that prevents this is the personal ego, which thinks itself to be complete and which has separated itself from the universal life power. The philosophical discipline is intended to overcome this egoism, or as Jesus said: "Give up your self if you would find it."

48

If he asks himself: What are the ultimate values of human life?—and if he clearly answers this question—he will find himself able to answer most of the immediate questions which concern the strategic policies, tactical details, and practical problems of human life. If he looks to final ends he will know the right means. If he finds out what is the larger purpose behind the smaller ones, it will be immensely easier to know what to do in any given situation when he has to choose between opposite courses.

49

One should not encourage psychic experiences nor attach undue importance to phenomena which are merely incidental to the true search. Instead, one should concentrate on self-study and objective analysis of ordinary experiences.

50

He must study his failures minutely, reflect upon them deeply, and ascertain the causes which led to those lapses. The more he understands them, the less likely is he to repeat them. He should not be downhearted, especially if he is young. There are few who do not make mistakes in youth. It does not so much matter how many mistakes he makes if they spur him on to try even harder and if they encourage him to determine to learn their lessons and root out their causes. Let him remember that he cannot conquer his desires nor subdue his animal nature by his own strength alone. In the final outcome, it is divine Grace which releases him from his bondage. Grace comes only after he himself has made every possible effort, after he has practised sacrificing his desires and has offered up his whole lower nature to the Overself. Until he is freed from the chains of his ego, his strength may fail him in times of need. But when he finally and fully realizes his inadequacies and has done the very best that he knows how, then Grace will appear and assist him.

51

Imitate the fowl. Have a moulting season. Once a year, preferably on your birthday, moult your stupidities, your illusions, and your foolishness.

52

The habit of wasting no time in neurotic self-pity, of squarely accepting one's conditions as largely the fruits of one's own growing, is a necessary part of the Quest's work.

53

To work faithfully day after day to attract a glimpse is not only worthwhile for the sake of its resulting joy and strength but also because it provides an image upon which to mold oneself and by which to correct oneself.

54

To re-create himself by himself alone is hard. He will be better advised to accept the tested counsel offered by cultures of the past and by discriminated wisdom of the present.

55

We must take to heart, and deeply believe, those values and ideals which follow from the announcements made by prophetic men of these higher laws. For the pains of life are quite enough without incurring additional ones by contravening these laws.

56

We have to find, and keep, this link with the divine in actual experience.

57

Not only are attachments to worldly things to be overcome, but also attachments to rules, regulations, spiritual and ascetic disciplines which in time have become obstacles when it is forgotten that they are means not ends.

58

A great distance separates the life of a disciple from the life of the unaspiring, where emotions are involved. To overcome or renounce such personal feelings is really to crucify the ego. Yet only by such crucifixion, whether voluntary or forced, can the serene contentment of the true self be found.

59

If the change of outlook is only a superficial one, then a change of circumstances will sooner or later appear.

60

Observation shows that the attempt to confine spiritual work in self-training to rigid patterns is to deviate from the way a human being is able to develop successfully. All patterns must be adapted and tailor-fitted to the need of each individual aspirant.

61

Those who seek to learn singing as an art, as also speakers who study voice production discover, if they have an enquiring mind, that several different systems and methods exist and that the advocates of each way often commend their own and criticize the others. Systems conflict, methods contradict, teachers disagree. Such a situation prevails also, to a certain extent, in the circles of spiritual and metaphysical theories and training. But most of these doctrines can, again to a certain extent, be reconciled if it is recognized that because human beings are not all alike, the approaches they use to the spiritual goal also need not be alike. Routes may differ, destinations remain the same. The belief that the seeker must restrict himself to a particular named way only, is a narrow one. It oversimplifies the truth at the cost of truth.

62

Intuition, inspiration, and even grace may come directly to him through prayer, meditation, and reading.

63

To increase his personal capacities for undertaking tasks demanded by his environment may be a worthy ambition but is not the primary aim of this work. To move away from such identification with the ego is now to be his purpose.

64

If any path, technique, exercise, or practice arouses his dislike, he need not engage himself in it.

65

Any aspirant who looks to a personal attachment or earthly love for a durable and ultimate happiness will find that sooner or later his illusion will be removed and his mistake corrected by the painful tutorship of experience. If good fortune brings it to him he may enjoy it, but only if he can enjoy it inside his Quest and not outside it. If it separates him from his ideals and lowers his values, then he cannot keep to it and to the Quest too—then in his hour of need it will be lost by him or it will turn from him.

66

He ought to ask as much of himself as he asks for himself from Life. Everything must be paid for. It is a delusion that anything can be had for nothing.

67

Neither the exercises recommended to him nor the disciplines advised for him are to be regarded as being rigid inflexible things. He himself must learn how to adapt them to his particular situation and special circumstances.

68

We need not step outside the house, the rooms, or the tent wherein we live to look for God. They, too, can become a holy place and a sanctuary provided we turn our mind inwards every day for a while and seek that which is beyond all buildings made by human hands.

69

It is true that we have duties and responsibilities where others are concerned; but we also have them where we ourselves are concerned, and the highest duty for each man is to become a man, to fulfil his development, to rule the animal in him by mind, and to find the angel in him through the same medium.

70

One must not take the intellectual approach too seriously. The Quest is really simpler than the books suggest. People pay more attention, perhaps, when there is a little ponderousness in the writing!

71

Frankly, and without shame, he will acknowledge the animal within him. He knows its place in the long growth which he underwent through many an earth-birth. It served its purpose. But a higher purpose has now shown itself and must in its turn be fulfilled. The half-human must next become the fully human. For this, the control of self *must* be learnt, hard though it be.

72

It is an error to believe that the awakening of faith is all he has to do. On the contrary, *it is only a beginning*. One does not get something for nothing.

73

That a man has to work on himself is an easily grasped platitude in all teachings and faiths concerned with his spiritual life. That he has also to work *with* himself is neither so well known nor so comprehensible. It requires intuition both to follow and to use in practice.

Its development

74

The subtler mental equipment must be energized and developed before he can use the subtler ideas of philosophy in the higher stages of this quest. First comes the idea of mentalism. Beyond that comes the idea of simultaneity—that he both is and is not a twofold being.

75

Intellectual definitions of transcendental states merely leave us in the dark. We must practise walking on the divine path, and not merely talk about it, if we would know what these states really are.

76

These studies, coupled with the persistent practice of meditation, bring help and comfort to the mind by showing that life is full of high meaning and lofty purpose.

77

The finest literature on a subject, the best books which one owns yield no advantage if left unread and unstudied.

78

To transfer what we know to what we do, the best way is to *be*.

79

We do not have to bear half the burdens that we carry, if, after we have done the required work upon ourselves that they call for, we will turn them all over to the Overself.

80

The best general attitude is to be mentally positive to the thought-currents that come from outside himself while being mentally passive to the intuitional currents that come from inside.

81

He should make his mind the host to beautiful thoughts and fine moods and thus keep it ready as a place where the soul can enter untroubled.

82

The potency of his thoughts will be upheld by the consecration of his faculties.

83

Your mental attitude tells the story. It will take you up to heights supreme or it will cast you down into a sea of unutterable despair. Whatever you do, fight for the proper mental attitude.

84

There are laws of higher spiritual development, but they reveal themselves only upon their own terms. The first is that he shall apply what he already knows, and not let it rest as mere theory.

85

The truth must then gradually be fixed in your mind, in the words of an old Asiatic sage, "like an iron spike driven into a living tree."

86

He who has done his best to the limit of his possibilities may patiently wait for the time when those possibilities will stretch themselves of their own accord.

87

"Contemplation of reality in a seeker is the best. Study of the scriptures is middling. Worship by means of set prayers is the lower one. And the least helpful is running about places of pilgrimage. The true joy of Brahman does not come through words without real experience, like the taste of the fruit of a tree which is reflected in a glass." —*Maitreya Upanishad*

88

It is his duty to watch that no negative thought slips past his guard and enters his consciousness, no false belief infiltrates into his outlook. Such thought control pays the highest profits, for its effects on his outer life will unfailingly appear.

89

It is important for the study of philosophy and especially for the practice of its Short Path to avoid negative thoughts and feelings, to rebut them as soon and as often as they arise. This is not only a moral necessity but also a practical one. Such avoidance helps the mind to reach or keep the delicate condition of intuitive transcendent understanding.

90

Let us have a joyous spirituality instead of a melancholy one. With such a treasure in our hearts and minds, we have the right to abort the heaviness which is too often associated with religion.

91

However pious a man may be, or however much he withdraws from the world, because of its distractions, into monasticism, if a man still believes that spirit exists, and matter exists, he is practising duality, and is still, in subtle ways, a materialist. The world will cease to disturb him if he looks upon it mentalistically—in the true way.

92

He has found the first traces of truth. But they were in words printed in books, heard in lectures. He has next to find them in himself.

93

If he remains faithful to the practice of these periods of daily reflection upon the Divine Affirmations or the inspired texts or the quest itself or the kind of non-discursive meditation which is really contemplation, he can say with truth that he continually receives his daily bread. Thus the Lord's Prayer has been answered, the Biblical cup which "runneth over" has been filled anew and anew.

94

If words alone could work this miracle of changing men's hearts then Jesus and Buddha would have worked it long ago.

95

There are a certain number of enquiries which the man needs to make. They are: What is the meaning of the Self, the world, God, life, truth, sanity, and health? These are essential if he is to function satisfactorily as human.

96

The reflective study of these books is essential to this Quest. The student needs to become familiar with the mentalist doctrine of the universe, the mystical awareness of his divine Overself, and the metaphysical concept of Mind as the unchanging, underlying Reality. It will not be enough merely to read the books, however. One must cultivate and develop one's own capacity for thinking out the leading ideas here expressed, while deliberately opening oneself and being receptive to them. Such thinking is, in fact, one kind of meditation exercise which may be very profitably practised.

97

A real understanding of the Truth can be developed in only one way, through activity on the intuitive level, as distinguished from efforts made on the intellectual or physical level.

98

If he wishes to get at Reality, he may follow *any* mental discipline that helps him sharpen reason, tranquillize the mind, develop moods of abstraction, and completely concentrate thinking. All the different yogas, religions, and so on are more or less imperfect steps in this direction, so he is at liberty to invent his own. They are all only means, not ends. Parallel with this, he must thoroughly master and make his own by conviction the strange truth that *All is Mind*. This he can get even from the Western philosophy of the school of Idealism. He can study the books of Berkeley and Eddington, the idealistic portions of Schopenhauer, and also good interpreters of Immanuel Kant—as he writes a most unintelligible style. But he should take care to seek only for the proofs of philosophic Idealism in their works, rejecting all their theological and other speculations. In this way he can build a foundation for the higher and more advanced work which must come later. He must think his *own* way to truth, for the aim is to develop insight and not to become a mere metaphysical speculator or bookworm. Once he grasps this, it will not be so difficult to penetrate to the secrets of the ancient sages, for they are all based on this fact: that the world which we sense through the five senses is purely a mental world, that we know only what the mind tells us, that matter is a supposition to account for the solidity and tangibility of our sense-impressions. The mystic and the yogi, when sufficiently advanced, each makes a somewhat similar discovery in his reverie or trance, but he makes it only as a *feeling* and a transient one at that. It is only by thorough reasoning that the permanent understanding of it can be got.

99

Whatever weakens or takes away good judgement is to be avoided; whatever enhances it is to be welcomed. Drugs, alcohol—useful sometimes as a medicine—and rage come into the first category.

100

He should keep the key truths always in his memory and refer to them as often as the time to do so can be taken.

101

Out of such compounded studies, those eager to pursue truth may get a broader outline and more balanced view of it than from traditional and narrower sources. Prejudice and sectarianism will be weakened, too.

102

It is a valuable practice to consider profoundly the basic paradoxes of life—especially the illusion of reality which we all feel, and secondly the inability to express the Truth which the sage alone feels.

103

Emotional aversion and intellectual bias will inevitably and imperiously push him toward a particular view of the facts, a particular arrangement of their importance and weight, and a particular interpretation of inner experiences—unless he has been trained to discipline the ego. In this case, the interferences will be diminished—largely with some and less with others—but they are unlikely to be totally removed.

104

Mysticism is not an easy study for most persons and metaphysics much less so. Prudence suggests taking in the subject a small fragment at a time.

105

The thoughts he takes into his consciousness should be of a kind to carry him farther on his quest of the Perfect.

106

It is better in the end to drop naïve illusions than to go on being deceived by them. It is more prudent to acknowledge realities in time, before they bring on disaster, than to cherish a grandiose but groundless idealism.

107

The Tibetans say that to arrive at the spiritual goal one requires both the eyes of knowledge and the feet of technique. Within the first they include discrimination and intelligence; within the second, self-improvement and meditation.

108

He learns to be completely collected within himself, all his faculties gathered up but without tension. This is possible only because they are held and checked by a higher force.

109

The faculty of memory, rightly used, can incite him to further efforts and sustain them despite discouragement.

110

Philosophy is best understood where it is most practised.

111

The popular myth of the materialistic nature of life must be fought by the private truth of the mystical purpose of life.

112

It is necessary to add the reflections of philosophy to the practices of yoga, if the glimpses of reality received during these practices are to become permanent.

113

The importance and emphasis which is, in the beginning, quite rightly attached to the question *What Am I?* will gradually be shifted to the more encompassing *What is the meaning of this world-experience?* and *What is the object of all existence?*

114

The very perplexities which life breeds in the mind of humanity call forth the effort to solve them. And such effort in its turn develops intuitional and thinking capacity. We are all involuntarily metaphysicians although we do not know it and however much be our antipathy towards metaphysics. Again, by making errors in everyday living we become aware of our own ignorance. By becoming aware of our ignorance, we take the first step to transcending it.

115

If he is practising philosophic reflection regularly, correctly, and coura-geously (for it hits at self-defenses and self-justifications), he will not ordinarily need to fight with his weaknesses and indisciplines. It will often be enough to let them die out as the inner being gradually changes and swallows them by its own power. But such counsel is not intended for those on other paths: for them it would be silly and dangerous.

116

The meditational aspect of the quest, one of its most important parts, is like a spiral: it goes down deeper and deeper, circling all the while, as in advancing from the level of "the world of maya," casting off the illusory, to "the world is Brahman, the Real." Growth accrues with each circulation and further penetration; it is a repetition of the same cycle, but on a deeper level.

117

It is necessary to find the spur within oneself for a better self-control and for a more continuous effort in meditation and the devotional attitude. Outward changes are in the end the result of such inner ones.

118

Those who are not satisfied with a vicarious experience of the Overself, who want their own direct contact with it, must turn to mystical practices.

119

It would be wrong to believe that it is sufficient for the aspirant to join right theory with self-correction and right action to secure the highest result. The fourth item needed to complete his effort is even more impor-tant. It is proper meditation.

120

A life in which there are no placid pauses for meditation is a superficial one.

121

To sit, completely immobile, for a half or three-quarters of an hour while attention and aspiration are concentrated and merged, is an exercise needing much practice if success is to come.

122

Those who shrink from the fatigues of meditation do not often shrink from the fatigues of pleasure. Therefore, a sense of values is the real question involved here.

123

How few Westerners know, how few could believe that stillness itself can make an impact that lingers long in memory?

124

We can discover for ourselves if these statements are true or not by actually leading the inner life. The importance of a little practice of mental quiet each day is high. It is this practice which brings definite results in time and this which gives one strength as well as understanding. Effort is required.

125

From one point of view, the work done on the Quest is simply an uncovering of what is covered up: thoughts, emotions and passions, unceasing extroversion and never-ending egoism lie over the precious diamond, like thick layers of earth. This is why the penetrative action of meditation is so necessary.

5

BALANCE THE PSYCHE

Engage the whole being

What we can do is to prepare favourable conditions for the Light of the Overself's appearance or for the manifestation of its Grace. This is the role and function of mystical technique and is as far as it can go. There is no technique which can guarantee to offer more than such preparation. If it does, it is quackery.

2

The impelling force of an ardent desire for self-improvement must unite with the attracting spell of the Overself's beauty to give him the strength for these labours and disciplines. On the one side, he reflects on the disadvantages of yielding to his faults and weaknesses—on the other, to the benefits of establishing the virtues and qualities of his higher nature.

3

A rich, many-sided personality may still be in the process of accumulating experience and unfolding potentialities. Experience alone is a hard path; it should be backed by reason, intuition, and correct counsel. But reason is useful for truth-finding only when it is detached and impersonal; intuition must be genuine and not camouflaged impulse or wishful-thinking; and correct counsel may be obtained only from the most inspired, and not the merely sophisticated, sources.

4

Whoever wishes to develop beyond the spiritual level of the mass of mankind must begin by changing the normal routine of mankind. He must reflect, pray, and meditate daily. He must scrutinize all his activities by the light of philosophy's values and ethics. He may even have to change his residence, if possible, for serenity of mind and discipline of passion are more easily achievable in a rural village than in an urban city.

5

He has to learn how to surrender his egotism and swallow his pride. He has to cleanse his heart of impurity and then open it to divinity.

6

He should never forget that in his metaphysical studies or mystical practices he is working towards an ultimate goal which lies beyond both metaphysics and mysticism. He is preparing himself to become a philosopher, fitting himself to be granted the Overself's Grace, unfolding passive intuition and critical intelligence only that the transcendental insight may itself be unfolded.

7

The philosophic life is a steadily disciplined, not a severely ascetic one.

8

The aspiration toward the higher self must be formally repeated in daily prayer, cherished in daily retreats, and kept vivid in daily study.

9

So long as man is imperfect in character, defective in intelligence, and mechanical in sense-response to his environment, so long must he seek to improve the first, perfect the second, and liberate the third. And there is no better way to achieve these aims than to pursue a philosophic course of conduct and thought.

10

It is a wise rule of aspiration not to seek for more power than you are able to use or more knowledge than you are willing to apply.

11

The inability to believe in or detect the presence of a divine power in the universe is to be overcome by a threefold process. The first part some people overcome by "hearing" the truth directly uttered by an illumined person or by other people by reading their inspired writings. The second part is to reflect constantly upon the Great Truths. The third part is to introvert the mind in contemplation.(P)

12

Make it a matter of habit, until it becomes a matter of inclination, to be kind, gentle, forgiving, and compassionate. What can you lose? A few things now and then, a little money here and there, an occasional hour or an argument? But see what you can gain! More release from the personal ego, more right to the Overself's grace, more loveliness in the world inside us, and more friends in the world outside us.(P)

13

This Quest cannot be followed to success without the quality of courage. It is needed at the beginning, in the middle, and near the end. It is needed to think for oneself, to act in nonconformity to one's environment, and to obey intuitive leading toward new, unknown, or unfamiliar directions.

14

He must develop emotional maturity, strong character, and a coura-geous attitude toward life. This positive strength is needed to face and master the many different trying situations of existence. The will has to be hardened so that it keeps him from being drowned in the wash of emo-tional reactions. Only after he has done this can he penetrate through to the deeper layer of being where his inner Self dwells. If this is not done in the early stages of growth he will eventually be forced to retrace his steps and learn, consciously and deliberately, the neglected lessons.

15

Because the quest is in part an attempt to raise himself to a higher level of being, he must change his attitude for a time towards those powers of the lower level which would keep him captive there. That is, he must liberate himself from the thraldom of the senses and the tendencies of the intellect. The first he may accomplish by ascetic disciplines, the second by meditative disciplines. The body must be mortified, the emotions purified, and the mind reoriented. He has, in short, to pursue the good with all the ardour and faithfulness that the world reserves for its lesser loves.

16

At least two urgent needs must be attended to. The first is self-awareness and control of our emotional and mental reactions. The second is the same, but in reference to our physical reactions, that is, the way we use our body. In short, we must learn how most efficiently to function both in rest and in activity.

17

By the use of will, of force of a decision made and kept, a man may strive against his animal self to win peace. By the practice of mental quiet, of turning inward, of letting his higher nature emerge, he may win it, too.

18

The mere flexion and extension of the body's muscles may be valuable to the man who wants to display how large and how thick he can develop them, but it is not enough for, and may be mere drudgery to, the man who wants the philosophic attainment. The latter must creatively join breath-ing, thinking, imagining, believing, worshipping, and willing to the physi-cal act and focus them upon it, if he is to gain that attainment.

19

So long as he lacks humour, he may tend to make the quest a heavy burden of disciplines, exercises, duties, and tests only—that is, he may confine it to the Long Path only, and miss its joyous releases, its happy discoveries.

20

There is no point on the Path where a man may cast goodness aside; neither near its beginning, the middle, or the end may he do so.

21

The quality of calmness is to be highly valued, constantly pursued and practised, until it becomes well stabilized. Philosophical knowledge and meditational exercise, plus application to everyday living, bring this prize.

22

After the necessity for self-improvement has been brought home to us, whether by peaceful reflection or painful experience, we begin to cast about for the power to effect it. We see that enthusiasm is not enough, for this having bubbled up may pass away again into lethargy. We need the effort to understand, and to organize our thought to this end as well as the will to apply in action what we learn.

23

He is willing to submit to the restraints imposed by the ideal because he wants the benefits gained by following the ideal, including the benefit of feeling that he is doing what is right. He submits cheerfully without regarding the restraint as being oppressive.

24

Life is grey enough without being made greyer by sacrificing the little colourful pleasures which art can bring to it or the little cheering comforts which invention can contribute to it.

25

Aesthetical starvation and emotional purity are not convertible terms.

26

Wisdom is needed to make the most of life. The discipline of character is needed to prevent avoidable suffering. The control of thought is needed to attain peace. Reverence for the highest is needed for spiritual fulfilment.

27

The man who takes his body for himself, misunderstands himself. Only a course of severe discipline will correct it and reveal to him by intense experience the power subtler than flesh, subtler even than intellect, which is at the vital centre deep within consciousness.

28

At first he will find within himself only a tiny spark of divinity. He will next have to strive to kindle this spark into a flame.

29

The aspiration has gotten into his bloodstream and every act, every thought follows inevitably from this one primal fact.

30

"The question of attainment depends only, in the last resort, on the thirst of the soul," Swami Vivekananda once told an aspirant.

31

It is true that the aspiration for Overself is also a desire and must eventually also go. But it is useful and helpful in getting free from lesser or lower desires.

32

The means needed for the quest have been listed in Buddha's eightfold path: (1) right belief, (2) right decision, (3) right words, (4) right dealings, (5) right livelihood, (6) right tendency, (7) right thinking, (8) right meditative immersion into oneself.

33

The student has to unfold a wider sense. He must begin to see the whole of which he forms a part, which means he must become more philosophical. His physical existence depends on the services of others, from the parents who rear him, the wife who mates him, the customer who buys his goods or services, the farmer who grows his food, the soldier who guards his country, to the undertaker who buries his body. No man can forever isolate himself from the rest of mankind. In some way or other, for one essential need or another, he will come to depend on it. The shoes he wears or the food he eats were prepared for him by somebody else. Thus he is mysteriously chained to his human kith and kin. Thus he is forced to learn the lesson of unity and compassion.

34

It must become something as central to his life as eating, as necessary as breathing, and as welcome as great music.

35

According to the Pali Buddhist texts, the three main requisites to be cultivated for enlightenment are Understanding, Concentration, and Right Conduct. These correspond to the Mahayana requisites of Wisdom, Meditation, and Morality.

36

The aspirant has such a task to perform that he must needs husband his strength for it. He must keep his fingers lithe and nimble for his starry work, untrammelled by the behests of other taskmasters.

37

Attentive study, faithful practice of the exercises given in my books, and the re-education of character and conduct along positive lines will help to prepare him for glimpses of enlightenment.

38

We must direct all our desire along this channel of a high aspiration, as the artilleryman directs all the force of an explosive within the steel wall of a gun, concentrating it into conquering potency.

39

He is not only to *seek* the Real, but he is also to *love* the Real; not only to make it the subject of his constant thoughts but also the object of his devoted worship.

40

It is the shortest step in humility that we can take to admit that we are all *en route*, and leave it to others to talk of final attainments. In an infinite realm of nature, the possibilities are also infinite.

41

When we feel the littleness of our ego against the greatness of our Overself, we become humble. Therefore it is that to those who feel neither the one nor the other, the first prescription is: cultivate humility.

42

Those who cannot or will not learn to bow their heads in reverence at certain times like sunsets, in certain places like massive mountains, or before certain men like sages, will not be able to learn the highest wisdom.

43

The refinement and evolution of a human being requires not only a cultivation of his intellectual faculties, not only of his heart qualities, but also of his aesthetic faculties. All should be trained together at the same time. A love of the beautiful in nature and art, in sunsets and pictures, in flowers and music, lifts him nearer the ideal of perfection.

44

There is a difference between aspiration and ambition as they are to be understood on this quest. The two easily get confused with one another. Aspiration tries not to surrender to the ego's tyranny whereas ambition directly strengthens it. I do not refer here to a young man's ambition to make a career for himself. That is another matter and ought to be encouraged.

45

It is right to go beyond admiration and honourable to rise up to veneration in a place where Nature gives us great beauty, or at a truth of being which redeems life from chaos and meaninglessness, or in finding a book which comes with a welcome opportune message at the right moment, and finally with a work of true art testifying to the noble, creative, or unworldly inspiration behind it.

46

It may not be an axiom in many teachings, but it is in philosophy: to purify emotion, to refine feeling, to control attitude, and to uplift mood by accepting help from art and nature *are* spiritual exercises.

47

This faculty of discrimination, called *buddhi* in the Sanskrit *Bhagavad Gita* and *chih* in the Chinese Confucian classics, is to be developed not only by studies and reflections but also by experiences of life: it is to be applied in observations, decisions, and actions. It is at first a rational faculty but later, on a higher level, is transfused with intuition.

48

The universal rule of all true spiritual teachers which calls for him to purify himself means simply that he shall remove the hindrances to clear awareness of his Overself. The passions are merely one group of these hindrances: there are several others and different kinds.

49

The man who is devoid of the eight qualities which practice of the Long Path eventually develops in him will not be able to succeed in practising the Short Path. These qualities are calmness, self-control, oriental withdrawal, fortitude, faith, constant recollection, intense yearning for the Overself, and keen discrimination between the transient and the eternal.

50

The attempt to use Spirit for personal ends cannot succeed, but the willingness to be used by it can be realized.

51

The recognition of one's limitations, together with voluntary annihilation of self-will at the feet of the Overself, are indispensable prerequisites on the part of the entire ego before the experience of Reality can transpire.

52

The aspirant who has to undergo deep changes and to learn how to humble himself must remember that this is for his own ultimate benefit. All experience of this kind is intended to promote spiritual growth.

53

The attitude of expectancy and hope in the matter of seeking illumination is a correct one. But the hour when this Grace will be bestowed is unpredictable; therefore, hope must be balanced with patience, and expectancy with perseverance. Meanwhile, there is all the work one can handle in attending to the improvement of character and understanding, the cultivation of intuition and practice of meditation, the prayers for Grace, and in self-humbling beneath the Will of the Overself.

54

In this study it is needful to maintain a discriminative attitude in every matter—then help and instruction can be obtained from all kinds of unexpected sources. Such an approach, however, should not be confused with mere credulity since this would delay progress.

55

Until the time his karma brings him the indwelling Master, the seeker must continue to prepare for what will then happen. He must seek to uncover and uproot all faults and characteristic weaknesses. He must resolve to achieve the best life—that is, one that exemplifies truth, goodness, and beauty. He must understand well the proper values to be attached to worldly matters and to spiritual ones. He must face the difficulties of everyday life with courage and with the knowledge gleaned from his study.

56

He must climb out of the dark pit of emotional resentment and self-pity into which the blows of life throw him. He should extirpate all the human and pardonable weakness which made him unhappy. He should be big-hearted and generous towards the failings of others who, he feels, have wronged him. It is a grand chance to make a quick spurt in his spiritual progress if he could change from the conventional emotional reaction to the philosophic and calmer one, if he could rise at one bound above what Rupert Brooke called "the long littleness of life." He should not continue to bear resentment against those who have wronged him, nor to brood over what they have done; let him forget the mean, the sordid, and the wicked things other people do and remember the great, the noble, and the virtuous things that he seeks to do. Follow Jesus' example and cheerfully forgive, even unto seventy times seven. By his act of forgiveness to them, he will be forgiven himself for the wrongs he also has done. In their pardon lies his own. This is the law. In this way he demonstrates that he is able to leap swiftly from the present self-centered standpoint to a higher one, and he deals the personal ego a single paralysing blow. This is without doubt one of the hardest efforts anybody can be called upon to make. But the consequences will heal the wounds of memory and mitigate the pains of adversity.

57

In a certain type of person the most important factor in the inner life is the cultivation of the harder qualities like will, decision, execution, endurance, determination, energy, and the like.

58

He must work hard at eliminating the faults in his character. Even though he may yearn for the Overself, he may actually stand in the way of his own light. If the ego is strong in him, he must try to learn from others the humility, devotion, and unselfishness which are so admirable and necessary. He should not be afraid to go down on his knees in prayer and confession, for pride, vanity, egotism, and self-assertion must be broken. Even if he has very good qualities he must forget these and concentrate on the eradication of his faults, to perfect himself as much as possible. Character is what counts in every sphere.

59

Ultimately he will have to rise into that pure atmosphere whence he can survey his personal life as a thing apart. And, still more difficult as it is, he will have to live in such a way as to use personality to express the wisdom and goodness felt on that height. The second part of this program is almost beyond human strength to achieve. Therefore he has first to establish the connection with the Overself so that its strength and understanding will then rule him without requiring any effort on his part. The moment of this event is unpredictable. It depends on the Divine Grace. However, if he sticks to the Quest, its arrival is sure. After that, Fate readjusts his external circumstances in what may seem to be a miraculous manner and life becomes more satisfying.

60

At last he finds that he must become as a little child and re-acquire faith. But this time it will not be blind faith; it will be intelligent. He must free himself from the pride, arrogance, and conceit of the intellect and bow in homage before the eternal Mystery; there is much that he can learn about himself, his mind, the laws of living, and the ways of Nature. Nothing is to be rejected. He needs to believe as well as to know. In the end, too, he has to drop all the "isms," however much he may have got from them in the past, and think, feel, and live as a free being.

61

His personal duty is to grow spiritually all he can as quickly as possible. He must concentrate on himself, but always keep at the back of his mind the idea that one day he will be fit to serve others and do something for them too. Spiritual growth entails meditation practices kept up as regularly as possible, metaphysical study, cultivation of intuition, and a kindling of an ever increasing love for the divine soul, the true "I." It is this soul which is the ray of God reflected in him and it is as near to God as anyone can ever get. God is too great, too infinite, ever to be completely comprehended; but the Overself, which is God's representative here, can be comprehended. Only it keeps itself back until he yearns for it as ardently as the most love-sick young man ever yearned for his sweetheart. It wants him to want it for its own sake, and because he has seen through all the material values and understands how imperfect they are in comparison. So he must cultivate this heartfelt love towards what is his innermost "me" and must not hesitate to pray for its Grace or even to weep for it. He must surrender inwardly and secretly all the ego's desires to it.

62

It is through heartfelt prayer and aspiration to become one with his own higher self that the student will eventually open the way for the further guidance he needs.

63

It is absolutely essential for seekers on this Quest to avoid becoming sidetracked by psychism and occultism and their devotees—and to place their faith and aspiration in the transcendental purity of the divine Overself alone.

64

The fact that one may not have had any apparent mystical experience, even though he has tried practising concentration, need not dismay him. Concentration alone is not enough. It is no less important to practise prayer and aspiration, unremitting effort at improving character and eliminating weaknesses, strengthening the will and purifying the emotions. If he applies faithful and persistent effort in these directions, he will not only cultivate a properly balanced and well-developed personality, but he will eventually call forth the Grace and Guidance of the Overself.

65

Intensified aspiration for the Way, Itself, rather than too much concern about the steps that lead along It, will act as a propulsive force.

66

Those who feel they lack the strength to restrain their emotional ego may vicariously, if momentarily, find it by immersing themselves in the creations, literary or artistic, of others who do have it.

67

In what way and by what means can a man discover the truth? By an aspiration active enough and intelligent enough to penetrate both mysticism and philosophy while saturating itself in reverence.

68

Counsel to a seeker: *First* hear or study, reflect and understand what you, the world, and God are. *Then* enter the Stillness, love it. The Stillness will take care of you, and of your problems.

69

There are two stages: (a) effort, and (b) cessation of effort while waiting for Grace. Without guilt and without the use of willpower, he watches his weaknesses and desires as a mere spectator. This nondualistic attitude, which refuses to separate body from soul, is metaphysically correct; but he must place within, and subordinate to, this larger acceptance the minimum disciplines and controls and exercises. Thus the latter are modified and their harsh, rigid, or mechanical character is eliminated. The teaching of acceptance is given by Krishnamurti, but it is not balanced by the disciplines; it is too extreme, it is not complete. The balanced philosophic approach eliminates the dualism of body and soul, so criticized by Krishnamurti, yet makes a proper limited use of asceticism.

70

The Quest uses the whole of one's being, and when enlightenment comes, all parts are illumined by it. To prepare for this, one should continue the self-humbling prayers for Grace, the exercise of sudden remembrance of the Overself, the surrender of the lower nature to the Higher, and the never-ceasing yearning for Reality.

71

It is not only character, capacities, faculties, and intelligence that are to be developed by mankind in the course of centuries as concerns his inner nature but also refinement. This is an attribute which he expresses chiefly through aesthetic feeling and artistic sensitivity yet also through speech, manner, dress, and behaviour. It betokens his quality and lifts him from a lower caste (by *inward* measure) to a higher one.

72

He must try to remain noble even in an ignoble environment, philosophical in an ignorant one.

73

Not infrequently a student asks, "Has anyone ever been in my position? How can I arrive at awareness of the Truth?" The Teacher could reply that he himself has been in many such positions. What he did was to ardently and prayerfully seek Truth through the fivefold path of religious veneration, mystical meditation, rational reflection, and moral and physical reeducation. There is, however, a certain destiny always at work in these matters.

74

It is necessary to explore, find, and face his problems before he can resolve them. This will require a ruthless impersonality and a maturity of experience which not many possess. Therefore, it is here that the wholesome books and the advice of friends may be sought.

75

Our human nature is so pitifully limited and imperfect that only its most rigorous discipline will bring the infinite and perfect enlightenment into consciousness without spoiling it in some way.

76

He needs a humbleness like that of the grass which is trodden by all feet, a patience like that of the tree which is exposed to all weathers.

77

The ego must aspire before the soul can reveal.

78

It is a work upon himself, his character and outlook, his knowledge and capacity. But especially is it a work upon his faculty of attention, his control of thought, his delicate awareness.

79

Enframed and conditioned as they are by the suggestions and influences from various outside sources, the first duty is to find liberation from them.

80

It is easy to express the wish to become an instrument in the hands of the Divine but hard to become one in actuality. Countless pious persons say countless times, "Thy will be done," but they seldom do it. They are not to blame, however. For they are ignorant of the fact that *before* their words can get any real meaning, they themselves must pass through a discipline, a preparation, a self-development, and a balancing-up.

81

Self-study and self-observation, a constant effort toward developing awareness, and a truly objective analysis of past and present experiences in the light of one's highest aspirations, will eventually lead one to the discovery of the Undivided Self; whilst meditation, accompanied by an intensified attitude of faith and devotion, will lead to deeper understanding of, and communion with, this Goal of Goals.

82

These ideas will have to become not merely his beliefs but his very life, will have to govern not merely his head but his deepest heart. He must live in them as naturally and continuously as he breathes in the air.

83

We are living in wonderfully momentous times and it is the task of those on the Path to become bearers of the light in a dark age. But first, before that can be, each one must purify, ennoble, and instruct himself. He must fit himself for the divine grace because nothing can be done by his own personal power.

84

Though you may be the greatest of sinners, do not be afraid to take up yoga. It is not for the good alone, it is for all alike. Take up this practice, give a little time to it regularly, and you will begin to see your sins gradually disappear. It will happen naturally, automatically. Did not Socrates somewhere say that "knowledge is virtue"? And we can guess that his favourite precept was "Man Know Thyself."

85

The sincere attempt to live out our highest intimations even among the most mundane of environments is essential if we are not to lose ourselves in a sea of vague sophistication. No metaphysical study, no pondering upon the fascinating laws of mind, no ambiguous wandering with a candle in the dark recesses of psychical life can ever atone for the lack of Right Action. We may harbour the loveliest dreams but we must turn them into realities by effort.

86

Some means of testing his faith and character, his ideas and motives, his values and goals must be found. Life itself provides that means.

87

The idea that being practical means being dead to all sacred feelings and holy intuitions is another error to be exposed. Everywhere men of affairs and achievement, both celebrated and obscure, have kept their inward being sensitive and alive amidst their earthly labours and worldly successes.

88

If daily work is accompanied by daily remembrance, and if detachment from the ego is practised along with both, this goal can be attained by a worldling as much as by a world-renouncer.

89

These teachings have first to become known, then understood, next accepted, and lastly made a part of day-to-day living.

90

Another excellent practice is to begin each day with some particular quality of the ideal in view. It is to be incorporated in the prayers and meditations and casual reflections of that day. A special effort is to be made to bring all deeds to conform to it.

91

Day by day and hour by hour it must be practised, must be brought into personal living. For it is not to be treated as something abnormal and unnatural or set esoterically apart.

92

He should ask of each day what it has yielded in this lifelong struggle for the realization of higher values.

93

Time may bring him more perception, experience may bring him more knowledge, but he will gain inner strength only as he uses his opportunities aright.

94

He need not torment himself trying to understand everything in the teaching, if he finds many parts too difficult. It is enough to start with what he can understand and apply that to daily living. This will lead later to increased intuitive capacity to receive such ideas as he had to pass by for the time being.

95

Those who do not feel ready, or inclined, to fulfil the disciplinary requirements and follow the meditational practices of the Quest, can still benefit in a practical way by using its ethical principles in daily life.

96

In the spiritualization of active life, through the deeds that come from him and the events that come to him, he has one effectual method of self-development. For a valuable part of the quest's technique is to treat each major experience as a means of lifting himself to a higher level. All depends not on the particular nature of the experience, but upon his reaction to it. It may be pleasurable or painful, a temptation or a tribulation, a caress by fortune or a blow of fate; whatever its nature he can use it to *grow*. As he moves from experience to experience, he may move from strength to strength. If he uses each situation aright—studying it analytically and impersonally, supplicating the higher self for help if the experience is in the form of temptation, or for wisdom if it is in the form of tribulation—his progress is assured. Thus action itself can be converted into a technique of self-purification instead of becoming, as so many monastics think it inevitably must become, a channel of self-pollution.

97

There is great profit in the coinage of spiritual self-growth waiting to be picked up at every turn. The method is a simple one. Consider every person who makes an impact on your life as a messenger from the Overself, every happening which leaves its mark as a divinely-sent teacher.

98

We must endeavour to find this divinity within, not merely at set times of meditation, but also amid the press of the marketplaces.

99

Learn how to live the teaching out in the midst of the world, yes! with all the temptations and trials; to shun cloistered virtues which, because they are untested, may not be virtues at all; to stay amongst suffering ignorant men who need enlightenment and not to leave them to rot in their darkness; to face the difficulties of worldly life as brave students of philosophy and not as cowardly weaklings; to be too big-hearted and tolerant, too broad-minded and intelligent to separate yourselves; in short, to follow Jesus' advice and be in the world yet not of it.

100

We must bring our philosophy to the test not only in the exalted stratosphere of inspired moods but also in the prosaic flatness of daily life.

101

Since most of us have to live in the world as laymen, or even prefer to do so, we must learn how to make use of the world so that it will promote our spiritual aspirations and not obstruct them.

102

What the poet or artist conceives is within himself, but what he creates is outside himself. Similarly, what the Quester conceives is within himself, but what he creates is the actual life that he creates in the world outside himself.

103

The beginner needs knowledge, needs to attend lectures, study books, discuss ideas, and even debate the criticism of them. But the man who has done all that needs to move on, to get into the testing ground where teachings and values must prove themselves—that is, into life itself.

104

To accept a high ideal during emotional enthusiasm is one thing; to live up to its guidance during the everyday routine life is another.

105

It is not easy, this living of two different lives at one and the same time, yet it is not impossible. The common everyday existence is not so unrelated that it cannot coexist with the uncommon mystical existence.

106

If his common activities are carried on against a background of philosophical endeavour, they will themselves tend to become in time a part of this endeavour.

107

It is necessary to strive increasingly for practicality and some measure of self-reliance in worldly life. This is not something separate or apart from the search for the higher self. On the contrary, whatever Truth is found and whatever changes are brought about in one's being should be reflected in one's participation in every activity and relationship, whether it be in the work done as the individual's share of world-labour or in his necessary ability to get along with others—not only with those of similar interests and understanding, but with all humanity.

108

Progress can be made not only in Egypt or India but anywhere. No matter who or where he is, each individual's own character, together with its participation in daily life, is the material presented to him for self-study and self-observation. An analysis of these experiences, both past and present, when carried on in the light of his highest aspirations and in his search for awareness of and attentiveness to God, will open the way to guidance from the Higher Self.

109

"The time of happiness does not differ with me from the time of prayer, and in the noise and clutter of my kitchen I possess God in as great tranquillity as if I were on my knees," said Brother Lawrence as he went about his work in the monastery kitchen. This is the reward—or rather part of the reward—which philosophy holds before us. It is worth striving for. And the *Gita* tells us that no efforts are in vain; all bring their fruit sometime, somewhere—if not in this birth then in another, if not in this world then in the next. For the man or woman busy with his bit in the world's work, the Quest must be carried on in the midst of activity. He must not let the difficulties which arise inevitably out of such work cause him to abate his trust in the divine laws. These should be his safeguard, his dependence, his armour, and his weapons.

110

It is sometimes asked whether it is better to retain a detached attitude in one's relations with others during the day, or to cultivate and concentrate on a feeling of unity with them and with the All. Since both are necessary, one should follow his inner promptings as to which phase needs to be developed at any particular time. By keeping his approach flexible, and by carefully heeding these inner promptings, his judgement of and dealings with all daily situations will be greatly improved. Such promptings— when free of and not influenced by selfish desires—will shift of their own accord when the need for balance arises.

111

He may call himself a follower of philosophy only when it has become a part of his daily life.

112

His mind having captured these ideas and his heart being captured by them, the next step is to apply them in daily living.

113

Do your duty to the best of your ability, but preserve mental equilibrium at the results, whether the latter be success or failure. This is karma yoga.

114

Until we learn to regard our environment and our contacts as means of rising spiritually, we remain on the materialistic level and do not get as much out of life as we could.

115

The student's "firsthand experience" is his daily life. This opportunity should be used, and through it will come a deepened and more complete understanding of what has been gained from intellectual knowledge.

116

Once his understanding is sufficiently mature and once he is achieving the correct results in meditation, the aspirant's progress will be assured and rapid. Before this stage is reached, however, his immediate need is to bring into his everyday life whatever fruits he has so far gathered from his studies. Spiritual growth, like physical growth, is a series of separate growing moments. Just as the child cannot become an adult overnight, illumination, too, is a long, slow process. The aspirant must actually and literally begin to *live* what he has already learnt; otherwise, he is unwittingly holding himself back, and limiting Reality to the realm of mere theory.

Cultivate balance

117

But if he overdoes the recognition of life's transiency he may upset the delicate balance needed in his self-training for attainment of the goal. For, thus overdone, it will turn into manic depressiveness and pathological melancholia, into groundless fears and hopeless worries. The remark of Emerson that the strength of the spirit is expressed in its joy is useful here.

118

Few beginners feel the need to keep their balance. Consequently most beginners have a chaotic inner life. It is well looked after in one or two aspects but neglected in others.

119

When a scientist like Darwin confesses that he was utterly impervious to poetry and another like Freud that he lacked any feeling for music, we must conclude that they are one-sided in their development, that is, unbalanced.

120

If the struggle for holiness becomes desperate, if the probing into his spiritual state becomes constant, then the effort is excessive and unbalanced.

121

Unfortunately, his virtues will throw dark shadows if they are not balanced by reason and restraint. Enthusiasm will be trailed by rashness and faith by superstition.

122

If we misapply the right or overdo the good, we may create new foolishness and fresh wrongs. If, for example, we remain patiently inactive when it is time to effect a positive change, then we fall into the sin of indolence.

123

Unbalance can take the form of an indomitable determination to attain the goal coupled with an equally indomitable determination to follow foolish procedures.

124

Whoever, in his ill-instructed ignorance, says that the physical, the intellectual, and the aesthetic are irrelevant to the quest of spiritual fulfilment or, in his fanatical bias, says they are even obstructive to it, merely shows up the incompleteness of his experience and the imbalance of his being.

125

One side of his character will respond less quickly than another. His development will be uneven and unequal.

126

When the will is feebler than the imagination, the life loses its balance.

127

Self-discipline must be balanced or it will become needless torment, fanatic self-injury.

128

To promote his idealistic tendencies and to neglect his realistic ones, to achieve a high level of intellectuality and to remain at a low level of morality, to be over-critical of others and under-critical of oneself—these are types of unbalance which he should adjust as soon as possible.

129

He may have difficulty in the world in generating the necessary ambition for pushing ahead with the business side of life. However, the strain and pain of his efforts will pass away eventually whereas the fruits in developed faculties and increased balance will remain as permanent possessions. He must stick to the task of rebuilding his personality on a more solid basis. He must take as his symbol the Great Pyramid with its huge square base but narrow pointed apex signifying that the broader and bigger the personality the more inspired the service that can be accomplished through it. For there is an invisible inverted pyramid resting on the visible one. This other unseen pyramid stretches away and can stretch away into infinity without limit whereas the lower visible pyramid can proceed no further than the earth's surface.

130

The very nature of man as a psycho-physical organism with spiritual possibilities and animal actualities, compels him to attend at some time or other to all his sides. No amount of denying or ignoring any one of them will succeed in the end, any more than exaggerating or over-emphasizing some other side will escape Nature's eventual attempt to correct the unbalance and regain equilibrium.

131

The ideal is the fullness and harmony of balanced qualities, wasting none, denying none: the active will companioned by the mystical intuition, the pleasure-loving senses steadied by the truth-loving reason.

132

Do not lose your sense of proportion and assume that your actions are going to make any difference to the Witness, the Overself which always remains unaffected.

133

Somewhere between undisciplined sensuality and uncontrolled asceticism there is the way of sanity.

134

Philosophy teaches that both aversion from, and attraction to, the world are to be avoided if the fine balance of mind needed to perceive truth is to be attained.

135

If on the one hand he ought not try to turn philosophy into sectarian dominated theology but keep it rigorously upon the wide bases of experience-supported Reason, critical judgement, and balanced synthesis, on the other hand he ought not desert the precinct of holiness: daily he should seek a reverent atmosphere and become suffused with divine feeling.

136

Only to be a scientist or an artist is not enough, just as only to be a very ordinary person is not enough: a fuller human being is life's silent, ever-pressing demand.

137

The ability to make this research successfully without ascending to the clouds and getting lost in them, is as necessary as the sensitivity which keeps itself alive, alert, and unsubmerged within the world-experience.

138

Balance cannot be separated from proportion.

139

We have to find our way between the optimist to whom life is a joyous dance and the pessimist to whom it is a sad dirge.

140

Risk and caution should pair each other, if he is not to be one-sided.

141

Goodness must be tempered by intelligence, for instance. How many misguided persons assiduously cultivate an inferiority complex under the misapprehension that they are cultivating a selfless character!

142

The Quest must become obsessive without becoming unbalancing.

143

Whatever faculty, quality, function, or aspect he is deficient in, he should seek to cultivate it. Whatever is present to excess, he should seek to curb or modify it. Harmony, Balance, and Completeness characterize the idea.

144

He must meet the demands of his whole psyche if he is to have the proper equipment with which to find the whole truth.

145

We must punctuate our philosophy with the periods and commas of action, or it will become somewhat stale.

146

There are different principles of man's being. Each has to be developed and equilibrated. Only after this is done can the energies of the Overself flow into them and thus transform them into expressions of itself.

147

The safeguard of balance prevents any single aspect of his development and any single function of his psyche from being cast for the role of supreme domination.

148

The virtue of balance is neither easily nor quickly bought, but its cost is repaid by the values it yields—greater security, more endurance, less error, and better progress.

149

"Sensible" and "balanced" are convertible terms.

150

He will have to bring into a fine balance the refusal to be satisfied with the man he is or the way he lives and the acceptance of life generally.

151

Without this proper balance, he may easily mistake being sentimental for being compassionate.

152

This need of balance may show itself in a hundred different ways. Where kindness compulsively overrules judgement, for instance, there may be a price to pay. And where kindness keeps beggars in self-chosen or socially enforced idleness, it may harm them, whereas where it finds and fits them for useful work, it must surely help them.

153

He has to train himself to catch what the soul intuits as clearly as he can already catch what the intellect thinks and the body reports.

154

Be and behave grown-up, not childishly. Understand something of yourself, your character, your strengths and weaknesses. Find and keep a balance, a common-sense, and a sanity. Value good health, good diet, good manners. Develop yourself, your talents, your knowledge, your calm.

155

If he himself is a quietist, temperamentally suited only to the studious and meditative pursuits, then he needs activists around to balance and compensate him.

156

Whenever he observes too much one-sidedness in his being or living, he must attend to its balance and make needed adjustments.

157

A sound protective balance must be held between the pressure of these different tendencies. It must be slowly learnt by experience as well as considered reflectively in the mind.

158

Balance is needed in all ways on this quest. The student must not overvalue his emotional experiences, nor overconcentrate upon his meta-physical studies. He must strive for poise in all things and at all times. To lose it is to lose that integrality of character which is the mark of the true philosopher. The mournful consequences which follow are apparent in the fantastic cults which pass for mysticism, as well as in the fantastic movements which distort modern art; they can be seen also in the dry barren field of academic metaphysics as well as in the ugly earth-tied materialism of utilitarian science.

159

The ideal of Balance keeps us from falling into dangerous extremes. The self-controls which follow detachment are meritorious but its lengthening into callousness is not.

160

The Sanskrit word for inner Balance is *samadham*, that poise which is maintained in all kinds of circumstances. By constantly thinking about the falsity of the ego and its phantom-like nature, it can be sublimated and its power divinely directed.

161

If intensity is achieved but other qualities neglected, then this very virtue may turn into fanaticism and balance lost. The Quest is a way of balanced thought and living, not a mania to unhinge the mind and disorder the emotions.

162

We exist on more levels than one, from the grossly physical to the finely ethereal. We have to take care of our body, of our vital force, our emotions and thoughts because we have to live with them and use them.

163

In the well-formed and well-informed aspirant the activities of both paths will be subtly blended. This is part of what is meant when it is said that he is properly balanced. And out of this union will come the "second birth," the new man who reflects at last the glorious consciousness of the Overself.

164

Even when one's deep sincerity and earnest aspiration are beyond question, and even though one may have already travelled fast and far in certain directions, this may not be enough to attain enlightenment. All sides of the psyche—including some previously neglected—must be evenly balanced and developed in order to lead one to a full and lasting illumination of the whole.

165

Energy and drive in action, calm and patience in meditation—this is the combination he ought to achieve.

166

To get this strength and gain this wisdom, he must paradoxically follow two opposed courses. First, he must retire wholly from all activities every day and contemplate them analytically as well as impersonally. Second, he must plunge into and use those activities as springboards whence to rise to higher levels. Hence, it is said that neither meditation nor action is enough. Both are necessary to him and to one another. The first inspires and aspires, the second expresses and tests.

167

Man wants certain things from life, but life itself wants certain things from him. It wants proper treatment of his body, it wants knowledge and understanding in his mind.

168

It is essential to keep a certain minimum balance in life and nature when thrusting forward to develop or improve on both; otherwise the over-doing will bring new evils and upset both.

169

Because we refute authoritarianism this does not mean we are to jump with the unbalanced into intuition and deny all value to the past, to books, and to the teachings of other men. Life would be empty indeed if each of us had to start his quest afresh without the help of great authors like Sankara. Because we deny that material inventions can alone give man happiness, we are not therefore to follow the fanatic and flee into asceticism.

170

Salvation does not depend on any one factor but on a balanced total of several factors. The devotional temperament is not enough. The disciplined will is not enough. The moral virtues are not enough. The trained intellect is not enough.

171

Aspiration and wisdom-knowledge are "the two wings which help the soul in the course of its spiritual flight" or as Professor Hiriyanna used to say to me "knowledge without devotion is as futile as devotion without knowledge."

172

The thoughts in the brain and the feelings in the heart need to be together; each side of his nature contributes to make a man what he is. Both are necessary to a full development. Why ignore or, worse, reject one or the other?

173

An equilibrium of mind and heart must be established, the deliverances of both must be respected and reconciled.

174

A well-balanced personality requires that he should be not less a sharp thorough observer, with feet kept well on the ground, than a rapt absorbed meditator.

175

No man is freed from the necessity of developing his thinking capacities merely because he is developing his mystical ones. The reverse is just as true. Nature is not satisfied if he is a good mystic but a bad thinker.

176

His intellect needs to understand what are the real facts of his situation, while his moral nature needs to be willing to fulfil the sacrificial and disciplinary demands made.

177

The goodness which must come into his willing is not separate nor separable from the truth which must come into his thinking.

178

One part of his being may yield obediently to the philosophic discipline but other parts may not. His thoughts may surrender but his feeling or his will may not. So struggle there must be until the ego's surrender is total and complete.

179

Although the emotions will provide driving force to secure action in giving up bad habits, for instance, the co-operation of the reason and the will is needed to secure lasting results.

180

Intuition leads the way in the philosophic quest and reason follows it; faith, feeling, and will are then obedient to, and balanced by, reason.

181

The wise student understands that the pattern of human existence is too complex to be drawn by any single straight-line movement. Therefore he will strike a balance between his feelings and his reasonings, between his mental life and his active life. He knows it is always foolish and sometimes dangerous to overdo the one and underdo the other. For the contradictions and disharmonies which are thus set up, the disproportion between aims and means, will hinder progress and harm experience.

182

If he seeks truth with his whole being, then it must enter into his whole being. Hence, if through inborn disposition he felt his way with the emotions toward it in the past, rather than knew it with the understanding, he will one day become aware of the need of adding an intellectual basis to his life. That which leads him into this awareness is his own higher self.

183

We have referred often to the need of balance but not so often to its importance. Yet this can be plainly seen from the picture of a broken- or clipped-winged bird trying to fly on its sound wing alone. It flutters round and round in the air, always returning to the starting point, to its own confusion. This is a picture of a creature without physical balance; a person without psychic balance, which follows completeness of development, whirls about just as vainly in his intellectual, emotional, and active life.

184

The more intellectual a man is, the more does he need to bring a devotional element into the studies and practices.

185

It helps to attain a measure of emotional balance, calmness and detachment if, in the midst of bright fortune, you remember the time of dark despair.

186

All influences, contacts, persons, or places which destroy our balance are to be shunned as undesirable, if not evil.

187

The ability to reason accurately must be balanced by the ability to live according to one's findings.

188

He may have studied under mystical teachers, lived in monastic ashrams, and wandered in mountain caves in former reincarnations gaining much bliss by the practice of meditation. That is why he may feel such a strong hankering for these things during the present incarnation. But the rhythm of progress has put him into a Western body and given him family life in order to develop another necessary phase of character and thus make him better balanced. Mysticism is only one side of life and a most estimable one, but life itself is many-sided. The true Quest must lead to a development of all these sides. Nothing narrower than this ideal will suffice. Any attempt to escape in the wrong way from the path which karma has outlined for him can only end in disappointment and disillusionment. However there is a way of escape from hard, external conditions and that is by fully learning their lessons, by mastering the problems of practical, everyday living, by developing intelligence and reasoning power, and by remembering to keep the mental picture of a fuller life of disinterested service ever before him.

189

A certain hardness of character in some students is not altogether a defect as there is no particular virtue in being soft. The world being what it is today a little toughness acts as a protective shield. The defect lies only in pushing this to extremes and in not balancing it appropriately with its opposite. For such persons, there is the need of evolving a gentler side of the character and the result will eventually be all to the good in a finer, better balanced personality.

190

Hard thinking is just as necessary on this path as gentle submission to delicate moods of mental stillness. Both are required.

191

A well-developed critical intellect in combination with over-concentration produces an exceptionally strong ego. Such a person should cultivate a little more humility so as to improve the natural balance of his personality. He must humble the ego. He should do this himself, secretly, and through calm, reflective meditation; then life will not do it to him openly and through bitter external circumstances.

192

It is one function of experience through action to correct our mistakes in thinking, as it is a different function of thinking to correct our mistakes in action.

193

Right feeling should accompany right thinking, right willing should complement right intuition.

194

So long as man lives in a fleshly body he is the compound of animal, human, and angelic beings. Nature does not permit him to destroy any one of these three parts of his personality. What she does require of him is to make the animal subject to the human and the human again subject to the angelic.

195

Evolution is working along three lines in the human being: the intellectual, the mystical, and the moral-physical. All must be attended to. Hence it is not enough to develop any single part of one's being alone. The threefold path is what philosophy asks for although religion, science, or mysticism is usually satisfied with a single path. Meditation is the most important of all as without it one cannot transcend the intellect, but it is not enough by itself. He has to practise meditation, cultivate knowledge, and shape conduct aright—all these being directed towards the quest of the Overself. The combination of all three will yield results far in advance of those which a separate development could yield.

196

Many a yogi will criticize this threefold path to realization. He will say meditation alone will be enough. He will deprecate the necessity of knowing metaphysics and ridicule the call to inspired action. But to show that I am introducing no new-fangled notion of my own here, it may be pointed out that in Buddhism there is a recognized triple discipline of attainment, consisting of (1) *dhyana* (meditation practice), (2) *prajna* (higher understanding), (3) *sila* (self-denying conduct).(P)

197

The quest is integral—a combined approach through formal meditation and study, analytic observation, reflection, moral endeavour, religious devotion, and constant self-recollection.

198

The objection is made that to engage in the total approach—*hatha*, *bhakti*, *raja*, and *gnana* yogas—is too large a program for any man outside an ashram, too impossible in the case of the average man in the world. Who, after the work of his business or livelihood, has the requisite energy for its study or practice? Who, with a family—wife and children—has the requisite time? My answer is: True! But you can do a little of each yoga. Make the best of the situation and thus tempt the Grace of the Overself to ease the situation.

199

He must not only do so far as he can all that the Long Path demands from him but he must also step outside it altogether and do those totally different things that the Short Path demands.

200

Three subjects of study: the natures of man, the universe, God. Three duties are owed: to yourself, to other living creatures—human and animal—to God.

201

The aspirant need not confine himself to any single approach, leaving out all the others. His greatest success lies in using and balancing the different techniques.

202

But finding the higher presence within the heart is only the first step. The next is to surrender oneself to it, to be passive in its hands, to let it direct the course of thought, feeling, and conduct. This is a task which is not less hard, and will take not less time, than the first one. It is indeed an art to be learnt by unremitting practice.

203

It is better nowadays to pursue the different paths side by side, whilst placing special emphasis on one of them.

204

The philosophic life accepts, combines, and follows all these four dictates: The Christian self-giving, the Roman-Stoic self-control, the Grecian self-balancing, and the Hindu self-knowledge.

205

The balance does not have to be exact.

206

He ought not to restrict himself to a single approach. His nature as a human being has different areas, each of which needs to be worked on. The body needs cleansing, the feelings need uplifting, the thoughts need calming. Especially in the contemporary individual the critical analytic intellect needs turning away from its destructive tendency and directing constructively, first, to discriminate truth from error, reality from appearance and, second, to discern the ego and its working, as well as its education by experience.

207

Each has its place and one need not be decried in favour of the others: homage and devotion to a guru, study and practice of the teaching. For from the first one gains inspiration and from the second, understanding and capability.

208

All this work upon the different sides of oneself does not have to be done by turns, for each does not exclude the others. One will benefit more by doing it at one time, even though it will be probably necessary to stress the work on a hitherto neglected side.

209

The Quest has two aspects. One is the constant accumulation of right thoughts, feelings, and acts, along with the constant elimination of wrong ones. The other aspect called the Short Path is the constant remembrance and contemplation of the Overself.

210

He should not discard meditation before he has completely mastered it. Yet, the balanced threefold path should be followed and not merely meditation alone. Otherwise mental and emotional defects will be magnified. Moreover the times in which we live today make practical service necessary.

211

The two processes, of on the one hand developing and on the other balancing his faculties, have to be carried on and perfected together so far as possible. The qualification is added because it is rarely possible to do so completely. Human nature being what it is, development inevitably tends to move in one-sided phases.

212

Here again the delicate balance of things which the total Quest demands must be brought into play. It is not only the long-drawn-out labour of the Long Path which must engage him, but also the continuous and fresh attempt to follow it in what he thinks, feels, and does here in this *very place*, *and now* at this very moment.

SELF-REFLECTION AND ACTION

Be objective

If he can bring himself to desert his habitual standpoint and begin to think as a sage thinks, his battle will be over bloodlessly. But if he cannot do so, cannot let go so abruptly of his old egoisms and animalisms, then there will be a long struggle, with its attendant wounds and inescapable sufferings.

2

The disciple should be ever alert to profit by his experience and, especially, to note where his own attitudes create his own ills. This profit will come to him only if he looks at the experience with ego-free eyes.

3

His aim being the contrary of most people's aims, he tries to depersonalize his attitudes and reactions. What relief he feels with even partial freedom from the burden of self-consciousness. How heavy a load is borne by those who see, sense, or react with ego-centered nervousness.

4

The inner work requires him to strive deliberately to keep on entering—and re-entering after each lapse—a state of awareness of what thoughts he is holding and what emotions he is feeling; and if any correction is called for to make it instantly. The work is to be continued until correct thinking has become habitual and settled.

5

At off intervals during the day, he is to pull himself up abruptly and note the nature and character of his thoughts. Then he is to ask himself *why* he is holding them or *what* is impelling him towards them. The purificatory worth of this practice is great. It gives him the chance to become aware of negatives and throw them out, but best of all it trains him in detachment. From this exercise he is to go on to its sequel, which applies the same attitude towards what the body's senses tell him and also towards what his emotions and passions make him feel.

6

In the end, the Quest becomes an effort to separate himself from his lower principles, to disown his lower nature, and to repudiate his lower self. He must consider the task a lifelong one, and therefore guard against premature complacency by making repeated self-scrutiny with humility and abasement.

7

As he studies his present life so impersonally, the past also comes back to him. He will then find himself more interested in its errors and failures than in its virtues and successes. He will search for, and try to recognize, the point of departure where, in such negative experiences, he first went wrong.

8

Unless you word your replies to criticisms carefully, cautiously, restrainedly, mildly, and with dignity, you will create violent and intolerant reactions, for few seek truth and most seek partisan opinions. You must demonstrate by the calm, dignified, temperate, and fair character of utterance, by its freedom from bitterness, that you have attained a higher level than those whom you criticize.

9

The philosophic aspirant must test the truth or falsity of the phenomena which present themselves as he advances, of the teachings he hears and the intuitions he receives and, especially, of the moral ideals involved in every situation. He should not take for granted his ability to distinguish true from false, right from wrong, whether in the inner or outer life. The safeguard of such a test is needed because he is, mentally and emotionally, so tangled up with his personal self that his experiences themselves are so interfered with, his interpretations of them so altered by the ego, that their correctness needs to be examined.

10

It is the earnest aspirant's duty to accept criticism. Provided it is not rendered in a spirit of personal malice, he should humbly, unemotionally, and impersonally seek to learn therefrom.

11

He will have to learn the art of standing aside from himself, of observing his actions and analysing his motives as though they belonged to some other person. He may cease to practise this art only when his actions reflect the calm wisdom of the Overself and when his motives reflect its detached impersonality.

12

Once the past is properly, impersonally, understood; once the logic of its consequences is traced; once the implication of all this is practically applied, especially in self-discipline: let it go.

13

He needs to recognize his strengths as well as his weaknesses, so as to have a fairer view of himself. He need not paint too sombre a picture.

14

It is hard for the civilized man to know what are his true instincts and what his false ones. What seems true may be merely what is habitual to him, what he is accustomed to. So he must get this knowledge from a revelation—either an external or an internal one.

15

Only he who is willing to regard himself entirely without partiality and his critics entirely without prejudice can hope for any success in this Quest.

16

We must learn to see more clearly, to separate our real needs from our fancied ones. Take a single example. Our real need is to be emotionally secure. Our fancied need is possession of or association with a particular person through whom we believe such security can be had. This person may be a marital mate or a spiritual master.

17

If he is to save himself he will need a relentless honesty about, and toward, himself. He must be uncompromising in getting at true appraisals of his motives, his actions, and his feelings.

18

Through attending to the deepest inner promptings that come to one in moments of relaxed calm, one may get valuable pointers toward the best direction of any needed changes or adjustments in his worldly life.

19

Take all criticism graciously, even smilingly. This means you are neither upset by it nor indifferent to it, but that you take it to heart to learn humbly, coolly, and impersonally whatever is true in it.

20

"Straight is the way and narrow the gate thereof," said Jesus. The Hindu *Upanishads*, the sacred and formerly secret works containing some of the highest wisdom of India, have a similar phrase: "The path which is as narrow as the edge of a razor." What do these words mean? They do not tell of a path to moral perfection, however desirable it may be to be morally perfect. No! the way they speak of is the Ultimate Path which demands from us utter and complete rectitude of thought and feeling. Every movement made in the heart and mind must be completely straight, undeflected, and undistorted. The mental activity must be true in every sense of the word. Life must become one-pointed, perfectly concentrated, moving always in a straight line. When ideas are warped by prejudices, or distorted by preconceptions, or clouded by illusions, or inflamed by excitements, then the movement of the mind is not straight but wavering from side to side. It may even turn round and move backwards. We inevitably approach life with a predetermined outlook which has gradually developed from the many influences played upon us since childhood. Rare indeed is the man who is immune to them. This bias tends to overload with personal feeling all judgement, and to raise selfish emotion to the status of a test of truth.

21

As if his own new negative creations plus the inheritance of older karmic carry-overs were not enough troubles for him, he has also to endure the buffetings of other persons' negative thoughts, feelings, and speech about him.

22

The obstacles which he has put in his own path can be removed by no one but himself.

23

It will be hard to ferret out the blunders into which his own egoism will lead him, for it will deceive itself as it will deceive him, by using the guises of virtuous feeling or logical thinking. His supposedly selfless motives may be, in reality, other than what they seem. His superficially sound reasoning may be an attempt on the part of his ego to retain its hold upon him by plausible self-justification.

24

Difficulties are always within the skull. Unless you can conquer them in there, you will never conquer them outside.

25

Some denigrate their own power by accepting the truth of mentalism but denying the possibility of realizing it in experience. For them the sages prescribed the study of texts, the thinking out for themselves of their deep meaning, and deep meditation. This done, the obstacles are removed and the way is opened for intuition to transcend intellect and lead the aspirants into Overself. It presupposes that they have earlier purified character and strengthened concentration.

26

If a person desirous of following this path has troubles and difficulties, which assuredly most of us have, he must learn to apply mental discipline to himself in dealing with these conditions. There are those who have a tendency to magnify fears unreasonably, and to throw themselves un-necessarily and unjustifiably into moods of acute anxiety or emotional disturbance. Such people must learn to apply their philosophy to the difficulties they are having and try to rise high above them, serenely and calmly, by refusing to worry and by turning them over in full faith to God. Isn't this the test of faith? They must show by the way they refuse to be drawn into merely personal attitudes towards these problems and by the way in which they instantly commit them to God and His powerful care that they have an appreciation of this teaching and seek to apply it. They must also overcome the habit of seeking, every time a difficulty crops up, advice from the mystics whose teachings and writings they strive to follow—or else they will rob themselves of true self-reliance. It is impossi-ble for the advanced mystic to undertake intervention in all such personal matters as that is really outside his province. Usually the way in which he gives help is general, not particular, impersonal and not personal, and it is through a prayer whose result spreads over long periods rather than through day-to-day separate thoughts. It is easy for the ego to mis-translate the help it receives, so these people must be careful to watch out for that.

27

As Tze Ya Tze wrote: "To hesitate when the occasion presents itself is to hinder Tao."

28

Those who limit themselves to the practice of meditation as the sole means of finding the spiritual self and who believe that this alone is sufficient, who never show signs of giving attention to the ennoblement of character or to magnanimous, generous, and compassionate aims, will not find the spiritual self but only a dull quiescence of feeling, a blank empti-ness of mind, that have no real lasting value since they will crumble away when meeting the hard struggles of worldly life.

29

The hidden resentments have to be unveiled, the open mental barricades have to be raised.

30

Concepts and procedures which served him on the Quest in the past—ideas symbols names and forms which helped him then—have become rigidly fixed in his mind and he himself has become so attached to them as to be dependent upon them. He has lost openness of mind and become dogmatic, the victim of his own jargon. Thus the very things which were of service to him are no longer so and, in fact, constitute barriers stopping his further progress towards the true freedom.

Apply the will

31

The right creative use of faith and will, exercise and effort can work wonders in leading us out of the enslavement, the blindness, and the ignorance of the lower nature back to the enlightenment, the freedom, and the wisdom of the higher self.

32

Practice is the first requisite. Day after day one must dig into one's mind. One cannot learn swimming from a printed book alone, nor can one learn to know the Overself merely by reading about it.

33

Few are willing to undergo discipline and deliberately reform themselves. Yet, some method of attainment is necessary, some exercises of the inner life must be followed, otherwise there will be inertia and stagnation. The resolute practice of some spiritual technique brings inner energy into everyday living.

34

If a man is to arrive somewhere on this Quest, he must gain his own respect by being strong, must have a firm mind and support his words by his will.

35

His spiritual fervour is not to consume itself in futile emotional sputters that end in the air nor waste itself in frothy sentimentalities that are shut-eyed to realities. If he finds himself strong in feeling but weak in action, he should take it as a sure sign that the will has to be exercised more, the body hardened and disciplined.

36

Only he who has taken one can know the value of a vow to help him struggle through inner conflicts of will against desire. The dedicated life can become also the fortified life, if a man swears solemnly to hold it to a specific discipline.

37

But men cannot master themselves solely by willpower. It can give them so much control and no more.

38

The cultivation of power must begin with the will, which must be used to impede desire and govern passion.

39

It is for him to determine how his thoughts and feelings are to be shaped, and how his forces are to be used. This calls for acts of the will to follow choices of the will.

40

At first he has to use his will to break away from undesirable or negative feelings, to move his consciousness out of them. But first he must recognize them for what they are, then he must react against them swiftly.

41

Anyone who pursued the Quest with the same zeal with which everyone pursues earthly things, would soon come within sight of its goal.

42

There is a weapon which we can place in our hands that will render us independent of external patronage and make us master of circumstance's ebb and flow. This is the power of persistent will.

43

Aspiration must express itself in action. The weak are forever wishing, but the strong take the plunge and act. There are three kinds of people in the world: the Wills, the Won'ts and the Can'ts. The first achieve everything, the second oppose everything, and the third are failures. Which will you be?

44

To make the result dependent on grace alone would be to deny the existence and power of the universal law of recompense. The need of effort can only be ignored by those who fail to see that it plays an indispensable part in all evolution, from the lowly physical to the lofty spiritual.

45

If we were static beings fixed and chained by Nature, nothing would be worth the effort of trying. But we are not. We are dynamic centres of intelligence. Most of us revolve at low speeds. All of us could revolve more quickly. Some of us could even revolve at high speeds. For we can will ourselves into anything. In the silence of our heart we must will that this thing be accomplished, and lo, it is. "I will" carries man onward and upward, and defeat only spurs to further endeavour.

46

We have to demonstrate by our lives and to exemplify in our attitudes not only the truth of the ideas which rule our minds, but also the inherent power of these ideas.

47

The iron strength of his purpose will shield him from temptations, the intense force of his loyalty to the truth will carry him through obstacles and barriers. He is astonished to find how easily the man who knows what he wants can conquer his way to it, if his will is able to go straight to its mark.

48

To enter into the inmost part of his being calls for a terrific struggle, a terrific strength, and a terrific concentration. All his powers need to be called to the task. They must therefore be brought up out of latency and developed to a sufficient degree before the inward journey can even be started, if it is to have any likelihood of success at all. Such development requires systematic working on himself and cannot be left to merely chance and random spontaneity.

49

The power to commune with the Overself is within us all, but most do not trouble to exert themselves in the nurture and cultivation of it. Hence they do not possess it in actuality.

50

The quest is a deliberate attempt to shorten the passage from life in the underself to life in the Overself. Therefore it involves a constant discipline of actions, feelings, thoughts, and words.

51

There is no room for spiritual lethargy and personal laziness in the philosophical aspirant's life. First he will labour incessantly at the improvement of himself; when this has been accomplished, he will labour incessantly at the improvement of others.

52

If some men succeed spiritually because they are destined to, most men do because they are determined to.

53

Form a plan of life and carry it out.

54

He has to oppose his own preferences when they stand in the way of progress. He has to drive himself to do what he fears to do.

55

Nothing is more fortifying to the will than to do something every day along the lines of a declared intention to which all habit and environment are opposed.

56

They must stir some strength into their wills. But if they were unwilling to do this, then it were better to wait and let evolution perform its slow process of education. Suffering and loss would not be absent from this process, but they would be spread out over longer periods and hence spread thinner.

57

To take up the practice every day afresh requires a certain strength of will, a certain stubbornness of purpose, and a certain appreciation of its worth. Few have this staying power.

58

Eckhart: "Sloth often makes men eager to get free from work and set to contemplation, but no virtue is to be trusted until it has been put into practice."

59

It is true here as in other fields that study of the history and theory of mysticism will never be a satisfying substitute for practice of the exercises of mysticism.

60

Philosophy uses sacrifice and discipline to train the practical will. For we are not only to hear its voice but also to obey it.

61

To believe that such a great task can be achieved without personal effort and self-control is merely to deceive themselves. It is to deny the biblical statement that only what they sow can they reap.

62

This is a work which calls for the interaction of two powers—man's will and Overself's grace. The will's work is to engage in some measure of self-discipline, and yet to surrender itself entirely at the proper moment.

63

If the fruits of philosophy are not to be plucked in the gutter and the tap-room, neither are they to be found in the dry leaves of printed books: they can be gathered only by those who attempt to live it.

64

Each man must want and will his own entry to communion with the higher power.

65

"IF . . ." is usually the symbol of failure, but "I can . . ." and "I will . . ." are powerful mottos that are always the sign of the success-bound.

66

"No man can serve two masters," said Jesus. Thus he rejected all indecision of will.

67

We must lay siege to our own soul. If the fort of mind is attacked with dogged determination, the victory is promised us. But the siege must be maintained until the day the gates open.

68

Ideas are born and die within our brains. Lofty thoughts and magnificent schemes for self-regeneration swim before our eyes like some new tortures of Tantalus. Yet we are unable to back them up in action. Our desperate need is the vital will necessary to give our ideas concrete expression in external life.

69

To all those students who complain of inability to get correct guidance on the problems and confusion in their worldly lives, answer: This is because they are not practising what they have studied. They are not applying the philosophy. They allow negative moods, emotions, and thoughts to take possession—instead of firmly exercising their will to resist beginnings and crush the danger in the bud. They want the guidance without having prepared the conditions which make guidance possible. If aspirants do not try to deny themselves in certain ways, they remain unprepared and therefore unfit for illumination. They must firmly resolve to lift themselves above the level of blind animal impulse or mere inert drifting. Otherwise, what is the difference between them and the multitude of ordinary folk who do not even know there is a Quest? This quest is not for weaklings. Let such go back to popular religion. It is only for those who are ready to be steeled in will and shorn of self-pity. Real aspirants show they are such because they do not weary in their efforts and remain uninfluenced by the setbacks and difficulties that they meet with on the way. There is good hope for a man no matter how much of a beginner he is, but only if he is eager to see his mistakes, if he is his own harshest critic, and if he puts forth a continuous and persistent effort to amend his life.

7

DISCIPLINE DESIRES

Renunciation

To deny himself is to refuse to accept himself as he is at present. It is to become keenly aware that he is spiritually blind, deaf, and dumb and to be intensely eager to gain sight, hearing, and speech. It is to realize that nearly all men complacently mistake this inner paralysis for active existence. It is restlessly to seek the higher state, the nobler character, a more concentrated mind: it is to be willing to withdraw from all that accumulation of memories and desires which ordinarily constitute the ego.

2

The heart should be kept free. For that, too, is a desire that binds, a longing that torments, like all longings, unnecessarily. Being bound brings disappointment, brings pain. Renounce the *desire* to live in any particular place, as you have renounced other cherished desires. Then happiness will not depend on its satisfaction. Nor will inner peace be lost at its nonrealization.

3

Disgust with life, recognition of the futility of all human exertions, is one common precondition of inwardly turning away from the world. The aspirant who feels this dies to the world and consequently to the personal self which was active in that world. After that, he is attracted only to that which is deep within him—to the utter Void of the Overself.

4

With simpler homes and fewer pleasures, with physical bonds and emotional attachments reduced to a minimum, it is easier for a man to fortify his life and cultivate his soul. When he denies satisfaction to his various desires, he eventually exhausts the desire to live itself. With this sterility the cycle of reincarnation comes to an end and the peace of Nirvana is his.

5

Professor T.M.P. Mahadevan said: "The truest Renunciation is to renounce belief in the world's reality." P.B.'s comment on above: This is the interpretation of Shankara given most commonly. Perhaps by altering the word "reality" to "materiality" we may help the Western mind.

6

This is not the fierce, tough, ruthless, forcible use of the personal will to gain some desired worldly thing or position, but the calm, mental-emotional letting go of captivity to it.

7

A single revolutionary act of renunciation rooting out the ego will take care of all the lesser ones. That done, they will adjust themselves in time. Some things he will not be required to give up.

8

It is not always and absolutely essential to remove from one's existence any thing, person, or habit to become detached from it. What is essential is to keep it at a distance emotionally.

9

The ideal may require sacrifice, in its name, of possession, love, ambition, desire. But unless he be a monk, this purifying experience may be an internal one. He may stay in the world yet not be of it.

10

If the inner reality of holiness or renunciation is missing, then the wearing of priestly robes or yogic loincloth merely camouflages hypocrisy and hides humbug.

11

If, on the inward journey from ego to Overself, a man has to give up everything, on the outward journey he may pick up everything again. If he has to become a little child in order to enter the kingdom of heaven, he will return from that kingdom and become a man again, yet without losing all that was worthy in the childlike faith. Whatever the aspirant has sacrificed for the sake of finding God, God may restore to him afterwards.

12

The theory of detachment may seem cold and heartless if applied to human relationships also, and its practice positively cruel. Yet life itself enforces it upon us in the end. There is no avoidance.

13

In the elderly man, desires are gradually outlived and dropped, ambitions begin to come to a natural death. But in the philosophic man they pass through the same process through his own deliberate choice and at an earlier age.

14

The man who embraces philosophy is not called upon to renounce the pleasures and comforts of this world, but he is called upon to re-evaluate his time, discipline his body, and train his will. This is not done out of a harsh and narrow austerity but in the need and name of the body's health and the will's strength.

15

Prince Rama wanted to withdraw from his position, title, duties, and family in pursuit of God. But the wise Vashistha, the great teacher of Mentalism, asked him: "Is He apart from the world that you wish to renounce it?"

16

Whether we acquire or renounce possessions is not really the main point. Renunciation is a dramatic and symbolic gesture whereby a man announces his change of course. No longer satisfied with worldly life, he will seek the kingdom of heaven in his heart. The physical manifestation will depend on circumstances, situation, family, country, and outer or inner guidance.

17

It is an inner emptiness gained by casting out desires and attachments, habits and tendencies, so that the heart is wide open to receive life's greatest gift—Grace. The craving to acquire personal possessions is a hard thing to still but once done we are rewarded a hundredfold.

18

It cannot be bought cheaply. Relinquishments of distracting activity must be made, disciplines must be brought in, the work on oneself must be done, the hands which want to hold others unclasped and solitude embraced.

19

It is not enough to renounce something by excluding it from your physical life. You ought also to exclude it from memory and imagination.

20

There comes a time when he has to turn his back on the past, for the old man is becoming a stranger and a new man is coming to birth. Memories would obstruct this process.

21

First let go of attachment, then let go of the ego itself. First let go of all things—physical and mental, all creatures, all that is past—in the end nothing is really yours. This inner separation, this detachment, is the true freedom.

22

The counsel about not being attached to results was never intended to mean being blind to results. It means that we should rise emotionally above them; it does not mean that we should not study their nature and take appropriate action accordingly. If we are to be blown emotionally hither and thither by favourable and unfavourable results, it will never be possible to attain any peace. On the other hand, if we are not to use our critical judgement about people in situations, we cannot deal successfully with the world.

23

It is better to realize that transiency is in the very nature of things. Man constantly deludes himself with the hope that some transient possession will become a permanent one. It never does, and the self-deception merely robs him of a peace he might otherwise keep. And this is true whether he wants to possess another human being or another hundred dollars, whether he wants to chain someone's love to himself or to chain more things to his home. Hence the student who is oppressed by the rapidity with which his years are waning away will seek all the more intensely and aspire all the more earnestly for that which is itself eternal and above the years.

24

We have come into incarnation for a purpose: life is our business here, not running away from it. When certain renunciations are called for, they are part of this preparation for life, because they are needed in the fulfilment of this purpose.

25

He who claims to have renounced the world and to own nothing must then beg, accept, or take from other people the things he needs to survive—food, clothes, shelter, and so on. While he has these things he is back in the world again, making use of it, in some kind of relationship with it.

26

This inner detachment from the world comes but slowly, so deep are the roots of desire. The young who value freedom to the point of rejecting home, parents, family, society, education, and tradition should enquire more deeply into what freedom is.

27

A double work goes on: the man slowly withdraws from the things which hold him, which make him theirs, while his higher aspirations attract the higher self to slowly take over the place in his heart which they filled.

28

He will discover that renouncing the world is only a stage on the way, that renouncing oneself is an even longer and much more austere stage.

29

If we are called by the Quest to give up everything for a time or for all time it is only that we may receive something infinitely better in exchange. The Quest calls us to renunciation of earthly desires not to make us miserable but to make us happy.

30

How to translate these philosophic ideas and spiritual ideals into terms of actual life is our problem. Here is the answer, from an Indian text: "One who relinquishes the fruit of action, is from the spiritual point of view, a true Sanyassi," says the *Gita*. This is plain enough. "One who remains unaffected by the fruit of action done in discharge of duty, is *not* entangled in the meshes of births and rebirths by such action!"

31

There is much confusion about this reiterated counsel to practise self-surrender, to give up the ego, and to become unselfish. Its primary meaning is not that we are at once to run out in the street and transfer all our possessions to other men. Indeed, it is not concerned with society at all. It is that we are to effect in consciousness a displacement of the lower by the higher self. Such a displacement cannot happen so long as there is any inner resistance on the ego's part. Hence the counsel warns us to avoid such resistance, encourages us to offer the ego willingly as a sacrifice to the Overself, stimulates us to let go of the animal and human complexes which retard the consummation of such a sacrifice. Each struggle passed through successfully builds up our higher will.

32

He finds in the end that he does not need to divorce himself from ordinary civilized society except for periodical and, perhaps, short daily retreats; that the work to which he is called is, primarily, an inner one; that the only asceticism he is called to is a simple self-mastery gotten in either the worldly order or the monastic order; and that his spiritual quest is in the end a personal, not an institutional, one.

33

Perhaps most people find it easier to graduate their renunciations but some find the oppositive way of drastic renunciation the simplest solution.

34

He may keep his likes and preferences, his attachments, if he must, but he should be prepared to drop them at the shortest notice.

35

Whatever purifying renunciations and ascetic disciplines are to be effected should be effected naturally, inevitably, and without strain from within.

36

"One is not to be called a renunciate for having merely given up his possessions. Unattached at heart even though attached in outward show, standing aloof from the world, having broken all his bonds, and regarding friend and foe equally, such a man, O king, is to be regarded as emancipate." —*The Mahabharata*

37

If he really wants to renounce them by doing without them, he ought to do without some of the things he *loves*. Only then will he understand the Oriental phrase, "God only is rich."

38

It is not by becoming a pauper that one demonstrates spirituality, as so many yogis think, or by becoming well-to-do, as so many "Right Thinkers" and Christian Scientists think.

39

The mind's detachment from the world will bring the body into line with it in time: this takes longer than the ascetic's way of forcibly imposing rigid renunciations, but it is more natural and less harsh—easier and philosophic. It softens the rigour of inescapable controls. What is more important, perhaps, is that it works in a deeper ground, so its result is more durable than the other way.

Asceticism

40

He may have to adopt a penitential way of living for a time, purificatory and reformative. It may even be required for several years. But fanatical extremes and foolish self-torments are not required.

41

He who is owned by things and no longer owns them should turn to asceticism and practise the virtue of renunciation. But he who is so enamoured of asceticism that he shrinks from comfort and shudders at the sight of pleasure should turn away from renunciation. Balance is required.

42

The drastic means used by some forms of asceticism are not suited to nor willingly accepted by most modern seekers. It is preferable to lead them by gentler and more gradual means.

43

How is he to achieve this inner freedom? Should the method include outer acts? Should he make the Herculean gesture of parting with all his possessions? Should he embrace voluntary poverty like a monk and henceforth live without receiving any regular income and consequently without paying any further income tax? This ascetic idea of not being fettered by any external thing is good as far as it goes. But it fails to take note of the fact that one may be just as fettered by an internal thought. The ascetic gives up the vices and allurements of the world in order to become free, renounces earthly desires and futilities in order to become happy, shuns pleasures because he associates them with guilt. But if he has not grasped the truth of mentalism, if he does not comprehend that thought is the next battlefield, he remains as tied as before, albeit by new chains.

44

His feet will have to tread the painful path of asceticism for a while. But whether it will be for a short or a long while, whether the pain will be little or great, whether the asceticism will be slight or extreme, will depend on the circumstances of each individual case.

45

This search for the road to God has been turned by many in the past into an impoverishment of human existence, a denial of human joy. Yet if the greatest rapture exists in the finding of God, why should the way to it be so cloudy and gloomy?

46

Have these men found peace in their world-rejecting hearts, won harmony in their womanless lives?

47

The logic of Buddhist asceticism is as relentless as it is comfortless.

48

Even Muhammed could not stop the arisal of ascetic ideas and practices, however plainly he banned them.

49

Science justifies itself insofar as it helps to make life on this planet more bearable and more pleasant. We are here to live. Fools make the rigours of renunciation the end of living.

50

Ascetic regimes, just like other spiritual practices, may become a source of spiritual pride. It is needful for him to watch out for the subtle desire to indulge them as glorifications of the ego. Instead, the proper desire is to submit to them as steps to the true consciousness.

51

Those who can only learn self-discipline by leading the restricted life of asceticism may do so. The wise, however, will rule themselves by reason—which is not something one suddenly calls up for the first time in one's life, but is the matured fruit of a gradually growing habit of thinking.

52

If we need not follow an extreme asceticism, we must obey a moral discipline that seeks to purify thought, feeling, and conduct. If we are not asked to become martyrs and heroes in the battle against lower impulses and calculating worldliness, we are called to the battle itself.

53

Ascetic panegyrics on the simple life find their logical conclusion in grinding poverty and utter destitution.

54

The notion that a woman cannot have a husband, bear children, and wear fine dresses if she wants to and still enter the kingdom of heaven, is as stupid as it is barbaric. Yet this is the constricted teaching which is propagated in the name of "higher" spirituality. But its proponents are usually monks themselves, men who, having found what suits the taste, temperament, or circumstances of their particular personality, would proceed to impose such taste on all mankind by raising it to the dignity of a universal law. My plaint against ascetics therefore is that they turn their very limitations into vaunted virtues.

55

It is to the extent that a desire stands in the way of pursuing this quest that it is to be negated, but only to this extent. This means that a total asceticism is usually unnecessary as it is often undesirable.

56

The true place of asceticism is at the beginning and in the middle of this quest, when a man becomes conscious of his weakness of will and slavery to sensuousness. In order to strengthen the one and neutralize the other, it is a part of yoga to practise hard austerity and painful self-denial. But this is done only for a time; it is a means not an end, a path to detachment and deliverance but not a goal for human life.

57

The practice of a wise and philosophic asceticism enables him to separate himself from a widespread illusion—identification with the body. When its self-denials are directed against fleshly appetites, passions, and desires for the purpose of compelling them to submit to intuition and reason, greater health for the body and greater truth for the mind are secured.

58

An intelligent asceticism is proper, even praiseworthy, for certain periods at certain times. It gives a man power over himself, his body, his passions, his appetites. It disciplines whereas the mad asceticism merely destroys.

59

The asceticism has its place, just like the Long Path, of which it is a component, but when it is stressed to an unnatural point, fanaticism is born, equilibrium is lost, and tolerance is destroyed.

60

A proper asceticism is concerned with the curbing of desire, the practice of self-denial, the overcoming of weaknesses, and the control of body, mind, and speech.

61

Proper asceticism ought to be not a torment or a punishment, but a purifier; it gets rid of bad habits and clears the way for good ones. It trains feeling, disciplines body, prepares a temple for "the Holy Ghost."

/ 62

The stringent rules of some monastic institutions may discipline the body and defy its senses, but the consequences may show in a harsher character and a colder heart.

63

Gautama found that imposing harsh denials on the body, ascetic pains and rigorous torments, gave certain valuable fruits—such as strengthening of the will—but did not give enlightenment.

64

But this said, it must also be said that philosophical mysticism does not desire to nullify our human joys with a lugubrious and somber asceticism. There is an unfortunate tendency among ordinary mystics to become so enthused about the way of asceticism as to regard it not as it should be, that is, only as a means to an end, but as a complete end in itself. The original purpose of ascetic discipline was fourfold: First, the victory of mind over body as a preliminary to the victory of mind over itself. This involved taming passions and disciplining appetites. Second, the solar plexus, the spinal nerve ganglions, and the brain nerve-centres were not only recharged with essential life-force but both the cerebro-spinal and sympathetic nervous systems were stopped from obstructing, and made to promote, the new and high ideals implanted in the subconscious mind by the conscious one. Third, the stimulation of the pituitary and pineal glands. Fourth, to straighten and strengthen the spinal column. This gave a clear unhindered path for and helped to evoke the currents of a mystically illuminating force fully evoked by special meditation exercises. Asceticism was like a remedy taken to cure a sickness. But in their unbalanced reaction against worldly life, its followers turned it into a permanent way of life. Medicine is most valuable as medicine, but not as food. Because quinine has cured someone of fever, he does not incorporate it in his diet for the remainder of his lifetime. Yet this is just what most ascetics did. They succumbed to intolerant manias with fanatical exaggeration and without understood purpose, and thus lost the balance of their psyche.

Clearly, the way of sanity lies between the two extremes of self-indulgent worldliness and of body-crushing mortification. Philosophy highly values asceticism when used with adequate reason, when sane, temperate, and balanced. It knows how necessary such a regime is to cleanse the body of poisonous toxins and keep it strong and healthy. But it despises the unnecessary misery and useless struggles with which the ordinary ascetic obsesses himself. It sympathizes with the modern seeker when he is not as attracted by the rigours of a forbidding asceticism as his medieval forebear was. It respects, indeed includes and advocates, an occasional and limited asceticism, but it rejects a permanent and excessive asceticism. It very definitely makes use of abstinence at a certain stage of the aspirant's career but then only as far as necessary, and for a limited time, and with the knowledge got from experience. It certainly bids its votary to practise some austerities, submit to some disciplines, but not to make a fetish of them, to use them only so far and so long as they are helpful to achieve self-mastery and bodily health and thus treat them as means, not ends. Lastly, it affirms that self-restraint and sense-discipline are always necessary, even though harsh asceticism is not.

The limitation of a merely physical asceticism is demonstrated by the fact that bodily habits are really mental habits. Desire, being but a strong thought, can be effaced only by an equally powerful thought, that is, by a mental process. No merely external discipline or physical renunciation can have the same effect, although it does help to bring about that effect and therefore should be used. Asceticism pronounces the pleasure we take in the experience of the senses to be evil in itself. Philosophy replies that it is the being carried away from reason and intuition by the pleasures, the being attached to them to the point of utter dependence upon them, that is evil. The fanatical and dogmatical kind of asceticism declares the physical things we touch and taste to be evil, but philosophy says touch and taste are really mental experiences and that their mental discipline will be more effective than abstaining altogether from their physical exercise. Hence, it leaves us free to enjoy the good things of this world, so long as we do not get too attached to them nor inwardly enslaved by them. Living in inward detachment from the world is much more important than practising outward contempt for the world.

65

The ascetic who retires from the sordid struggles, gnawing insecurities, and dangerous discontents of our time, like a rabbit into its hole, gains ease at the cost of conscience. The philosopher must think of others as well as himself. If the message to the world of this ancient wisdom were only a call to its inmates to desert it, then would the outlook for mankind be a sorry one indeed.

66

The ascetics who seek to kill out desire are themselves inflamed with the desire to kill it out. They may lull, refine, purify, or exalt desire—but its root always remains.

67

In so far as ascetic regimes clip our worldly desires, they also clip the illusions and deceptions which are bred by those desires.

68

The wise and well-disciplined man will be able to put on asceticism or take off luxury like a suit of clothes, that is, at will, at any moment and in any place.

69

A temperate asceticism hardens the will, fortifies against temptation, and profits character. Such self-imposed discipline of animal desires and earthly aggrandizement pays high dividends.

70

We need not a fussy asceticism but an inspired humanism.

71

The ascetic who wants to dodge experience in the belief that it is either valueless or vile is the unfortunate victim of a widespread inability to distinguish between means and ends in these matters of yoga, renunciation, and the like.

72

The modern man is predisposed to want too much of the comforts and too many of the pleasures of the world. A little asceticism will therefore do him no harm and may bring him much benefit.

73

A self-tormenting frustration, imposed from without, is not the same as and not to be mistaken for a self-improving asceticism, imposed from within.

74

There is an asceticism which blights life and exhausts man, which shrivels his sympathies and freezes his humour. This he ought never be willing to accept, nor does true philosophy ever ask him to accept it. There is another asceticism which expands life and renews man, which confers the benediction of good health and tends towards a warm, cordial, and cheerful disposition.

75

Men with energy crushed it by ascetic practices until the state of a hibernating toad became their highest goal. Men with good will denied it by withdrawing from society and leaving the fields of activity, guidance, and leadership free for more selfish men, so that the general welfare inevitably suffered!

76

We do not honour the soul by imposing tortures on its tabernacles.

77

The weakling who is incapable of resisting whatever can bring him pleasure, who has never learnt discipline from the results of his weaknesses, has no other way to harden his will than the way of ascetic withdrawal.

78

Contemporary society is apt to laugh at and even to hinder these aspirations. We are not likely to become saints. All the likelihood runs in the opposite way. So let us not hesitate to practise a little self-denial, a little self-discipline, yes! even a little asceticism.

79

The Jain yogis even make the severest asceticism the chief feature of their path to the spiritual goal.

80

The discipline of the will must be practised against one's weaknesses and passions. This is where the ascetic finds his proper justification. But he need not push his effort into absurdities, for then he becomes a fool, or to extremes, for then he becomes a masochist.

81

It is not suggested that he become the kind of mystic who remains on the outside of life, unattached and rootless, a mere onlooker while others act and work and move and love.

82

To withdraw ascetically from worldly affairs and let go one's grip on worldly things quite deliberately, and not through old age or chronic illness or repeated failure, is something that many active-bodied or keenly intellectual people find difficult to understand.

83

It is not fully helpful to us, creatures of modern civilization and metropolitan cities as we are, that most of the information which has come down to us about this subject has come from monks, nuns, abbots, and hermits too often given over to excesses of asceticism. This has given us their point of view, but we ourselves are not placed at the same point as they are.

84

We dislike the idea of becoming saints and fear the idea of becoming martyrs, just as we are averse to the idea of becoming ascetics. The spirituality of an antique period is not for us. We agree to learn a subject only when it is made easy, or to become spiritual only when the disciplines and dangers are first removed. We want the Quest but without the cross, the Overself without forsaking the ego.

85

Nobody need be frightened away from the quest by unnecessary fears and imaginary obstacles. Complete asceticism and full retirement are not asked for by philosophy. It asks instead for a spiritualizing of life in the world. It is realistic even when being idealistic. It leads men on from where they already are, not from where they find it impossible to be.

86

Philosophy does not encourage the escapist in his evasion of morally obligatory responsibilities or in his illusion of merely external asceticism.

87

The notion that, in order to live a spiritual life or to attain spiritual salvation, a man must always flee from the world arises from several different causes, as well as from certain understandable confusions. It is not baseless although in a number of cases it is useless. One of the causes is disgust with the evil that surrounds us. One of the confusions is failure to perceive that mental flight is far more important than physical flight.

88

The Hindu-Buddhist monastic sects which consider life in this world to be an evil, and the world itself to be an inexplicable mistake to be endured until we can escape from it by a transcendental attainment, are not supported by all their own sages. Some, and they are of the best, reject such statements.

89

It is sinful to throw away or destroy what Nature or man has taken the trouble to produce, and what some other person can use. Life attaches a penalty to such a sin, the penalty of loss or privation in the thing concerned. It is not generally known or recognized as a sin but then not all of the higher laws are known or recognized.

90

Like the celebrated Abbess of Port-Royal, some thought that by living in squalor they were actually living in poverty, to which they were vowed. But this was a ghastly mistake, a confusion of definitions which brought about lamentable results.

91

To accept such values and to act in accordance with them would lead society back to a primitive stage and deprive it of the benefits of invention, the progress of civilization, and of the inspirations of literature and art.

92

Such temporary ascetic practices are an unmistakable gesture to the Overself that he is willing to make some sacrifices in return for dominion over his animal nature, that he is prepared to pay with the coin of self-discipline for liberation from slavery to his lower appetites, that, in short, he really has elevated his values.

93

Among Orientals the popular association of poverty with holiness is undeniable. The *fakir* begged his way as he wandered, the *dervish* begged at the door—both had given their lives to religion.

94

A reasonable ascetic abnegation may well become necessary at some stage, but it is he who must judge and test himself.

95

You are to hate nobody but to extend to everybody the sincere hand of goodwill, to bless all because in your own heart the conscious presence of the Overself has itself blessed you. Hence to purify your personal feelings from hate, resentment, anger, or malice, it is always needful to lift the problem of your enemy or your critic onto that plane where divine love and forgiveness can be felt and bestowed. But to discharge the social duties of the world in which we live, it is also needful to deal with him according to reason. The two attitudes are not conflicting ones. For whatever practical action you will then take will be taken calmly, nobly, and justly.

96

There are certain vital differences between the harsh asceticism of ordinary mysticism and the balanced discipline of philosophy. The first is an effort to arrive at a spiritual state by physical means, by forcible suppression and by mechanical obedience. The second is an effort to arrive at the same state by mental means, by gradual self-training, and by intelligent response. That is, the philosophical aspirant waits for the inner call to impose a bodily renunciation upon himself. He does not impose it arbitrarily merely because some external authority commands him to do so or because he seeks blindly to imitate the saints.

97

An occasional and limited austerity, intended to help and strengthen the growing will, is valuable to everyone. It is even more valuable to the spiritual aspirant because it teaches him to dissociate the self from the body.

98

Our objection is against that kind of asceticism which on the one hand merely expands vanity and increases egotism and on the other is only outward, formal, and physical.

99

Ascetic self-discipline must precede spiritual self-realization. We must let go of the lesser things of earth if we would find the greater ones of heaven.

100

The philosophic discipline makes use of physical austerity at certain periods and in a limited way. But it does not prescribe it arbitrarily. The prescription must come from within the aspirant himself. This ensures the right time, the mental readiness for imposing whatever outward discipline may be required.

101

The simple life advocated quite understandably by saints and mystics as a means of detaching people from too much worldliness is to be welcomed. But two points should be made and then kept clear. It should not be confused with the monastic life, with vows of poverty imposed on laymen. It should not be opposed to the cultural life and deprive us of the gifts of art, beauty, colour, and replace them by utter bareness or drabness. It should not be fanatical and push its dislike for the products of man's invention to the extreme. The cave is the simplest habitation. Are we to stop only there? And scratch on the walls instead of printing on paper?

102

Since they are so irrelevant to our times, why should we not soften the harsh rules of asceticism, so long as such softening does not minify the ultimate purpose itself, does not prevent a man from attaining the highest self-fulfilment?

103

When asceticism becomes a form of ill-treating the body, it renders no useful service—neither to religious aspiration in the best sense, nor certainly to the body itself, its health or well-being.

104

Buddha drew attention to the unpleasant parts and functions of the body and the unpleasantnesses associated with it, in order to get people disgusted with the body so that they might become less attached to the desires associated with it. The Hindu teachers instructed their seeking pupils to live near cremation grounds and burial grounds with a somewhat similar purpose in view, except that here there was emphasis upon the brevity of incarnation. But for those whose minds can function on a higher level, there is no need for such a one-sided outlook. Neither fanatical asceticism nor an utterly bare, so-called simple life should obscure the fact that the body also brings satisfactions. The pleasures of eating need not be disparaged; appreciation of beautiful song need not be missed.

105

Buddha tried the fanatic's way of asceticism but in the end gave it up for the Middle Way.

106

The body, passions, and undesirable emotions must be perseveringly disciplined. Whilst ungoverned and running wild, they constitute the lower nature that is symbolized in so many myths as a dragon, lion, or serpent which has to be slain before the guardians of the divine gate permit entrance. Such purification is a necessary preliminary to and prerequisite of the higher training, which opens the individual mind to spiritual consciousness. This does not mean that total asceticism is demanded, and, indeed, in the present era, such a demand would often be an impractical one. What *is* demanded is *inner* asceticism, that is, inner purification of thought and feeling. External measures may be adjusted later, according to the individual circumstances and personal inclinations.

107

Asceticism is not identified with philosophy but only with mysticism. Nevertheless there comes a period in his life when he has to go through the battles of Hercules, fight and overcome his lower nature before he may be initiated into higher realizations. Sex must and can be conquered. Only when this is done can rapid spiritual advancement be in order.

108

To take a single instance, the asceticism which marked those two Oriental messages (Buddhism and Hinduism), will not be a suitable feature of the new message. The new one says that we are to live in the world but not to become worldly, and that we may enjoy the good things of this world so long as we do not forget also to enjoy the good things of the Spiritual Quest.

109

He is here to understand life; and it can be understood just as well in business as in a cave. Moreover if he stays in the world he will have a far better opportunity to serve mankind than if he runs away. The time for withdrawing from business in order to have more time for meditation and study will come when it is right later on. He will gain little by withdrawal unless he does so under the orders of a competent teacher, whereas he will be able to benefit by the invaluable lessons and practical experience that business affords him. It is not a matter of finding time, this business of self-realization, but of finding the right tuition.

110

The ascetic physical regimes such as strict celibacy, total abstention from alcoholic liquor, living apart from worldly people, and not engaging in worldly business, were planned to keep the novice away from distracting environments and obstructing temptations. To concentrate successfully in meditation the mind must first become moderately settled. If it is excited with any passion, or agitated by any anger, then the aspirant finds it impossible to meditate properly. What he loves, longs for, or desires may come first before him when he sits down to meditate. The picture of that thing appears before him and makes his effort to concentrate more difficult. He may remove this unequal emphasis by strengthening his will through the deliberate renunciation of that thing for a time. This quietens the mind before he begins and thus there is a gradual, if temporary, dropping-away of the desire which might otherwise intrude and interfere. This is the theory of asceticism. Its defect is that the result is too often either a temporary repression or a total failure.

111

It is not at all necessary to emulate the emaciated self-hypnotized anchorite or the sombre intense ascetic.

112

If the Chinese ideal of the Harmonious Whole enters deeply into his thought, a one-sided attitude toward life seems too restricted. He can see no reason why a temporary and narrowing ascetic concentration, necessary though it was for most persons, should become a permanent imposition of austerity.

113

To reject a fanatical asceticism is not to plead for a free self-indulgence. The sybarite has no place on this quest. Moral, mental, and physical health needs the support of will and discipline.

114

Some practise asceticism, others merely pretend to do so.

115

Neither penance nor asceticism need be permanent. They are but stages, after all. The aspirant will receive an inner prompting when to bring them to an end. If, however, he is unintelligent, excessively obstinate, or emotionally unbalanced, he may disregard the prompting and turn what should be a means into an end.

116

If we want to understand why so many men have pursued ascetic ideals in a large part of the world and since before the Christian era, we have only to glance at those who have not pursued these ideals but rather the very opposite ones. What have ambition, wealth, power, pleasure and fame done to the character of those who placed the highest possible value upon them? How often have they weakened finer feelings, strengthened ignoble selfishness, or kept the mind on shallower levels?

117

A man may quite properly seek his material welfare without in any way being a materialist. The kind of ascetic mysticism which confuses the two is based on mere surface readings, not inner realities. The modern Westerner quite rightly has no use for that medieval outlook, that spurious holiness which praises the spiritual man only when he is also a starved man. He will prefer to follow Jesus' injunction to be in the world, but not of it.

118

They commit the mistake of going too far when they combat asceticism. They rightly object to its fanaticism, but this does not justify its total denunciation. It has a place, however limited, and a very necessary place, however temporary, in the life of all those who seek to rise above a merely animal existence. Because so many ascetics have been ignorant and extremist and unbalanced, this is no reason for refusing to honor the need of a prudent, sensible, and balanced restraint of the lower nature.

119

The ascetic belief that comfort is a spiritual hindrance, luxury a spiritual sin, and art a spiritual tempter is not entirely groundless. Much depends on the definitions made, the standards set, but more especially on the circumstances fixed by destiny.

120

The kind of asceticism which turns its votaries into human cabbages or living corpses is unattractive in theory and uncomfortable in practice.

121

The denial of comfort is not necessary to a simpler life, although grim ascetics may think so. Sitting on soft cushions need not make anyone more materialistic as squatting on bare earth, cemented or tiled floor has not made any Western visitor to Indian ashram more spiritual, if he dares to ignore his discomfort and think a little for himself.

122

Excessive surrender to the physical senses, instincts, desires, and appetites has created the need in most religions of codes, systems, and schools of the opposite, that is, asceticism. This is why more stress has been laid upon asceticism in a system like yoga than is really required, and why fanaticism so often accompanies it when it is excessive.

123

Those who wish to respond to the quest's silent invitation must begin by repentance, continue by self-discipline, and end by surrender.

Possessions

124

If a sceptic asks, "Why should I be detached from the things and creatures which make me happy?" the answer is a multiple one. First, their transiency—all and everyone are subject to change, thus making possible a change in the happiness you get from them. Second, their brevity—next year they may not be present for your enjoyment, whether through death, accident, illness, or ill-fortune. Third, life is like a dream; its solid reality is a borrowed feeling not really there but in the deeper being of yourself. Fourth, and final—to discover this being is why you are here anyway, what you have to do in the end, even if you put it off for many a reincarnation. Nor will you miss out on happiness if you do respond to the idea of detachment. It does not mean living like a caveman. It does not mean denying life, art, comfort, humanity.

125

The same possessions which enslave one man may set another free. For where the first uses them to strengthen desires, nourish passions, increase selfishness, and exploit humanity, the second may use them to build character, improve intelligence, foster meditation, and serve humanity. The very things which captivate the first man help to liberate the second one.

126

The belief supported by Rousseau that living simply and on a low income improves character or promotes spirituality is correct only in the case of those who have renounced the world, that is, of monks and nuns. In the case of the others, who constitute the mass of mankind, it is correct only for exceptional persons who know how to live in the world and yet not be of it. But most people are in the grade of life's school where they need to acquire experience and develop the faculties of human individuality. The spurs to that are first, responsibility, and second, ambition. These and the need to discharge family obligation must in the end force them to improve themselves and to improve their position.

127

It is possible happily to enjoy the pleasures of life in the world, the sense of power which position gives in the world, the securities afforded by properties and possessions in the world, without clinging inordinately to their ownership in the mind. It is possible to hold them without uncontrolled attachment, to take or leave them as fate or inclination dictates. This is not to say that human feelings are to be expunged and human nature crushed, but only that they are to be freed from avoidable and unnecessary miseries by the practice of philosophy.

128

We hear much counsel from the Orient bidding us relinquish career, fortune, and family. Is the pauper to be an aspirant's ideal type? Even Tiruvalluvar, a man whom South Indians revere as one of their greatest saints and poets, in his most celebrated classic, *The Kural*, rated poverty not only as painful but as a great evil. He abhorred begging.

129

When he lets himself get cluttered up with an excess of possessions, each demanding his attention, interest, and care, not to speak of his time, his needs get confused with wants, reality with illusions.

130

Possessions should not become prisons. The aspirant's mental attitude toward them must be vigilant lest he lose his deeply hidden independence. The ideal is to move through life with inward detachment. The thought of the impermanence of all things is one which should spontaneously arise in his mind whenever he comes into good fortune.

131

The way of decreasing possessions as a means of increasing spirituality is necessary at certain times to certain persons, but not to all persons at all times.

132

It may be a help to some in the attainment of inner freedom if they stop using the possessive pronoun "my" in reference to anything that belongs to them except their weaknesses.

133

If we could learn to hold things less possessively and people less adhesively, we would enjoy the things and give joy to the people much more than we do now.

134

The more he brings himself to let go *inwardly* of his possessiveness, the less he will suffer. It is easier to do so at first in abstract meditation and later in actual everyday life.

135

Yang Chu who was a Taoist, but such a strongly individual one that he did not hesitate to modify the teachings where necessary, thought that neither being poor nor being wealthy was desirable, that a better condition was the middle one between the two. The sage argued that they brought their own special kind of anxieties with them and so were not conducive to peace of mind.

136

If the religionist declares that man cannot live by bread alone, the materialist retorts that he cannot even survive unless he seeks, obtains, and eats bread. Moreover if too little money may bring a lot of misery, a lot of money may still accompany a lot of misery. But on the other hand if, as it is often said, money does not bring happiness, neither does poverty. The reasonable man is not tricked by such generalizations. He looks deeper and longer and more into those individual circumstances that are not so obvious.

137

The fifth of the *yama* restraints laid down in yoga discipline is variously translated as avoidance of "avarice," avoidance of "abundance of worldly goods," avoidance or non-taking of "gifts." The original word is *parigraha* (in Jaina texts). The philosophical view is that it means both "miserly hoarding of possessions," and "non-taking of gifts conducive to luxury."

138

If a man will not get this inner attitude toward possessions while he owns them, he may still fail to do so if destiny snatches them away.

139

Freedom means being able to make money without contracting into the sense of anxious possession which goes with it.

140

Although decried by the yogic and Vedantic texts, what is wrong with eating tasty food? Does not its enjoyment promote secretion of digestive juices? And although decried by the same texts, how is character harmed by comfortable surroundings or by artistic and intellectual culture? And finally, in what way could any of these things be discreditable to truth or the quest?

141

Wittgenstein gave away a large inheritance because he believed that money is a nuisance to a philosopher! The result was that he had to take a job, working among people who made him miserable.

142

To suggest, as philosophy does, a standard of living that rejects equally the exaggerated narrowing down to primitive and monastic conditions or the exaggerated expanding up to incessant acquirement of possessions is simply to suggest a healthily balanced life.

143

The simple life is rightly advocated as an accompaniment of the spiritual life. But the purpose of this advocacy should not be forgotten—to save time and thought from becoming too preoccupied with physical things. Yet those who draw help from beauty in art or nature, who are affected by colour and form, should not throw aside this cultural heritage in favour of bare, dull, dreary, and sometimes squalid surroundings in the name of *simplicity*.

144

It is easy to fall into the error that spirituality means stagnation, that transcending the worldly life means abandoning it. This error arises because it is not clearly comprehended that the operative principle is what one does with his thoughts, not with his things. For the second activity is always a result of the first.

145

The attitude taken up in preaching or writing that material things are worthless and on no account to be sought for, is not only nonsensical but often hypocritical. It is seldom put into practice by its advocates.

146

It is common for religious preachers and mystical authors to condemn the effort to acquire money. It is uncommon to find one who defends it. But the correct attitude toward money ought to be determined by the way in which it is gained and by the use to which it is put. The young man who nourishes honest ambitions and puts them to work without injury to other men but rather in service of them, until he is able to command sufficient wealth, and who then retires and puts his wealth to work in a way which enables him to command the kind of surroundings and life conducive to spiritual ideals, has attained true balance. The processes of money-making can destroy those ideals or promote them. Ignorance and greed bring about the first result, but wisdom and balance the second.

147

Inner security can be gained by anyone anywhere, but in Europe and America it can be gained with less difficulty and more speed if the seeker has just enough outer security to enable him to do the things he needs to do to foster spiritual growth. Money will corrupt him and delay or even stop his quest only if in its acquisition he does not know when to stop.

148

Must I add this new possession to the others? Is it a help toward living or really an encumbrance? If it can replace an existing one by being more efficient, better for health, comfort, work, or elegance, it may be permissible. But if it merely multiplies the number of objects needing care or using up attention, I will do better without it. Acquisition run to excess is the modern disease.

149

The gospel of the simple life, as preached by the Tolstoyans, the Gandhians, the Yogis, and the Fakirs, rejects every beautiful thing because, in its view, all art is distracting, unnecessary luxury. It rejects most of the inventions, developments, and creations brought about by modern science and industry because man can live without them and did, until recently, do so. It demands that he acquire the barest minimum of goods, food, clothing, and shelter which he can manage to maintain existence. Philosophy, while appreciative of the virtue of being unpossessed by possessions, of the advantage of some simplification of our pattern, sees no need why we should go so far as these ascetic extremists go. It rejects their rejections and turns away from their demands. In short, it accepts the reasonable enjoyment of life, art, possessions, and the physical world, so long as we do not forget the quest while we are enjoying them.

150

The attempt to cling to possessions or persons after they have been lost is the craving for what is past and the refusal to live in what is already here. It can only lead to frustration and dissatisfaction.

151

When a thing, a position, or a person is no longer an obstacle to his interior work of purification or meditation, then he has achieved the detachment from it which philosophy seeks. The possession of it will then be acceptable and harmless.

152

When the spirit of inner detachment has really been gained, whatever things were discarded during the struggle to attain it may again be taken up and used if they are needed.

153

In the end the things he appreciates are more his own than those he possesses.

154

It has yet to be shown that any wealth beyond what is needed for decency of living makes anyone any happier, or that owning more possessions and property than others have makes him really better off in the end than they are.

155

My true wealth lies not in the extent to which I possess things but in the extent to which I can cheerfully dispossess myself of them.

156

Those who complain of the burden of having too many possessions should remember the misery of having too few possessions.

157

The best of all possessions is to have this inward and secret possessionlessness.

158

It is not in the actual owning of things that the wrong lies; it is in such blind attachment to them that their ephemeral character and hidden penalties are left unrecognized. The beautiful and the useful have their proper place in home and life. Their offering may be accepted if it is kept within our understanding of truth and does not displace it and if our sense of values is not smothered by it.

159

If he lacks the material things and possessions to provide for essential requirements, his mind will constantly recur to them. In that sense he finds that poverty does not let him attain peace of mind.

160

With money one can disdain the inferior and purchase the best, cultivate the art of beautiful living, raise the quality of this human existence above the merely animal one, improve and refine surroundings. But without money, the only satisfactory alternative is the simple desireless life of a yogi.

161

The purification of the heart from worldly attachments is not easily achieved. A simpler life, setting a limit on the number of possessions, is a proven help to such an achievement.

162

The money he earns or possesses and the material benefits which he desires, pardonably occupy his mind. There is nothing wrong in this from the philosophical standpoint although there may be from the fanatical ascetic-mystic standpoint. But when they preoccupy his mind to the exclusion of all higher things, then the imbalance is certainly wrong.

163

The more possessions the more time we have to give to them, and therefore the more energy. There is then proportionately less of both available for higher studies, meditation practice, and metaphysical reflection.

164

Many of those things which we eagerly collect or gratefully accept as possessions in the beginning, we ruefully recognize as encumbrances in the end. For the responsibilities and consequences which follow in their train are often not to our liking.

165

The monk who takes the vow of personal poverty and renounces the possession of worldly goods is not superior to, but only on a parallel plane with, the householder who decides to simplify his life and discard superfluities or inessentials.

166

Earthly things are to be regarded as possessing a secondary value and offering a limited satisfaction. Where they have such a grip on the heart that this attitude cannot be taken up, then they are to be deliberately renounced to the extent and for the period necessary to set the heart free. Thus philosophy is somewhat ascetical but not wholly ascetical.

167

The simple life opposes itself to the abundant life: philosophy reconciles these opposites. Its full development of human faculty passes through an alternating rhythm, using both of them. But enlightenment itself is independent of either condition. It comes from grace, not from poverty and austerity nor from possessions and elegance. The austerity draws out self-control. The possessions, which include mental and artistic ones, enlarge the outlook. Both are merely for training the human entity. They are means, not ends.

168

The simplicity which is advocated in the name of asceticism, taking the original definition of the words as "training," is unobjectionable. It is part of the work of bringing the body and the physical senses under control, making them obey mind and will. It is an attempt to rule the acquisitive instinct which demands more and more belongings, more and more possessions, and in the end more and more luxuries: this leads into attachments to them and dependence on them for one's happiness. Buddha pointed out that cravings and desires were insatiable and block the way to *durable* satisfaction. These facts have been used as part of the justification for monastic existence. The monk does not have to take care of more objects than he can pack into a single small suitcase. This leaves his mind and time freer for its religious pursuits. But for those who have elected to stay in the world and follow the layman's supposedly lower and certainly less harsh way of life a wider view is permissible, and a little latitude may be given to the need of comfort and the sense of beauty. Bleak, shabby, or ugly surroundings do not promote spirituality. Cheerless and comfortless furnishings may dull sensitivity. It is not far from these things to regard art, music, poetry, colour, fine literature, and general culture as hindrances to the spirit at best, or enemies to the seeker after God at worst. But in the enlargement of life, mind, thought, feeling, and intuition for which philosophy becomes the agent, there is space for all these things. They are turned into helps on the way, feeding and promoting the spiritual life.

169

The Hindu sadhu and the Franciscan monk would applaud Roman Seneca's assertion that "property [is] . . . the greatest cause of human troubles." But would it not be more just to counterbalance this with the comment that the *lack* of property is one of the great causes of human troubles and crimes? Can there be contentment before basic human needs are met? Can we return to the caveman's propertyless and primitive way of life? Are not physical well-being and healthy surroundings necessary to satisfactory existence, and living decently necessary to the transition from the merely animal to the properly human order? Did not Epictetus put it in a phrase: "There is a difference between living well and living profusely"? Ought we not learn something from the sadhu's attitude of non-attachment without falling into his extremism? Should we not esteem control of thoughts and command of desires and passions for the inner peace they give to a man? In short, it is not only things but not less the mental attitude which matters.

170

How can he escape? There are but two ways. The first is to gather sufficient wealth into his bins to enable him to snap his fingers at conventional society, or at least to stand aside and laugh at the world whenever he likes. But by the time he has succeeded in this purpose, he is unlikely to want to free himself. The grip of routine will be greater than ever before. This method of liberation is a problematical one, after all. The second and certain way is to cut down his wants and needs so that his call on this world's goods is small.

171

A minimum of possessions must be set unless a man is to go about completely naked. A minimum of shelter must also be set, otherwise he may lose his health or soon die off. A minimum of food and drink likewise has to be set, or the body will perish even quicker. Where then is this minimum to be placed? Is it to be the same for every man? Is it to be the same for men in utterly different climates—such as the tropics and the arctic? The higher individuality is one, and unchanging, whereas the personal self may take different forms at different times, and certainly changes.

172

"Blessed are the poor," said Jesus. Jesus could not have meant that there is spiritual advantage in living in a slum. It is more likely to breed discontent, or why do those who increase their income move to a better neighbourhood? The phrase is not to be taken literally but metaphorically, as were so many utterances by Orientals. To live inwardly ever detached from things—whether they are owned and used or not—is a blessed state, giving peace of mind.

173

The disadvantage of having possessions is that they dissipate our energies and use up our time, either in making use of them or in taking care of them. These energies and this time and especially the attention involved in them, make it more difficult for beginners, I repeat—for beginners—to reorient their mind towards the Overself.

174

There is nothing wrong, but, rather, everything right in aspiring to a certain amount of success in worldly life along with one's spiritual development. But one must make sure that the worldly attainments are not gained at the expense of neglecting his inward development, and that they do not infringe upon the ethical principles which govern discipleship.

175

After an active, aggressive business life one does reach the time when more emphasis should be placed on inner development. Outer acquisition can become largely a distraction as that period emerges.

176

This is also true as respects personal attainments, whether intellectual, scientific, or otherwise. When the time has come for more intensive inner seeking it may be wise to consider if one's further activities in these other fields should not be left to others.

177

Money can be regarded as a symbol which represents, among other things, two which are quite important although unequally so. They are power and privacy.

178

It is usually the moneyless aspirants who decry wealth and praise poverty (calling it simplicity). If money can chain a man more tightly to materialism, it can also give him the conditions whereby he can set to work freeing himself from materialism.

179

If he feels the urge to discard superfluous personal possessions, he ought to obey it!

180

It is doubtless quite pardonable for a man to regard as permanently his own what he has possessed for a long time and to believe that life not only will let him have it always but ought to do so. To him, the idea of detachment must be an irritant.

181

How many of our possessions are, in reflective analysis, mere toys for adults! We expend so much effort and desire to get them, we cling so desperately to them, and we make ourselves so unhappy to lose them— when they are really toys, playthings. We take their arrivals and departures too seriously, hence we are overmuch elated or overmuch depressed quite needlessly.

182

Why must it be assumed that *only* the beggar, moneyless and homeless, can acquire this knowledge, this truth? Surely the privacy needed for meditation is easier got by the wealthier man? Getty, oil millionaire, summed up the chief benefit of his wealth as "privacy." Again, why must it be assumed that because most seekers in the past as in the present join a religious order, or mystical organization, all should become followers of some guru or leader? Has not history told us of those who found their own way after having passed beyond the beginning stages of joining or following?

183

To use possessions while being inwardly detached from them, to work as actively as if one had the ambition to succeed while all the time as indifferent toward success as toward failure—this is part of the freedom he seeks and gains.

184

If a little extra comfort leaves one's thoughts untroubled, one's feelings undisturbed, why not indulge in it?

185

It is not for everyone to accept the rule that to be civilized is to be sinful, that to make the furnishing of a house comfortable, tasteful, and agreeable is to betray spiritual standards. Does spirituality vanish if we go beyond making the house humanly habitable and make it aesthetically pleasing also?

186

It is true that every unnecessary possession may become a hindering fetter, obstructing the inner life. But what is unnecessary to a man in one set of circumstances or in one position of life may be quite necessary to a man in a different one.

187

The attachment to worldly goods and family life must be delicately balanced by the consciousness of their impermanence. It is impossible to get such a balance when the attachment is excessive.

188

Lao Tzu: "Which is the most to you, your person or your goods? Much hoarding must be followed by great ruin. He who knows when he has enough suffers no disgrace."

189

When we consider the care, the anxiety, the distraction, the time and energy associated with possessions, it may be a relief to shed some of them, and not a grief.

8

THE QUEST AND SOCIAL RESPONSIBILITY

On time and solitude

We lament the lack of time. But if we critically scrutinized our actions, and even made some kind of schedule beforehand, we would find that some activities are unnecessary and others are useless. These not only rob us of time but they deprive us of some of the energy needed for meditation, rendering it harder or even impossible.

2

Do not imagine that because the mystic frequently seeks seclusion he does this because he is bored with life and hence disdains the drawing rooms of society; rather is it that he is intensely interested in life and is therefore short of time, for drawing rooms are usually places where people go to kill time, because *they* are bored.

3

The quest calls for strenuous endeavours and the right use of time. Those who are indifferent to its disciplinary demands should not complain about the slow-motion character of their progress. Those who give little should not expect to get much.

4

It will not be enough, if he wants to find time for graver pursuits, to throw out of his life all harmful pleasures; he will also have to throw out time-wasteful and useless ones. Such exercise of self-denial proves a profitable one in the end, whatever it costs in the beginning.

5

If heart does not radiate silently to heart, then talk is idle dissipation of time and energy, even though it be continued for hours.

6

People who do not know how to get rid of time except by getting involved in time-using activities, cannot know the value of contemplation.

7

He may succeed in his aim only if he succeeds in not getting entangled by irrelevant activities and intruding persons.

8

Time is like a great treasury. Put nothing of value into it and you will get nothing out. Put philosophic study and self-training into it and at the very least you will draw out a measure of peace and understanding, at the most you may enter into realization of the Truth.

9

He should sometimes ask himself for how many more years may he hope to be given the chance which every lifetime gives a man to transcend himself.

10

To give time is to give life. To be master of one's time, for an hour or a week, free and independent, is to be master of one's life for an hour or a week.

11

It is a necessary rule of the aspirant's life, laid down by the yogic manuals of old and proven by experience today, that regularity should be faithfully observed in meditation practice and at least attempted in the other important duties of his spiritual career.

12

Those who object to contemplation as a waste of time and life, need to learn that it is also a form of activity—inner activity.

13

He will be forced to admit, with sorrowful head, that he had been too busy with the trivial matters of the moment to break through the mysterious barriers that bar our human way out of the prison of time and space.

14

Fritter—and fail.

15

The Quest does not demand the renunciation of worldly business but only the renunciation of a small daily fragment of the time hitherto devoted to such business. It asks for half or three-quarters of an hour daily to be faithfully given to meditation exercises. It asserts that the fullest realization of the Overself can be attained without becoming a whole-time yogi.

16

No man can escape responsibility for the way he uses his day. He can either carefully organize it to serve his highest purposes or he can carelessly fritter it away in trivial activity or idle sloth.

17

The day must be definitely apportioned and scheduled beforehand, its routine prearranged and left undisturbed. Chance visits by friends must be discouraged; he must refuse to fit them in.

18

The excuses given for this failure may be serious and sincerely meant, but the fact remains that those who make them can still find time to eat their meals and, perhaps, to make love. The essence of the matter lies in how important meditation is to him.

19

He is also too much aware of his own precarious mortality to permit useless involvements and irrelevant commitments to waste his life.

20

The ordinary person does not have the time to search intellectually or the desire to search adventurously for truth. This is partly because his other personal activities absorb his day. But a man who dedicates his entire time to this quest, who is willing to pay its cost, is more likely to find the truth. Yet time is only part of the price; he must also be willing to sacrifice dishonesty in his thinking.

21

He will find, on a strict self-examination, that he has allowed himself to be drawn into currents of time-wasting worldliness or attracted into whirlpools of time-eating frivolity.

22

Once he recognizes his responsibility toward the fulfilment of this higher purpose, for which the Infinite Wisdom has put him here, he will have to recognize also the obligation of devoting some time every day for study of, and meditation upon, it. The philosophic standard of measurement enables him to see plainly that however fully he has fulfilled all other demands made upon him—to the point that all his time is engaged—if he has neglected this single one, he is still at fault.

23

To find the time required for meditation may call for a little planning of our time and a lot of revision of our values. But this in itself is a worthwhile self-discipline. For we rush hither and thither but have yet to ask ourselves where we are rushing to. What better use could we make of the treasure of leisure than soul-finding?

24

Those costly hours when we abandon pleasure or deny sleep that we may take counsel of our better selves, are not wasted. They too bring a good reward—however deferred it be—and one that remains forever.

25

Our daily occupations and preoccupations keep our time, energies, and consciousness identified with the external world and external activities to such an extent that we have little left for reversing the situation and discovering—or at least exploring—the deeper layers of self. Yet, unless something is done about this situation, and at least simple exercises and pre-studies made as a beginning, we shall remain ignorant throughout life of what is actually of high importance to us. Twenty minutes a day at whatever time is convenient should at least be given for this purpose.

26

If the student finds his time fully taken up in caring for others, this must take first place. He must care for all victims of man's ignorance as though they were members of his own family; he must be as clearheaded and practical in dealing with his work as any worldly minded person, but underneath he will know that earthly life is fleeting, transient, never permanently satisfying, and therefore only the outer face of his life; deep within must be a persistent quest of truth and reality which alone confer everlasting peace.

27

His withdrawal from common gossip, tittle-tattle speech, and negative conversation must be deliberate until by habit it becomes natural. Such talk is unnecessary, extravagant, and harmful to his inner work.

28

It is not a moral endeavour, although that may enter into it, but a worthwhile plan to cut out time spent on adulterous theatre plays, "risqué" stories, and trivial television. The mental attention thus saved can be transferred and used more constructively on a higher level.

29

Half an hour is not enough for his high purpose. Only the whole day, all his waking hours will suffice for it.

30

If he values his life he will have to value his time. This means he will have to select the quality and limit the quantity of his experiences.

31

The man who seeks more free time for spiritual pursuits may find it by withdrawing from the fullness of human experience. By refusing to work at a job or to rear a family, he may achieve his aim.

32

You can throw your time away on the waste-heap, or you can transform it into a result-producer.

33

If you think you have not the necessary time for the practice of mental quiet, then make it. Push out of the day's program the least important items so as to make room for this, the most important of all activities.

34

Whoever is interested in making the most of his life and doing the best for his character needs two things among several others: he needs time and he needs seclusion. The time may vary from a few minutes a day up to a couple of hours. Seclusion may be in an attic or in a forest. A third thing needed is silence. With these three conditions he can begin the very important inner work: first of reflection, second of thought-control. The time is needed to withdraw from the hustle and bustle of the world, from the triviality and futility of so much social life. It is a good thing to come out of that for a while every day, to be sequestered from society and make the effort to be in himself—that is, in his true self, his spiritual being. These few minutes of detachment from the world can become in time very valuable to him if he uses them in the right way.

35

The little seed from which a great tree will one day grow makes no noise as it busily germinates in the dark earth. In such silence and with such reticence, the aspirant should begin his quest and wait patiently for the day when he shall receive a mandate to speak of these things. To speak prematurely is not only ineffective but likely to arouse unnecessary and avoidable opposition.

36

The real work on the Quest has to be carried out within and by the mind, not the body. The aspirant must try to live his outward life as normally as possible and avoid making a public spectacle of the fact he is following the spiritual path.

37

The quest is his secret which he can better carry in the depths of his heart.

38

Holiness or spiritual greatness or a dedicated life is a secret between a man and his God. He does not need to advertise it by any outward show, by a particular kind of dress, or by the professional sanctity of the monk or yogi.

39

The intellectual and intuitional and mystical sides of his real spiritual life will cause him to withdraw a part of himself from social communication. He will learn to live alone with it.

40

The student who rushes to narrate to everyone his inner experiences, his occult visions or messages, his high glimpses, may fall into the pit of self-advertisement, vanity, conceit. He may then lose through the ego what he has gained through his efforts.

41

He should not mention his mystical experiences to unsympathetic persons nor discuss them with incompetent ones. It is better to keep them to himself and talk about them only to a spiritual director or an aspirant much more advanced on the road than he is.

42

He should try to follow this quest and to practise its regimes as unobtrusively and as quietly as he can. By doing so he will reduce to a minimum the attention attracted from those persons who are likely to criticize his faith, or worse, to obstruct his path.

43

It is only the novice, enthusiastic but inexperienced, who loudmouthedly tells all and sundry about each one of his surface-scratching spiritual experiences. The man who is very far advanced on the quest acquires great discretion. In fact, the more advanced he is the more secretive does he become about such matters. He will not speak a word upon them unless he is bidden by the inner Voice to do so. The Overself does not live in public but in secret. It is totally outside the world's activity. Therefore the closer you approach it, the more secretive you are likely to become concerning the event. And when you do succeed in finally uniting yourself with it, your lips will be completely shut—not only because of the ego's greater humility but because the Overself desires it so. There is a further feature of this question of secrecy which deserves comment. Those who are very far advanced tend also to withdraw increasingly from the social circles or vocational activity which formerly engaged them. They vanish into retreat and withdraw into solitude for longer and longer intervals. Unless they are charged with a public mission, the world seldom hears of them.

44

This need of privacy to follow one's quest in one's own way is best satisfied by the wide open spaces of ranch life, next best by the vast impersonality of large city life. It is hardest to satisfy in a small town where watching eyes and intruding feet seek to mind everyone else's business.

45

It must live quite hermetically and secretly in his own mind and feelings, not because he wants to conceal truth but because it is still a tender young plant needing shelter and protection.

46

Where emotional guidance would bid him disclose his inner affiliation with the divine order, intuitional guidance bids him move unobtrusively and quietly.

47

The gossip who meddles with other people's private lives, the journalist who uses the excuse of professional practice to invade other people's privacy—these unpleasant repulsive creatures should be avoided or if necessary rebuked.

48

You must remember that everyone without exception stands in life just where the evolutionary flow has brought him and that his outward life is the result of all those previous experiences in many, many incarnations. His outlook and his beliefs, his attitude towards life are all part of his evolving growth. Therefore you will not try to convert him. If, however, doubts begin to arise in his mind and he asks you questions, then it is right for you to speak to him of a higher viewpoint. But say just what needs to be said to give him the light you see he needs, and no more. If you go too far you will confuse him. If you give him just enough to carry his mind a step onward you will help him. Until then every effort you make is wasted; it is throwing seed on to stony ground. Therefore, unless you are asked in this way it is unnecessary and often unwise to advertise that you are following spiritual practices or believe in spiritual truths. If you live with others and make a fuss about these things you may arouse their hostility. If you really have something to give them they will come to you one day and ask for help. You must learn discretion in dealing with people. You must learn when to be silent and when to speak, and when you do speak how much to say.

49

One reason why this silence about inner experiences is enjoined upon novices is that speech about them tends to spiritual conceit; another is that it identifies the novice with his ego from which it is the very purpose of those experiences to separate him. In learning to keep them secret, he is learning to keep himself out of the subtlest forms of egoism.

50

The seeker is warned not to talk about his inner experiences. They have to be well-guarded by silence if they are to be kept or repeated.

51

It is not a reprehensible selfishness to become, for the purposes of his inner work, more seclusive, more withdrawn, more conscious of the value of privacy. The more he obeys this higher will the more will others benefit.

52

If others laugh at him because he does not go with the herd, he must include it in the quest's cost. But it would be well to screen those things which need not be displayed, or refrain from drawing attention to them if this is possible. The world being what it is, negativities muddying so many characters, the less he lets them put their thoughts upon him the better.

53

The high value of secrecy in preparation and surprise in attack is well known to those who plan military operations skilfully. But those who want to succeed with their efforts for a higher kind of life can also profitably use these two approaches.

54

Most novices make the mistake of talking too freely to friends and relatives about the Quest. This is a serious error, and can lead to needless suffering on both sides. The aspirant must learn that it is a test of faith to trust in the workings of the Overself to spread these ideas in Its own time and way.

55

All must cherish secrets and the farther anyone advances on the path of knowledge the more he must cherish in this manner, not because of their value alone but because society is not usually ready to receive them. The sage, who is full of the loftiest secrets, does not suffer in the slightest from their possession. Restrained emotions are good as signs of attempted self-discipline but bad when they are set up as a goal of living. Asceticism can only bloom successfully when it arises out of genuine, reasoned understanding. Until such understanding comes one often has to restrain himself forcibly. But nothing ought to be overdone. The overdoing of asceticism produces cranks—unbalanced, illogical, and self-deceiving persons. Confession and sharing help to relieve the soul only insofar as they are connected with the right persons. To confess to the wrong persons or to share with them only makes matters worse.

56

The younger people of today who are knowingly embarking on the Quest should make some effort, within reasonable limits, to appear outwardly as being not too different from those who are not embarking on it—thus avoiding the stigma of being regarded as eccentric or, even worse, insane.

57

Such secrecy as he is expected to maintain about his quest is also due to the utter seriousness with which he must take it. It is something too sacred and too intimate to be talked about or argued about.

58

The impulse to speak may be obeyed or resisted; only each individual case can determine which course is correct.

59

To gain more friends at the risk of losing more privacy is a move which requires the fullest consideration.

60

Unlike most beginners, the proficient will never speak of his inmost spiritual experiences to other aspirants except in special cases. He will, however, drop such reticence with a teacher.

61

The rule of secrecy does not mean that he is never to talk about the Truth to others. It means only that he shall not talk prematurely about it. He must wait until he can talk with correct knowledge and at times when it is prudent to do so, and to persons who are ready for what he has to say. He must wait until he is himself strongly established in Truth, and will not be affected by the doubts and denials of others. He should learn and remember that speech opens his private purposes to their negative thoughts or antagonistic emotions and may thus weaken him. It needs firmness and discipline but by keeping his spiritual work and goals locked up inside himself and revealing them only when the right occasion arises he will show true practicality and foster real strength.

Spiritual service

62

He must defend his right to an inner life against all disruptions, however well-meaning the disrupter may be. What he owes to others, to society, friends, or family in the way of devotion, attention, or intercourse can and should be given. But there is a point where his self-giving may have to stop, where his responsibility to the higher purpose of living must cancel all other responsibilities.

63

When a man begins to think of what service he can render as well as the common thought of what he can get, he begins to walk success-wards.

64

All the great prophets have made special mention of the fact that the task of spiritually enlightening others is the most important and most beneficial activity in which any man can engage. He who wishes to stimulate others to start on the spiritual Quest, to help those who have already started to find the right direction in which to travel, and to make available to the public generally the leading truths of spiritual knowledge, feels that this is the most worthwhile activity. The effective and enduring preparation for this is first to spiritualize oneself and therefore it is up to him to carry on even more ardently with his efforts than he has done hitherto.

65

Philosophy bids him follow its quest and practise its ethics in his own person *before* he bids others do so. Only after he has succeeded in doing this, can he have the right to address himself to them. Only after he has discovered its results and tested its values for himself, can he guide them without the risks of deception on the one hand or hypocrisy on the other.

66

He may seek, when better equipped to do so, to render service to many people. But until that time comes, it is better to go on working upon himself, improving his moral character, increasing his knowledge of the philosophic teachings, humbling himself in daily prayer and worship, and cultivating that thread of intuition which links him to the Soul.

67

The seeker who follows this path is and will be of some service as a channel for the inspiration and enlightenment of others less advanced than he—within, of course, his own capacity and subject to his own limitations. Because of this, he should make every effort to acquire accurate knowledge of what the Quest is, what Philosophy contributes to it, and what—in everyday language—these mean and offer to the individual's everyday life.

68

The acts of service are yours, the consequences of service are God's. Do not be anxious where anxiety is not your business.

69

He must not only apply the teaching but he must apply it intelligently. His acts must either be inspired ones or, when they cannot attain that level, considered ones. Only in this way will he avoid the reproach so often levelled at mystics, that they are impractical, fanatical, and inefficient.

70

Service, in its purity, must be the first as well as the last thought behind his work. He is not unconcerned about rewards but he knows that they are always the natural accompaniment of, or sequel to, such service.

71

You talk of service. But you cannot really become a server of God before you have ceased to be a server of self.

72

The serious aspirant soon discovers that he has so much work to do on improving himself that he has little time left to improve others.

73

A novice in meditation ought not expect that he can give himself with impunity to the fully active life as an advanced practitioner can. Practical service of humanity ought therefore be limited within much narrower degrees by the former than need be done by the latter. The sphere of service should be widened only as the server develops his mystical faculties and should not outrun them. The sensible rule is that with the beginner emphasis must be laid upon self-development first and service last, but with the senior this order must be reversed. This is not to say with the reclusive minded that the beginner should be concerned wholly with himself and attempt no service at all.

74

Before we can help others or influence the world, we need to possess three things: knowledge, experience, and power.

75

It is an error to place too much stress on unselfish activity as an element in the aspirant's qualifications. We did not incarnate primarily to serve each other. We incarnated to realize the Overself, to change the quality of individual consciousness. Altruism is therefore always subordinate to this higher activity. The sage's compassion is not primarily for other people's troubles, although he certainly feels that too, but he knows that these will continue without end in some form or other—such being the unalterable nature of mundane existence. His compassion is for the ignorance out of which many avoidable troubles spring or which when they are unavoidable prevents people from attaining inner peace. Hence he economizes time and energy by refraining from devoting them merely and solely to humanitarian work and uses them instead for the root-work of alleviating spiritual ignorance.

76

Serve in sublime self-abnegation.

77

There is a common delusion that giving up selfishness in the sense of becoming utterly altruistic is the highest call of the quest. It is believed that the sage is simply a man who no longer lives for himself but lives wholly for others. Getting rid of one's own ego, however, does *not* mean taking on someone else's. It means taking on or, rather, being taken up by, the deeper self.

78

The divine power to help, heal, guide, or instruct others begins to show itself when we begin to turn our face towards it humbly, prayerfully, and thus make the necessary connection through meditation and study, through altruistic action and religious veneration.

79

They have no *adequate* idea of what they mean when they use this term "service." And in its absence they are liable to do as much harm as good. For they do not know in what consists the real good of other persons.

80

This does not mean that one is to renounce all ideas of rendering service. It merely means that one is to withdraw from premature acts of service, to withdraw for a time sufficient to prepare oneself to render real service, better service. One is to become possessed of patience and to wait during this period of preparation.

81

To refrain from premature service whilst developing oneself for better service, is not selfishness but simply unselfishness made sensible. He who has demonstrated his capacity to solve his own problems may rightly set forth to solve other people's.

82

Although the Buddha agreed with the mystical view that to seek one's own spiritual welfare and not that of another was a higher aim in life than to seek another's spiritual welfare whilst ignoring one's own, he said it was the highest of all to seek *both* one's own and another's at the same time.

83

But before he embarks on such service, such entry into the hearts and lives of others, he should be sure that neither personal egotism nor the desire for personal reward has mixed itself up with his altruistic impulse. If this surety is not present, he had better wait until it does arrive.

84

If you feel you want to spread this teaching, then do so; but do it in the right way. You don't have to organize a society or indulge in loud propaganda. Truth is not something which can be imposed on other people. They must grow through experience and reflection into the right attitude of receptivity and then they will look for whatever they need. It is only at such a critical moment that you have any right to offer what you yourself have found, just as it is only at such a moment that your offering will be successful and not a wasted one.

85

Another reason for not making meditation the sole path is that in these times of world crisis we deliberately have to emphasize self-forgetfulness, to stop looking so much at our own selves and start looking a little more at mankind, to forget some of our own need of development and remember others' need of development. The spiritual enlightenment, however humbly we are able to do it, of the society in which we find ourselves is at least as vital in this crisis as our own enlightenment through meditation. If we will faithfully recognize and obey this, then God will bless us and grant grace even though we haven't done as much meditation as in normal times we ought to have done.

86

We cannot save others until we can save ourselves. And yet the altruistic desire to share this self-salvation with others should be present from the beginning. Otherwise, it will not manifest itself when success comes.

87

If he begins to think what impression he is making on others, how spiritual his speech or appearance, his silence or personality must appear to them, then he is worshipping his own ego. To the extent that he does this, his value or service to them is diminished.

88

His first duty is to himself; only when this has been properly attended to is he free to consider his second duty, which is towards mankind. Nevertheless, he is not to fall into the error which would defer all consideration of such altruism until he has completely realized his Overself. If he does so, it may be too late to create a new attitude. It ought always to be at the back of his mind; it should be the ultimate ideal behind all his immediate endeavours.

89

That is pure service where the server feels no importance in himself, where he effaces the gratifying egoism that good deeds may bring to the doer. But where the opposite prevails, then the very act of service itself strengthens self-importance.

90

It is a human failing to wish to appear the possessor of important knowledge, and the desire to rise in the estimation of the curious may easily lead to loss of discretion.

91

There are those who sacrifice themselves to others under the belief that this is a virtue. But if the sacrifice is not linked with wisdom and righteousness, if it is foolish and cowardly, then it becomes the opposite of a virtue and brings harm to one's self and the others.

92

Only wisdom, not emotion alone, can show him how to help without becoming personally entangled. Otherwise he becomes caught in a web of lives, and no longer free to live his own.

93

By identifying emotionally with another's suffering, when this is based on futile, vain, or unwise demands, one does not really help him by supporting, or seeking to satisfy, those demands. One merely prolongs the fog of error around him. It is better to engage in the unpleasant duty of pointing out their unwisdom, of throwing cold water upon them. But this should be accompanied by positive suggestion, by pointing out the benefits of a self-disciplined attitude, by explaining how this is the correct way to heal the suffering emotions and bring peace to the agitated mind, because it is the harmony with the higher law.

94

The need of self-help precedes the duty of service. He must lift himself out of the errors and weaknesses of the flesh before he can safely or effectively lift others. He will be able to serve others spiritually precisely in proportion to the extent he has first served himself spiritually. There are profounder forms than the merely intellectual or merely muscular, too subtle for the materialists to comprehend, whose power is based on mentalist truth. Service does not primarily consist of repeating parrot-like what he has read. It consists of so deepening his consciousness and so developing his character that he can speak with authority, make every word count because of the spiritual experience behind it. If a man can deepen his consciousness, he will discover the instrumental means whereby he can help others to deepen their own. Power will flow from his mystic "heart" to any person he concentrates upon and will get to work within that other's inner being. It will take time for the results to show, however.

95

He who has helped himself to inner strength and knowledge, outer health and spiritual energy, becomes a positive force in the world, able to assist others instead of asking assistance from them. Self-salvation must come first.

96

Because your world is contained in your consciousness, as mentalism teaches, you can best help that world by improving and correcting your consciousness. In attending to your own inner development, you are putting yourself in the most effectual position to promote the development of other persons. Philosophy is fully aware of, and concerned with, the misery and the suffering which are rampant everywhere. It does not approve of selfishness, or indifference to the welfare of others. Yet, at the same time, it does not permit itself to be swept away by blind emotionalism and unreasoned impulsiveness into doing what is least effective for humanity. It calls wisdom in to guide its desire to serve, with the result that the service it does render is the most effective possible.

97

So long as there still adheres to his conscious mind even a fragment of the conviction that he is destined to serve humanity spiritually, much less save it messianically, so long should he take it as a sign that the ego is still dominant. With true humility, there comes abnegation of the will—even the will to serve or save.

98

The disciple who exposes himself too prematurely to the world as a would-be teacher, exposes himself also to new perils and dangerous temptations. It will not be easy for him to reorient himself toward the concept of pure service done disinterestedly, but without it he will fall into traps that will injure him.

99

Those who have been given a mission to perform, however small or large it may be, too often fall into the arrogant error of extending it beyond the proper limits. They let the ego intrude, overplay their hand, and thus spoil what might otherwise have been a good result.

100

What is the best charity, the truest philanthropy? It is so to enlighten a man that thereafter he will find within himself all the resources he needs to manage his life so as to bring him the greatest happiness.

101

Love is to be given as a first duty to our own higher self, and only then to other men. We are here on earth to find the soul, not to better the social relationship nor to construct utopia. These are highly desirable things, let us seek them by all means, but let us not make the mistake in thought of calling them first things. The two ideas are not mutually exclusive. They ought to be, and can be, held side by side, but one as primary and the other as secondary.

102

The feeling of compassion and the doing of service help to cleanse the human mentality of its innate egoism and to release the human heart from its inborn selfishness. Thus they are useful to the aspirant who is treading the path of purification.

103

Those who criticize this refusal to engage in service prematurely, this seeming mystical isolationism—and most Occidentals do criticize it—should ask themselves the question: How can people who are unable to live in harmony with themselves, live in harmony with others? Is it not wiser, more practical, to establish harmony within oneself first and then help others to do so?

104

To recognize that the conventional world is ruled by monstrous stupidity and malignity, to realize that it is useless, vain, and to no purpose to fight these powerful rulers—since failure alone can be the result—is practical wisdom. Let it be called selfishness and escapism, but to refuse the sacrifice of energy and the spending of time in so-called service of humanity is simply an acknowledgment partly that no good can come from meddling in other people's affairs that would not have come anyway, and partly that the character of humanity cannot be changed within one man's lifetime but only by the slow long processes of evolution. It is delusory to believe that anything effectual can be done to perceptibly weaken the real rulers of the world, the stupidity and malignity against which prophets have spoken and sages have warned mankind since thousands of years ago. The fruit of their denunciations hangs on history's tree before us—more stupidity and more malignity today than ever before! Time has not evolved virtue; it has only accumulated folly.

105

To rush out into the service of enlightenment too prematurely at the bidding of the emotion of pity unrestrained by the balance of reason, may do nothing worse than waste time, but it may also do something more serious. It may create confusion in others, pamper vanity in oneself.

106

He should certainly think of his own welfare, it would be foolish not to do that. The mistake or sin is to think *only* of himself or to make the welfare of others entirely subservient.

107

People will begin to come of their own accord for help and guidance when this higher power is using him.

108

He who waits until he penetrates to his innermost being before he begins to play with the notion of service attains depth in the character of that service, whereas he who hurries hastily into the arena may attain width in his service, but he will lack depth. Moreover, the first will work on a world canvas, because space cannot bar the efforts of the spirit, whereas the second, using the method and manner of the body and the intellect alone, may not reach farther than his own town or land.

109

The only kind of service he may render is unpaid service. This condition he cheerfully accepts. For whatever he does to help others, he does out of love of the deed itself.

110

Service must be thoroughly practical as well as conceived in a spirit of noble and generous endeavour.

111

But although premature service of this kind is to be discouraged, the attempt of an advanced disciple to help a beginner is not necessarily a blunder. That depends on confining the help given to proper limits and on abstaining from treading where there is no sure-footedness. He may rightly share his knowledge, experience, and findings.

112

If his efforts to serve mankind socially are made to the utter neglect of the need to serve his own self spiritually, then they are as unbalanced and unwise as the efforts to pursue personal salvation in utter indifference to the fate of others. The proper solution has been given by *Light on the Path*, which counsels the aspirant to kill out desire and ambition but to work as those work who are impelled by these two great forces. But if he does do this, the impelling forces within him can then only be duty and altruism.

113

Offers of service which have unseen strings attached to them, should not be made.

114

The snubs and rebuffs he will meet will cure him of the delusion that society is filled with people who would eagerly take to the quest if only they were told about its existence. Thus he will be brought face to face with the problem of the general uncomprehension of mysticism, the common unsympathy to philosophy. He will discover that his own feelings, his own intuitions, cannot be communicated to others through the medium of words where neither experience nor reflection have prepared a way for them. So he cannot share them with the crowd but must perforce keep them to himself.

115

To improve his corner of the world is good but to improve himself is still better. Unless he receives a mandate from the higher self to set out on such reforming activities, it may be mere egoism that drives him to meddle with them.

116

The field of service will widen in range as the fields of capacity and aspiration themselves widen.

117

The attempt to improve other people's lives can easily mask a presumptuous interference with them. This is especially true when the hidden realities and long-term causes of a situation are not known, or are misread, or when the higher laws which govern mankind are ignored. In all these cases, the old evils may merely be replaced by new ones, so that the improvement is entirely fictitious. In the early Christian times, Saint Cyril saw and said what, much more than a thousand years later, Ananda Metteya the Buddhist and Ramana Maharshi the Hindu told me—that one best saves society by first saving oneself. This is why the philosopher does not try to impose on others the Idea or the Way which he has espoused. For the itch to improve them or alter them is, he now knows, a form of interference. He minds his own business. But if the higher power wants to use him to affect others, he will not resist it!

118

If anyone becomes idealistic and wants to help others he is told to "start a movement" and to persuade as many people as he can to dedicate themselves to it. This is excellent advice in the world of politics, economics, social reform, and material philanthropy. It is of some use even in the world of organized religion. But it cannot be applied in the world of spiritual truth without self-deception. For there a movement must not be started by a man but only by the higher power. It will then select the man it can use, and will guide and inspire him.

119

To dedicate life to spiritually uplifting and guiding others, to the extent one is capable of, is to make certain of receiving the same help from those beyond oneself.

120

If you take another man's duty off his shoulders and put it on your own, or lift his responsibility and leave him without it, because you have a laudable desire to serve mankind, you may in the end render him a disservice as well as put an unnecessary obstacle on your quest.

121

Do not attempt to make people act on a level beyond their comfortable traditional one if they neither want nor understand the higher one. They will resist or resent your attempt, which necessarily must fail.

122

The best form of social service is the one which leads others to the higher understanding of truth. For from that single cause will issue forth various effects in higher moral character, better human relations, and finer spiritual intuitions. Interfering with the freedom of others and meddling in their affairs, while the true laws of man's being and destiny are still hardly understood, leads always in history to unfortunate results.

123

Moreover, whatsoever we give or do to others is ultimately reflected back to us in some form by the power of karma, and if he frequently nurses the ideal of serving mankind he will attract to himself the spiritual help of those who themselves have this same aim.

124

Although it is true that the help we give others always returns to us in some way, somewhere, somewhen, nevertheless he is not motivated in this matter by the desire of reward or return. He will engage in the service of humanity because compassion will arise in his heart, because of the good it will do.

125

The desire to help the unfortunate and to uplift the depraved is a noble one, but it may also be a misguided, premature, or even dangerous one. Misguided, because some men must pay for their criminality before they will be willing to renounce it. Premature, because the philanthropist may have nothing worthwhile of a worldly or spiritual kind to give others. Dangerous, because the mental atmosphere which surrounds low circles of society is haunted by vicious and perverse unseen entities which seek to influence sensitive or mediumistic minds.

126

That alone is pure authentic service which asks for no return.

127

He is warned not to get involved in the personal problems of others, not to assume responsibility for their own duty of forming decisions, and not to believe that he is helping them when they try to evade the necessity of using their own powers and judgement. At his present stage it is safe only to communicate what he knows of the general laws of the spiritual life. Beyond this he should not usually attempt to go, but should let each person apply them for himself to his individual problems. The effort thus called forth will be more valuable to that person's own evolution than blindly obeying someone else.

128

In what way can the student fit himself for greater service to humanity? Usually his first need is to acquire or improve balance between the various functions. It may be that he is overweighted on the side of feelings and psychic sensitivity, and underweighted on the side of caution, practicality, worldly wisdom, and personal hardness. He ought in that case to develop the qualities which he lacks. This he can do during meditation by logically pondering upon them and by making them specific themes for his creative imagination. He can also deliberately seek opportunities to express them in practical day-to-day living. The task is a hard one and certainly not a pleasant one, but it is necessary if he wants to render real service of a tangible nature and not merely indulge in vivid fantasy about it.

129

If one's greatest desire is to serve God, he must first understand that he will serve Him best by making himself a constantly fitting testament of his faith.

130

Students frequently carry over some remnant of the religionist's urge to convert others to their own belief. Self-disciplines must be applied to curb this tendency. Actually it is a product of wishful thinking combined with ignorance. Why ignorance? Because efforts of this sort are more likely to repel than to attract others, to set up what the doctrine of relativity calls an "observational interference." One's contribution should simply be to be available for some discussions of metaphysics and mysticism in general, and to answer questions—provided one is qualified to do so. If the person is really ready for this Teaching, he or she will become aware of it through higher forces than the student's. These work through the subconscious or over-conscious mind. Usually the individual builds up artificial resistances, and time is needed to overcome them. Then, some results will begin to appear in the conscious mind. This is the way the Overself "works." It is also the way the true Master teaches.

131

After the student has sufficiently prepared himself—that is, after he has undergone the philosophic discipline for purifying character, subjugated his lower nature, developed his intellect, and cultivated his intuition—he will then be able to use his gifts in the practice of a higher order of meditation, which will bring him the bliss of communion with the Overself. Others, who may have benefited hitherto by association with him, will find that the earlier benefits were superficial compared with those following his transformation. Thus, one's first duty is always towards oneself—although the idea of service may and should be held in the background for later use.

132

There is more than one way of doing some good to suffering humanity. He should find the way which suits his own temperament, qualifications, and karmic possibilities. For instance, he must not regard a trade or a business as an activity that is neither useful nor necessary. Business is so broad that it is possible to find branches of it that are superior enough to fulfil the double function of making a livelihood and helping others.

133

It is incumbent upon each of those on the Quest to play his or her part in the world in a courageous manner in accord with the teachings of this noble philosophy.

134

As to the time taken for attainment, one has certainly to go through many incarnations before becoming a fit channel for the Overself. But this does not mean that he is not used by the higher power until then. The student who has not yet been purified of egoism can only be used brokenly, in patches, and at intervals, whereas one who has made and implemented the requisite inner delegation of self to Overself is used continuously.

135

By humble prayer and aspiration one may attract that kind of Grace from the Overself which manifests as a power to heal those in unhappy states of mind, bad nervous conditions, and emotional unbalance. But first, he must work on himself and develop the requisite poise, strength, and wisdom from within. The intensity of devotion to the Divine, the desire to be used as a channel for it to others, and the faith which carries on ·with the Quest through both dark and bright circumstances, moods, or times—these things are equally necessary to such self-cultivation.

136

In trying to help others in these unsettled times—perhaps one's own children—one should try to think of them in their larger relation to God, rather than in their relation to familiar surroundings, filial attachments, or the unexpected, disturbing situations which have come up, over which one has limited or no control. Prayer and positive thinking will be as much of a help at these times as anything else one can say or do.

137

Until the aspirant has been notified that he has attained sufficient inner knowledge, purity, and strength, he should not attempt to engage in any outward service, such as entering into meditation with others, holding classes, and so forth, and he should restrict to a minimum the number of people with whom he discusses such matters.

138

Whenever the aspirant volunteers spiritual help to another, or seeks it for himself, he ought not to take money in return on the one hand, nor give it in payment on the other. Such needs will be attended to by the Infinite Intelligence at the proper time.

139

The weak spot in his attitude is its failure to achieve full purity, its pretension to a virtue which remains partially lacking. For his altruistic service wants to take something back in return for what it gives. Such service has hooks in it.

140

If he seeks the realization of his mystical aims only and for his own gain and no one else's, then it is quite proper and necessary for him to concentrate all his attention upon them and upon himself. To indulge in any form of altruistic service—even if it be spiritual service—is to go astray from this path and be led afar from his goal. But if he seeks humanity's benefit as well as his own, it is not proper and necessary to do so. For he will then have to divert some compassionate thought and meditation and feeling to humanity. The kind of mystical attainment which fructifies at the end of the quest depends on the kind of effort he previously put forth in it. If his aim has been self-centered all along, his power to assist others will be limited in various ways; but if it has been altruistic from the start, then he will be able to assist them adequately, easily, widely, and differently.

141

If he finds that the Overself is using him at any particular time as the personal instrument for its guidance, blessing, or healing, he must take care to be detached and keep ego out of the relationship.

142

The student must work for the welfare of the world, yes, but he must do it in his own way, not the world's way. He must not only do the right thing at the right time, neither too early nor too late, but also in the right way. He will not desert the world, but rather transfuse his little corner of it with truer ideals.

143

The right move made at the wrong time may no longer be a right one. If made too late, it may lose much of its effectiveness; if made too early, it may meet with failure.

144

A wise man will seek to study himself, a fool will be busy meddling with others.

145

All are not called to act as, nor are personally equipped to be, teachers and apostles, preachers and helpers, healers and expounders.

146

It is no use talking vaguely of service to humanity when he lacks the capacity to render any specific service at all. In such a case it is better first of all to set to work to develop within himself the necessary capacities.

147

Wisdom always relates service to need whereas ignorance relates it to desire.

148

The philosophic suggestion to be active in the service of mankind does not mean, as some think, that we have to be active in politics nor, as others think, to give away propagandist pamphlets.

149

Let it not be forgotten that goodwill towards mankind does not exclude goodwill towards oneself. The way of martyrdom, of dying uselessly for others, is the way of emotional mysticism. The way of service, of living usefully for others, is the way of rational philosophy.

150

If, at the insistence of other persons or of an over-tender conscience, a man takes too much on himself, he becomes less able to help those for whom he does so.

151

Why this eagerness to run about and set society right? If there is a God, then He has not run away from His creation and left it to fend for itself.

152

The *Bhagavad Gita*'s warning about the duty of another being full of danger runs parallel with the *Tao Teh Ching*'s advocacy of the practice of non-interference. Both Indian and Chinese wisdom thus tell us to mind our own business! Lao Tzu's words are: "The sage avoids the very popular error of endeavouring to assist the processes of nature, which is what he never ventures on doing." The wisdom of minding our own business is not only validated by such teaching: it is also confirmed by experience.

153

Those men who have known this inner life, that other Self, and who have the talent to communicate in speech, writing, or action, have a duty laid on them to tell others of it. But if they lack this talent, they do no wrong to remain in silence about it. For, as Ramana Maharshi once said to me, "Silence also is a form of speech."

154

He who attains even a little power to help others cannot measure where that help will stop. If it gives a lift to one man whom he knows, that man may in his turn give a lift to another person, and so on indefinitely in ever-widening ripples.

155

Reflection reveals and history shows that it is impossible to save the whole world. So he prudently keeps his energies for the task that holds much more favourable possibility—saving himself. It is only the individual person here and there, not the entire mass, who is ever led out of ignorance and slavery to wisdom and freedom.

156

It is bitter indeed to be strong and wise in oneself yet, by identification with another person, to share his weakness and his blindness. For the suffering that inevitably follows them must be shared too under a feeling of helplessness, of inability to change the other and save him from his self-earned destiny.

157

Those who are searching for truth are only a small number but still they are a growing number. Each of us may repay his own obligation by saying the *right word at the right time*, by lending or giving the right book to the truth-hungry person.

158

The minor conventions must be practised if we would serve mankind and achieve our major aims thereby. We can make the world in our own image only by mingling harmoniously with it.

159

Who can save the sick world from itself? Possibly an Avatar but there isn't one in sight at present, so what can we do? Each can save himself, can look to himself. He can tell or show others what he is doing for himself but cannot save them.

160

Even though one is headed in the right direction and is most earnest, his progress, sometimes, is slow. This may be Nature's way of encouraging restraint in his attempts to help or enlighten others. Discrimination is absolutely essential in such matters and they must not be undertaken before one is ready.

161

There is a proper time for everything. When he has reached the age when he has to consider his own spiritual interests he should lessen his activities and save his energies for a higher service, first to himself and then to others.

162

Rather than placing over-emphasis on vocal propaganda, students should, instead, silently exemplify in their own persons and conduct the fruits of such acceptance of this doctrine.

163

Sometimes it becomes necessary for the student to drop all thought of service for a while, in order to demonstrate in his own life what he can do for himself—both inwardly and outwardly. Before this time, any talk of service to others, especially to the Teacher, is premature. The philosophic ideal of ultimate service is agreed upon; however, there is no need to concern oneself about this until one has achieved enough knowledge and experience to make such service worthwhile.

164

The noble and beautiful teachings of old Greece, from the Socratic to the Stoic, harmonize perfectly with the age-old teachings of the higher philosophy. Although they taught a lofty self-reliance they did not teach a narrow self-centeredness. This is symbolized vividly in Plato's story of the cave, where the man who attained Light immediately forsook his deserved rest to descend to the help and guidance of the prisoners still living in the cave's darkness.

9

CONCLUSION

The development of the work

The aspirant will receive personal knowledge from within, as apart from mere teaching from without, only to the extent that he has inwardly prepared himself to receive it. The fruits of the quest cannot be separated from the disciplines of the quest. He is considered capable of grasping philosophic truth when, either now or in a previous existence, he has to some degree purified his understanding by self-discipline, introverted it by meditation, and tranquillized it by reflection. When his mind has habituated itself to this kind of keen, abstract thinking and in some measure has developed the capacity to rest absorbed in its own tranquil centre, when the emotions have purified themselves of personal and animal taints, he has prepared himself for the highest kind of knowledge. For then he is able to use this highly concentrated, well purified, efficiently serene consciousness as an instrument with which to engage himself in a quest to understand in true perspective what the ego really is and to look deep into the nature of the mind itself. For then his self-examination will be free from the emotional distortions, the materialistic impediments of the unpurified, unstilled, and unconcentrated consciousness. The truth about his own existence and the world's existence can then be seen as never before.

2

When the changes in habit come unbidden as the natural result of a more sensitive nature, a deeper outlook, a more compassionate heart, they come rightly. There is then less strain, less likelihood of lapse than when they come artificially or prematurely or through someone else's insistent pressure.

3

The setting of rules and the chalking out of a path are only for beginners. When a man has made sufficient advance to become aware of inner promptings from his higher self, he should allow them to become active in guiding him and should let them take him freely on his spiritual life course.

4

A true spirituality is not aware of itself and therefore is not portentous and heavy. It is "natural."

5

How increasingly difficult and dangerous the path becomes with every advance and how fragile is the attainment of the fourth, fifth, and especially sixth degrees is pictured by the Tibetan Masters who liken the disciple to a snake climbing upward inside a hollow bamboo tube. It can just barely turn around and a single slip may easily throw it all the way down to the bottom of the tube again.

6

Only at a well-advanced stage does the disciple begin to comprehend that his true work is not to develop qualities or achieve tasks, to evolve character or attain goals but to get rid of hindrances and pull aside veils. He has to desert the false self and uncover the true self.

7

Shen-Hui declared, in a sermon, that Enlightenment came as suddenly as a baby's birth. But what about the nine long months of *development* which precedes the birth?

8

The practice of systematic self-discipline will bring a man more and more to complete self-reliance and free him more and more from dependence upon sources outside himself.

9

Once the transition period comes to an end, a subtle change enters into his attitude toward the old habits. They lose their tempting quality and instead begin to acquire a repelling one. This feeling will increase and become firmly established.

10

A mind permeated with such lofty thoughts, constantly renewed by such lofty ideals, gradually empties itself of the baser ones—or rejects them if they appear.

11

The path is a progressive one and therefore the recognition of response to his prayer for enlightenment will be progressive also. At first he will have doubts and uncertainties about the response, but if he perseveres with his efforts it will become clearer and clearer—provided he makes proper use of the help which has been given him. His desire for spiritual attainment is not in the same class with all the earthly desires. It is aspiration and therefore entitled eventually to Grace.

12

This is the severe apprenticeship which philosophy requires, the progressive discipline which it imposes. Nor could it ask less, if it is to win the unshatterable poise and impeccable mind which provide the correct atmosphere for its last and highest revelations of truth.

13

If the changeover is suddenly made, it will be heroic, violent, forceful. But those of a different temperament, who make it gradually, will necessarily make it gently, peaceably, cautiously.

14

What is right at an early stage of development may not be right at a later one. The fitness of an ethos depends also on its time and place. It is better to define the concrete task of the moment rather than revel in abstract phrases about the distant future.

15

There are two occasions when it is necessary to define one's aims to and for one's self. The first is when one starts out to seek their realization. The second is when what one believes to be the realization itself is in sight.

16

If the seeker finds himself called upon by his higher ideals or by the necessities of his quest to make a decision involving financial sacrifice to the point of leaving himself with insufficient resources, he need have no fear about the ultimate issue. His higher self will permit him to fall into grievous want only if such a condition is really essential to the particular phase of spiritual discipline his ego needs just then. Otherwise it will use its power to protect him and to compensate him, for it can always adjust financial conditions more favourably by releasing portions of good karma to ensure his support.

17

He who wishes to pursue truth to its farther extent, which a man will usually do only under a concentrated compulsion from within—that is to say, under a driving urge from his higher self—will travel quicker than others but must expect to pay a heavier price than others.

18

The problem of philosophic attainment is one which man cannot solve by his own unaided powers. Like a tiny sailing boat which needs both oars and a sail for its propulsion, he needs both self-effort and grace for his progress. To rely on either alone is a mistake. If he cannot attain by his own strivings, neither is the Overself likely to grant its grace without them.

19

There is a proper time for all acts and attitudes. The improper time to drop mystical technique and quit meditational exercises is when you are still a novice, still aware only of thoughts and emotions on the ordinary plane. The proper time to abandon set practices is when you are a proficient, when you have become adequately aware of the divine presence. Then you need engage yourself only in a single and simple effort: to persevere in paying attention to this presence so as to sustain and stretch out the welcome intervals of its realization.

20

Those who have matured in the Quest, who have gone beyond the early fluctuations and confusions, who have found some equipoise beyond the adolescent reactions with their ardours and despairs, are alone entitled to, will be readier for its higher metaphysical revelations.

21

Hence the more he becomes aware of these frailties, the more he should discipline himself to get rid of them—otherwise the forces he has invoked will bring the pressures of pain upon him to effect this end. This is the first hidden purpose of the "dark night." The second is to develop the neglected parts of his human make-up and thus bring his personality into a safe balance. The light which originally dawned in his soul successfully illumined his emotions. He felt goodwill towards all men, nay all living creatures. But this illumination did not bestow practical wisdom or higher knowledge, did not affect his intelligence. Hence the light has still to shine down into the neglected regions of his personality. They are not automatically perfected. For the higher Self always seeks to enlighten the whole of the man. Hence the threefold-path character of the work of this quest. He may have to build more intellect or develop more will, for instance. He has to reorganize his whole personality, in short. The emotional perfecting is easiest and occurs first; the intellectual is harder and occurs second; the moral reeducation through right actions is hardest of all and occurs last. He has gained right feeling. He has yet to gain right insight. But this cannot be got without the co-operation of the full man, of all his faculties. So the higher Self turns towards his intellect and transforms it into intelligence, towards his will and transforms it into active moral work. This process, however, takes years. When all this preparation has matured him, the dark night will suddenly, even unexpectedly, come to an end and he will receive the long-sought illumination.

Such is the commoner form of the "dark night of the soul." A rarer and sadder kind may come, not to novices but to the highly advanced ones who are already within sight of their goal. For it is just here, when he has only one more step to take before the end is successfully reached, that all may be lost and he may fall headlong from this great height. The Biblical phrase, "Let him that standeth take heed lest he fall," is appropriate here. This terrible lapse is explained by the adepts as always being possible and especially probable when the sixth or penultimate stage of their seven-staged path is attained. Hence they call this the stage of "carefulness," because the mystic must now be extremely careful to preserve the delicate inward condition he has developed. He must guard this position per-severingly for a sufficiently long period and then the final, complete, and permanent merger into divine existence will be achieved.

22

Before he reaches a certain stage he will necessarily have to seek guid-ance from without, from books and teachers, because of his uncertainty, lack of confidence, and ignorance. But after he reaches it, it will be wiser and safer for him to seek guidance from within. The higher self will impart all the knowledge he needs, as and when he needs it.

23

He feels distant, bloodless, aloof, unemotional. The world appears as if in a dream, seems unreal on awakening. He is unable to take it seriously, to be moved by its sights with any feeling let alone with passion's force. He is indifferent to its drama. Life in it is a weary round. The description of these feelings corresponds to the Dark Night of the Soul.

24

The desire to get at the soul must become so predominant and so anxious that a continuous tension is created within him.

25

Whatever regime he follows, a time will come when momentous changes will become necessary in it. They may be dictated by external events, contacts, or environments. Or they may be quite voluntary, made under a compulsion rising from within himself.

26

If he makes sufficient advance, the time will come when he will look with horror and detestation upon the smug attitudes of his early spiritual life and the smug acts of his early spiritual career.

27

The experience of being gripped and physically shaken by some extraor-dinary power will also occur at certain intervals along this path. This is not to be feared but rather to be welcomed. It always signifies a descent of grace and is a herald of coming progress of some kind or other.

28

When the intervening stages of approach have been passed through one by one, truths which once seemed incredible now appear quite credible.

29

Those first appearances of the soul's presence must be carefully guarded and assiduously nursed. They are symbolized by the Christ-babe which has to grow until it is mature in virtue and wisdom.

30

When he feels the gentle coming of the presence of the higher self, at this point he must train himself in the art of keeping completely passive. He will discover that it is endeavouring actually to ensoul him, to take possession of him as a disembodied spirit is supposed to take possession of a living medium. His task now is purely negative; it is to offer no resistance to the endeavour but to let it have the fullest possible sway over him. The preliminary phases of his progress are over. Hitherto it was mostly his own efforts upon which he had to rely. Now, however, it is the Overself which will be the active agent in his development. All that is henceforth asked of him is that he remain passive, otherwise he may disturb the holy work by the interference of his blind ignorant self-will. His advance at this point no longer depends on his own striving.

31

In time, when the beginning state is well past, he will become intellectually free. There will be no theories, no ideologies to hold him captive and colour his judgements. This is not only because he realizes how the widening of his study, outlook, knowledge, development, has produced a succession of varied theories but also because he is coming nearer to truth, which exhilarates and liberates the mind.

32

Again and again one hears from aspirants that in the heat of the day's activity, in the turmoil of the day's business, and under the pressure of the day's work they tend to forget the Quest. At the beginner's stage this is inevitable; he has to attend to these other matters, and if he is to attend to them properly, effectively, and efficiently they need his whole mind. This is why the practice of having withdrawal periods each day for meditation, for study, or for relaxation is so well advised. It is only when a more advanced stage of the quest is brought under consideration that the matter becomes really serious. The aspirant is then trying to practise thought-control as often as he can. He is trying to practise self-awareness and he is trying to practise spiritual remembrance. But still he finds that what he's doing tends to carry his mind away from all these practices so that he forgets the quest. What he has been practising has not been wasted: it will bring its fruit in due course, but it is not enough to give him the success he seeks. The reason is that all this inner activity has been taking place in the realm of thought; he substitutes aspirational thoughts for the worldly ones from time to time. The way out is to deepen both his knowledge of mentalism and his practice of meditation. If he does not do this, he may split his personality and become a mere dreamer.

33

It is a matter of levels: at the beginning effort is necessary and efficacious. Its nature and result will of course be governed by the fixed conditions of his inner and outer life. But later, at the proficient's level, with its newly awakened recognition of the ego's presence in all this, he lets up, practises Lao Tzu's "Way of non-doing," abandons the old customary attitude.

34

Any form which can still be useful to the growth of others, or helpful for their support, should be thrown away only by the man who has finished the Quest. If these others throw it away also, out of imitation of such a man, they will only harm themselves and create anarchy in the domain of spiritual seeking.

35

If one has the capacity to make progress and to tune in to the True Divinity, he must—if he is to continue and not become sidetracked— renounce all interest in mediumistic or other so-called spiritualistic practices. Such an individual should strive to better his own character, cultivate his intuition, and increase his knowledge about the higher laws by studying inspired and reliable books.

36

That mysticism has its dangers is frankly admitted; and certain individuals should be warned of the seriousness of these dangers, otherwise they may later suffer mental disorders. First, at a certain stage, meditation can be overdone. When this has happened, it is advisable for the individual to withdraw from the practice altogether for several weeks at least, and devote his attention to practical, day-to-day activities in order to acquire better balance. Second, fasting at a particular stage of his development should be avoided, since it can open the way to a mediumistic condition and to the possible influence of mischievous entities. Any person thus affected by fasting definitely should not attempt it until such time as he has met with one much further along the Path than he is.

37

A time will arise when the student may feel it advisable to go away for a period of intensive meditation. It is imperative that he should learn that, such being his feelings, he has done quite enough meditating for his stage of development. It is not wise to overdo meditation.

What he needs now is to balance all the many profits hitherto gained from his meditating by bringing them into intellectual life. Although he may rightly believe the intellectual life to be inferior in value to the mystical life of meditation, nevertheless, it has its place and is needed for balanced development. It is necessary to stimulate the thinking faculties and critical judgement.

Therefore, the aspirant should study from a purely intellectual point-of-view all those teachings which he formerly grasped from an intuitional or emotional viewpoint alone. If he does anything at all in the devotional line, at this time, it should be Prayer.

38

When a seeker has developed sufficient mystical intuition, it becomes necessary for him to balance up by cultivating intellectual understanding. In this way he will be able to deal more effectively with the problems of the present age. At first, his progress in the new direction may seem slow and disappointing; but he should be cheered to know that he is, in fact, working and co-operating with Higher Forces. There is Infinite Intelligence always at work on this planet, and the seeker's own sense of being, motivated as it is by his individual intelligence, is a microcosmic facsimile of the Great Cosmic Workings. One day he will see the whole of the picture, not just the lower part of it, and he will understand that it is his own Overself which has brought him to—and led him safely through—the disheartening experiences of his present incarnation.

39

It may become necessary for the individual to withdraw for a time from his studies and meditation, in order to devote all his attention to problems of a worldly nature and to finding a way out of them. It is quite possible that these problems carry with them a special significance which is intended to develop the practical side of the student's nature as well as to dispel certain fantastic notions. Once he has resolved the problem and taken its message to heart, it will be permissible for him to resume his mystical studies.

40

Such actions as fits of weeping, accompanied by intense yearning, are, for many aspirants, emotional upheavals of an agonizing kind; but, fortunately, neither the demonstration nor the suffering lasts long. They are usually followed by a feeling of deep peace and surrender, which helps to loosen the hold on life-long, worldly characteristics that may be impeding one's spiritual progress.

41

The condition of spiritual dryness about which he may complain is a common phenomenon in the mystical life. It arises from various causes but he need not doubt that it will pass away.

42

If he once has an experience of his divine soul he should remember that this was because it is always there, always inside of him, and has never left him. Let him but stick to the Quest, and the experience will recur at the proper time.

43

It is through meeting and understanding the difficulties on the path, through facing and mastering them, that we grow. Each of us in this world lives in a state of continuous struggle, whatever outward appearances to the contrary may suggest. Repose is for the dead alone—and then only for a limited time. We must study the lessons behind every experience, painful or pleasant, that karma brings. We lose nothing except what is well worth losing if we frankly acknowledge past errors. Only vanity or selfishness can stand in the way of such acknowledgment. Earthly life is after all a transient means to an enduring end. The worth or worthlessness of its experiences lies not in any particular external form, but in the development of consciousness and character to which they lead. Only after time has cooled down the fires of passion and cleared the mists of self-interest are most people able to perceive that these mental developments are the essential and residual significance of their human fortunes. With the seeker after truth, the period of meditation must be devoted, at least in part, to arriving at such perceptions even in the midst of life's events.

44

It is not possible for a student to know the changes which are going on in his subconscious mind and which will eventually break through into his consciousness at some time. If he feels he is failing in some way through his attachment to material things, the very recognition of this is itself a sign that he has half-progressed out of this condition and is not satisfied to remain inside these attachments. Of course, the struggle to free himself from them is at its worst when he does not have the feeling of the Divine Presence. But when that feeling comes the struggle itself will automatically begin to die down.

45

He should not worry about his lapses from meditation or his inability to study deep books. There is a time for all things and the keynote for such a period is action. He can take up further meditation and study again later.

46

The integral ideal of our path is threefold: (a) meditation, (b) reflection, and (c) action. The passing over from one phase of development which has been over-emphasized to another which has been neglected is necessarily a period of upheaval, depression, and unsettlement. But it draws to an end. After the storm comes peace.

47

A teacher may inform his pupil that it is unnecessary to read any more for the time being. This is not an injunction to stop reading but a hint that the next step forward will not arise out of the reading itself. The fact that he finds new inspiration in the books does not alter the truth of this hint. For the change that has come arose within his mind first and enabled him to find fresh material to digest in these books. If this inner change had not first started into activity, the books would have remained the same as before to his conscious mind. The spiritual movement starts in the subconsciousness first and later breaks through into the everyday consciousness. This is merely an academic point. What really matters is that he should become aware of progress.

48

Feelings of inward peace, moral elevation, and divine presence are immeasurably more valuable and significant than visions.

49

Sometimes, at a certain stage of development, a reorientation of outward life does become necessary. The aspirant must then study the situation to see how this can be worked out satisfactorily for all concerned, remembering that the wishes and feelings of those who share his life must also be considered and respected.

50

A time will arise when nearly all questions constitute an intellectual probing, which, in many cases, defeats the purpose of spiritual progress. It is better to wait patiently for the individual's own development to bring what is really needed at each stage.

51

The blind gropings of those early days give place, after many years, to the clear-sighted steps of these later ones. The completion of his quest now becomes an impending event; the quintessence of all his experience now expresses itself in this fullness of being and knowing which is almost at hand.

52

Little by little, at a pace so slow that the movement is hardly noticeable, his mind will give entrance to thoughts that seem to come creeping from some source other than itself, for they are thoughts irrelevant to his reasonings and inconsistent with his convictions. They are indeed intuitions. If he submits to their leading, if he surrenders his faith to them, if he drops his blind resistances, all will be well with him. He will be guided out of darkness into light, out of materiality into spirituality, out of black despair into sublime hope.

53

A few years earlier these defects would have excited little attention. It is because he is now more morally advanced that he is so dismayed by them. Therefore, there is cause here for a little satisfaction surely.

54

If weeping comes, be it in sound or in silence, it will not be to express unhappiness nor to express joy. For it is very important, and on a deeper, more mysterious, level. So let it continue if it chooses.

55

These formal patterns of behaviour set forth as examples to learn and imitate are, after all, mainly for undeveloped or immature beginners. They are commandments to be obeyed. But evolved maturer types may not really need them, because they instinctively act in such a way.

56

The imposition from outside of any rule or regime or discipline is rarely successful in its results unless it gains the assent of the innermost feeling or intuitive mind.

57

There will come a time when this early need of explicit instruction is felt less and less, when what he already knows must be worked out more and more.

58

The timetable of a seeker's advance depends on several factors, but without doubt the most important of them all is the strength of the longing within his heart for the Highest.

59

He must pass through the Egyptian pylons of self-subdual and enter the straight and narrow path beyond them.

60

When the acceptance of these truths becomes instinctive, even if it remains inarticulate, he will begin to gather strength from them, to feel that the little structure of his life has nothing less than cosmic support beneath it.

61

There is a time in his progress when he should put aside all intellectual problems for the time being and concentrate on the two most important tenets of mystical philosophy. They are: that man in his deepest being is an immortal soul, and that there is a path whereby he may discover it for himself.

62

Desire and peace, passion and repose, will alternate in his heart like the sun and moon.

63

When he has gone through some training in yoga or meditation, he is fit to ascertain Truth . . . emotionally and mentally fit. His mind can be held for a long time on a single theme without wandering; he can *concentrate* his thoughts upon the pursuit of Truth to the exclusion of everything else. His power of attention is made needle-sharp and brought under control. Thus equipped, he can begin to find Truth.

Everything up till now was but preparation. With this extraordinary sharpness of intelligence and attentiveness, he has next to discriminate between pure Consciousness *per se*, and everything that merely forms the content of consciousness. For Consciousness is the ultimate, as science is beginning vaguely to see. With concentrated, sharpened mind he can pierce into his deepest self and then endeavour to *understand* it; he can also pierce into the external world of matter and understand that too. Unthwarted by the illusions of the ordinary man, who takes what his eyes see for granted, he can probe beneath appearances. And when he can at last *see* the Truth, his spiritual ignorance falls away of its own accord and can *never* come back to him again, any more than a man who has awakened from dreaming can relapse back into his original dream.

Thus, the actual finding of Truth, which is the same as Nirvana, Self-Knowledge, Liberation, is really a work of brief duration—perhaps a matter of minutes—whereas the preparation and equipment of oneself to find it must take many incarnations.

If this presentation sounds unorthodox, he will find that in chapter 13, verse 2, of the *Bhagavad Gita*, Krishna distinctly asserts that *both* the knowledge of the *Kshetrajna* and *Kshetra* are required before a man may be deemed to possess the truth. In plain English, this merely means that he must know both himself and his body. But as the body is a part of the external physical world and represents it in miniature, the meaning must be extended to include the whole physical world. Merely going inwards and enjoying emotional ecstasies will not do. It may make him happy, but it does not give the whole truth. He has to come outside again, and lo and behold! there is the material world confronting him—yet not understood.

If however, the yogi takes his sharpened, concentrative mind and applies it to such understanding, he discovers that the world of matter is ultimately space and that all material forms are merely ideas in his mind. He discovers, too, that his inmost self is one with this space, because it is formless. He perceives the unity of all life and he has found Truth, the whole Truth. This is maha-yoga, the higher path that awaits every yogi or mystic, and which alone leads to Truth.

The working of Grace

64

You may believe in a religion, but it is not enough to believe in philosophy; you have also to learn it. Nor can it be learnt through the head alone, it has also to be learnt through the heart and the will. Therefore, do not expect to master it within a few years but allot your whole lifetime for this task.

65

Lao Tzu said, "Do nothing by self-will but rather conform to heaven's will, and everything will be done for you." The whole of the quest may be summed up as an attempt to put these wise words into practice. However, the quest is not a thing of a moment or a day; it extends through many years, nay, through a whole lifetime. Therefore, merely to learn how to "do nothing" is itself a long task, if it is to be truly done and if we are not to deceive ourselves.

66

To take such sentences from Lao Tzu's book as, "The way undertakes no activities, and yet there is nothing left undone," and to assume, as so many Western commentators assume, that it means complete retirement from the world as a way of life because everything will be done by the Higher Power is to confuse the minds of aspirants. The virtue and power lie not in the retirement but in the linking up with the higher force which flows through the adept, a force which is unable to flow through the beginner. To take another sentence from Lao Tzu, "The Sage manages his affairs without assertion and spreads his doctrine without words," would again be foolish or dangerous if applied to the beginner. It is natural for the ego to assert itself and it will continue to do so even if he retires from the world. Only when the ego loses the power to rule the affairs of a man does the Overself step in and rule them for him, but this position is not reached merely by saying or wishing that it should be reached. It represents the culmination of a lifelong struggle. Then again, unless a man has become completely united with the force which lies within the depths of silence, he must necessarily depend upon words to spread a doctrine: only the adept who has united himself with that force, which is immeasurably more powerful than the intellect, can afford to remain silent with the perfect confidence that the doctrine will spread despite it.

67

Essay: The Progressive Stages of the Quest (The Working of Grace)

"On the day of life's surrender I shall die desiring Thee; I shall yield my spirit craving of Thy street the dust to be."
—Humamud Din (Fourteenth-century Persian mystic)

In these poetic lines is expressed the lengths to which the mystic must be willing to go to obtain Grace.

Only if a man falls in love with his soul as deeply as he has ever done with a woman will he even stand a chance of finding it. Incessant yearning for the higher self, in a spirit of religious devotion, is one of the indispensable aspects of the fourfold integral quest. The note of yearning for this realization must sound through all his prayer and worship, concentration and meditation. Sometimes the longing for God may affect him even physically with abrupt dynamic force, shaking his whole body, and agitating his whole nervous system. A merely formal practice of meditation is quite insufficient although not quite useless. For without the yearning the advent of Grace is unlikely, and without Grace there can never be any realization of the Overself.

The very fact that a man has consciously begun the quest is itself a manifestation of Grace, for he has begun to seek the Overself only because the Overself's own working has begun to make it plain to him, through the sense of unbearable separation from it, that the right moment for this has arrived. The aspirant should therefore take heart and feel hope. He is not really walking alone. The very love which has awakened within him for the Overself is a reflection of the love which is being shown towards him.

Thus the very search upon which he has embarked, the studies he is making, and the meditations he is practising are all inspired by the Overself from the beginning and sustained by it to the end. The Overself is already at work even before he begins to seek it. Indeed he has taken to the quest in unconscious obedience to the divine prompting. And that prompting is the first movement of Grace. Even when he believes that he is doing these things for himself, it is really Grace that is opening the heart and enlightening the mind from behind the scenes.

Man's initiative pushes on toward the goal, whilst divine Grace draws him to it. Both forces must combine if the process is to be completed and crowned with success. Yet that which originally made the goal attractive to him and inspired him with faith in it and thus gave rise to his efforts, was itself the Grace. In this sense Paul's words, "For by Grace are ye saved through faith, and that not of yourselves," become more intelligible.

The Grace of God is no respecter of persons or places. It comes to the heart that *desires it most* whether that heart be in the body of a king or of a commoner, a man of action or a recluse. John Bunyan the poor tinker, immured in Bedford gaol, saw a Light denied to many kings and tried to write it down in his book *Pilgrim's Progress*. Jacob Boehme, working at his cobbler's bench in Seidenburg, was thrice illumined and gleaned secrets which he claimed were unknown to the universities of his time.

If a man has conscientiously followed this fourfold path, if he has practised mystical meditation and metaphysical reflection, purification of character and unselfish service, and yet seems to be remote from the goal, what is he to do? He has then to follow the admonition of Jesus: "Ask and ye shall receive, knock and it shall be opened unto you." He has literally to ask for Grace out of the deep anguish of his heart. We are all poor. He is indeed discerning who realizes this and becomes a beggar, imploring of God for Grace.

He must pray first to be liberated from the heavy thraldom of the senses, the desires, and the thoughts. He must pray next for the conscious presence of the Overself. He should pray silently and deeply in the solitude of his own heart. He should pray with concentrated emotion and tight-held mind. His yearning for such liberation and such presence must be unquestionably sincere and unquestionably strong. He should begin and close—and even fill if he wishes—his hour of meditation with such noble prayers. He must do this day after day, week after week. For the Overself is not merely a concept, but a living reality, the power behind all his other and lesser powers.

No aspirant who is sincere and sensitive will be left entirely without help. It may appear during temptation when the lower nature may find itself unexpectedly curbed by a powerful idea working strongly against it. He may find in a book just that for which he has been waiting and which at this particular time will definitely help him on his way. The particular help he needs at a particular stage will come naturally. It may take the form of a change in outward circumstances or a meeting with a more developed person, of a printed book or a written letter, of a sudden unexpected emotional inspiration or an illuminating intellectual intuition. Nor is it necessary to travel to the farthest point before being able to gather the fruits. Long before this, he will begin to enjoy the flavour of peace, hope, knowledge, and divine transcendence.

In the moment that a man willingly deserts his habitual standpoint under a trying situation and substitutes this higher one, in that moment he receives Grace. With this reception a miracle is performed and the evil of the lower standpoint is permanently expelled from his character. The situation itself both put him to the proof and gave him his chance.

The factuality of Grace does not cancel out the need of moral choice and personal effort. It would be a great mistake to stamp human effort as useless in the quest and to proclaim human inability to achieve its own salvation as complete. For if it is true that Divine Grace alone can bring the quest to a successful terminus, it is likewise true that human effort must precede and thus invoke the descent of Grace. What is needed to call down Grace is, first, a humility that is utter and complete, deeply earnest and absolutely sincere, secondly, an offering of self to the Overself, a dedication of earthly being to spiritual essence, and, thirdly, a daily practice of devotional exercise. The practices will eventually yield experiences, the aspirations will eventually bring assistance. The mysterious intrusion of Grace may change the course of events. It introduces new possibilities, a different current of destiny.

Our need of salvation, of overcoming the inherently sinful and ignorant nature of ego, isolated from true consciousness as it is, is greater than we ever comprehend. For our life, being so largely egotistic, is ignorant and sinful—a wandering from one blunder to another, one sin to another. This salvation is by the Overself's saving power, for which we must seek its Grace, approaching it with the childlike humility of which Jesus spoke. No man is so down, so sinful, so weak, or so beaten that he may not make a fresh start. Let him adopt a childlike attitude, placing himself in the hands of his higher self, imploring it for guidance and Grace. He should repeat this at least daily, and even oftener. Then let him patiently wait and carefully watch for the intuitive response during the course of the following weeks or months. He need not mind his faults. Let him offer himself, just as he is, to the God, or Soul, he seeks. It is not indifferent nor remote.

The forgiveness of sins is a fact. Those who deny this deny their own experience. Can they separate from the moon its light? Then how can they separate forgiveness from love? Do they not see a mother forgive her child a hundred times even though she reproves and chastises it?

If the retribution of sins is a cosmic law, so also is the remission of sins.

We must take the two at once, and together, if we would understand the mystery aright.

We humans are fallible beings prone to commit errors. If we do not become penitents and break with our past, it is better that we should be left to the natural consequences of our wrong-doing than that we should be forgiven prematurely.

The value of repentance is that it is the first step to set us free from a regrettable past; of amendment, that it is the last step to do so. There must be a contrite consciousness that to live in ego is to live in ignorance and sin. This sin is not the breaking of social conventions. There must be penitent understanding that we are born in sin because we are born in ego and hence need redemption and salvation. It is useless to seek forgiveness without first being thoroughly repentant. There must also be an opening up of the mind to the truth about one's sinfulness, besides repentance, an understanding of the lesson behind this particular experience of its result.

This primary attribute is extolled in the world's religio-mystical literature. "Despair not of Allah's mercy," says the *Koran*. "What are my sins compared with Thy mercy? They are but as a cobweb before the wind," wrote an early Russian mystic, Dmitri of Rostov. "Those who surrender to me, even be they of sinful nature, shall understand the highest path," says the *Bhagavad Gita*.

Yes, there is forgiveness because there is God's love. Jesus was not mistaken when he preached this doctrine, but it is not a fact for all men alike. Profound penitence and sincere amendment are prerequisite conditions to calling it forth. It was one of the special tasks of Jesus to make known that compassion (or love, as the original word was translated) is a primary attribute of God and that Grace, pardon, and redemption are consequently primary features of God's active relation to man. When Jesus promised the repentant thief that he would be forgiven, Jesus was not deceiving the thief or deluding himself. He was telling the truth.

The Divine being what it is, how could it contradict its own nature if compassion had no place in its qualities? The connection between the benignity which every mystic feels in its presence and the compassion which Jesus ascribed to that presence, is organic and inseparable.

The discovery that the forgiveness of sins is a sacred fact should fill us with inexpressible joy. For it is the discovery that there is compassionate love at the heart of the universe.

We may suppress sins by personal effort but we can eradicate and overcome them by the Overself's Grace alone. If we ask only that the external results of our sin be forgiven, be sure they won't. But if we also strive to cleanse our character from the internal evil that caused the sin, forgiveness may well be ours.

The aspirant's best hope lies in repentance. But if he fails to recognize this, if he remains with unbowed head and unregenerate heart, the way forward will likewise remain stony and painful. The admission that he is fallible and weak will be wrung from him by the punishments of nature if he will not yield it by the perceptions of conscience. The first value of repentance is that it makes a break with an outworn past. The second value is that it opens the way to a fresh start. Past mistakes cannot be erased but future ones can be avoided. The man that he was must fill him with regrets; the man that he seeks to be with hopes. He must become keenly conscious of his own sinfulness. The clumsy handiwork of his spiritual adolescence will appall him whenever he meditates upon its defects. His thought must distrust and purge itself of these faults. He will at certain periods feel impelled to reproach himself for faults shown, wrongs done, and sins committed during the past. This impulse should be obeyed. His attitude must so change that he is not merely ready but even eager to undo the wrongs that he has done and to make restitution for the harm that he has caused.

We do not get at the Real by our own efforts alone nor does it come to us by its own volition alone. Effort that springs from the self and Grace that springs from beyond it are two things essential to success in this quest. The first we can all provide, but the second only the Overself can provide. Man was once told by someone who knew, "The Spirit bloweth where it listeth." Thus it is neither contradictory nor antithetic to say that human effort and human dependence upon Divine Grace are both needed. For there is a kind of reciprocal action between them. This reciprocal working of Grace is a beautiful fact. The subconscious invitation from the Overself begets the conscious invocation of it as an automatic response. When the ego feels attracted towards its sacred source, there is an equivalent attraction on the Overself's part towards the ego itself. Never doubt that the Divine always reciprocates this attraction to it of the human self. Neither the latter's past history nor present character can alter that blessed hope-bringing fact. Grace is the final, glorious, and authentic proof that it is not only man that is seeking God, but also God that is ever waiting for man.

The Grace is a heavenly superhuman gift. Those who have never felt it and consequently rush into incautious denial of its existence are to be pitied. Those who flout the possibility and deny the need of a helping Grace can be only those who have become victims of a cast-iron intellectual system which could not consistently give a place to it.

It was a flaming experience of Grace which changed Saul, the bitter opponent, into Paul, the ardent apostle.

This is the paradox, that although a man must try to conquer himself if he would attain the Overself, he cannot succeed in this undertaking except by the Overself's own power—that is, by the Grace "which burns the straw of desires" as *Mahopanishad* poetically puts it. It is certain that such an attainment is beyond his ordinary strength.

All that the ego can do is to create the necessary conditions out of which enlightenment generally arises, but it cannot create this enlightenment itself. By self-purification, by constant aspiration, by regular meditation, by profound study, and by an altruistic attitude in practical life, it does what is prerequisite. But all this is like tapping at the door of the Overself. Only the latter's Grace can open it in the end.

The will has its part in this process, but it is not the only part. Sooner or later he will discover that he can go forward no farther in its sole dependence, and that he must seek help from something beyond himself. He must indeed call for Grace to act upon him. The need of obtaining help from outside his ordinary self and from beyond his ordinary resources in this tremendous struggle becomes urgent. It is indeed a need of Grace. Fortunately for him this Grace is available, although it may not be so on his own terms.

At a certain stage he must learn to "let go" more and allow the Overself to possess him, rather than strain to possess something which he believes to be still eluding him. Every aspirant who has passed it will remember how he leapt ahead when he made this discovery.

At another stage, the Overself, whose Grace was the initial impetus to all his efforts, steps forward, as it were, and begins to reveal its presence and working more openly. The aspirant becomes conscious of this with awe, reverence, and thankfulness. He must learn to attend vigilantly to these inward promptings of Divine Grace. They are like sunbeams that fructify the earth.

With the descent of Grace, all the anguish and ugly memories of the seeker's past and the frustrations of the present are miraculously sponged out by the Overself's unseen and healing hand. He knows that a new element has entered into his field of consciousness, and he will unmistakably feel from that moment a blessed quickening of inner life. When his own personal effort subsides, a further effort begins on his behalf by a higher power. Without any move on his own part, Grace begins to do for him what he could not do for himself, and under its beneficent operation he will find his higher will strengthening, his moral attitude improving, and his spiritual aspiration increasing.

The consciousness of being under the control of a higher influence will become unmistakable to him. The conviction that it is achieving moral victories for him which he could not have achieved by his ordinary self, will become implanted in him. A series of remarkable experiences will confirm the fact that some beneficent power has invaded his personality and is ennobling, elevating, inspiring, and guiding it. An exultant freedom takes possession of him. It displaces all his emotional forebodings and personal burdens.

Grace is received, not achieved. A man must be willing to let its influx move freely through his heart; he must not obstruct its working nor impede its ruling by any break in his own self-surrender. He can possess Grace only when he lets it possess him.

Philosophy affirms the existence of Grace, that what the most strenuous self-activity cannot gain may be put in our hands as a divine gift.

As at the beginning, so at the end of this path, the unveiling of the Overself is not an act of any human will. Only the Divine Will—that is, only its own Grace—can bring about the final all-revealing act, whose sustained consciousness turns the aspirant into an adept.

In seeking the Overself, the earnest aspirant must seek it with heartfelt love. Indeed, his whole quest must be ardently imbued with this feeling. Can he love the Divine purely and disinterestedly for its own sake? This is the question he must ask himself. If this devotional love is to be something more than frothy feeling, it will have to affect and redeem the will. It will have to heighten the sense of, and obedience to, moral duty. Because of this devotion to something which transcends his selfish interests, he can no longer seek his selfish advantage at the expense of others. His aim will be not only to love the soul but to understand it, not only to hear its voice in meditation but to live out its promptings in action.

68

Whether the world was brought into existence as *lila*, a theatrical show, as one important Hindu theology says, or as a universal joke, as some important Western metaphysicians conclude, it still remains that the humans in it must suffer; whether they are puppets in a play or victims of divine fun, sooner or later they have to endure loss, illness, bereavement, and death. The practical attitude is then to minimize the suffering where possible and where self-caused, on the physical level, and to develop inner strength, composure, and understanding on the emotional-mental one so as to be less vulnerable. This is to apply philosophy.

Part 2:

RELAX AND RETREAT

The world clamours for attention and participation. God alone is silent, undemanding, unaggressive.

It is not that the soul cannot be found in populous cities but that it can be found more easily and more quickly in solitary retreats. Its presence comes more clearly there. But to learn how to keep it, we have to return to the cities again.

1

TAKE INTERMITTENT PAUSES

Perhaps these pages may impart a flavour of that unforgettable quiet which counters the tumult of today's existence.

2

He must make two demands on society if he is to accomplish his purpose—solitude and time. And if society is unprepared and therefore unwilling to grant them, he must take them by force. If this leads, as it may, to the false criticism that he is self-centered and proud, he must accept this as part of the cost of growth.

3

A modern way of spiritual living for busy city-dwellers would be to carry out all normal duties but to retreat from them from time to time into rural solitude for special meditation and study. In the town itself, they should manage to find a half to one hour every day for prayer and mental quiet.

4

If you begin the day with love in your heart, peace in your nerves, and truth in your mind, you not only benefit by their presence but also bring them to others—to your family or friends, and to all those whom destiny draws across your path that day.

5

This withdrawal from the day's turmoil into creative silence is not a luxury, a fad, or a futility. It is a necessity, because it tries to provide the conditions wherein we are able to yield ourselves to intuitive leadings, promptings, warnings, teachings, and counsels and also to the inspiring peace of the soul. It dissolves mental tensions and heals negative emotions.

6

We need these interludes of mental quiet.

7

Lucky is the man who, in these days, can extricate himself from society without passing permanently into the cloister. Yet luck is only apparent, for no one can do it without firm determination and stubborn persistence.

8

The aggressive world of our time needs to learn how to get out of time. The active world needs to learn to sit still, mentally and physically, without becoming bored.

9

If we give a part of the day to the purposes of study, prayer, meditation, and physical care, it may begin as a duty but it may end as a joy.

10

To begin the day with such high thoughts, such metaphysical reading, such meditative calm, is to begin the day well. All his reaction to its coming events will be influenced by this wise procedure. He is a far-sighted man who refuses to be carried away by the speed and greed of our times but insists on making a period for elated feeling and exalted mind.

11

He can do nothing better for himself and, in the end, for the world than to step out of its current from time to time. If he uses the occasion well, he will bring back something worth having.

12

In these periodical retreats from society he finds the best part of himself. In society, he finds the other part.

13

The earth will continue to turn on its axis, with or without him. He is not so important as he thinks.

14

If human life is to achieve intelligent awareness, it must find time, privacy, and quiet.

15

He must do whatever is possible within his karmic limits to arrange times for such retreats. Otherwise the pressure of habit and routine, of other persons and social, family, or professional demands, will provide excuses for their neglect.

16

If, to find this leisure, he has to shorten working or sleeping hours, it is still well worth the price.

17

At certain periods they feel a need to get away from each other. There can be merely physical, nervous, emotional, or mental reasons for it, but on the highest plane it is the need of that undistracted aloneness in which God can be found.

18

Before the day's business starts, attend to your business with the Over-self.

19

The man who makes no time for thought about God or contemplation on God is to be pitied. For on the scale of real values his actual business is mere idleness if it remains unguided, unprotected, and uninspired by the truths, laws, or intuitions drawn from such retreats.

20

When he can retreat within his own mind and enjoy the peace he finds there, how little can the busy thrusting beckoning world attract him?

21

In these periods he retreats for a while from the outer role he is playing on the world-stage. He is letting it go, no longer to play the "personal self" role but to rest from it and simply "be."

22

The principle of temporary withdrawals and occasional retreats from the world is a valuable one. It clears the mind which has become too fogged with its own desires. It calms the heart which has become too agitated by disturbing events.

23

These intervals of retreat give us the chance to lift the mind above all the hates, fears, and greeds of negative suggestions from our surroundings.

24

It is good to forget for twenty or thirty minutes each day the world and its affairs in order to remember the Overself and its serenity. This forget-fulness is exalting and uplifting in proportion to the distance it carries us from the ego.

25

A day begun with mental quiet and inner receptivity is a day whose work is well begun. Every idea, decision, move, or action which flows out from it later will be wiser better and nobler than it otherwise would have been.

26

Those who keep their leisure too busily occupied with too many unes-sential activities, useless gossip, or excessive entertainment to have any time left to spare for the higher purposes of life, will have only themselves to blame if, later, the outer crises of life find them without the inner resources to meet them.

27

To sit down and literally do nothing except to abstain from mental and physical movement would seem to an unknowing onlooker to be another way of being idle. Perhaps. But there is paradox here, for it is also the best way of being busy!

28

Nature's rhythm of energetic activity and recuperative stillness offers us an ancient lesson, but too many are either too slow to learn it or too impatient willingly to reduce the speedy tempo and busy thought of the modern mind. So they fail to return to their centre, fail to profit by the great ever-present Grace.

29

The failure on the part of most people in the West to give a little of their time to personal and private holy communion—bringing no priest or clergyman into the period but seeking in their own solitude to take advantage of the usually well-camouflaged fact that man is essentially alone—brings its inevitable consequences. Their lives may be good or bad, their careers may be successful or failing, but with no consciousness of Consciousness, they remain only half-men. They have so little competent guidance from those who are professional spiritual guides that most do not even know the sin through omission they are committing, do not recognize the failure in duty, and are not troubled by the incompleteness of their knowledge.

30

A life which contains no interludes of stillness can possess no real strength.

31

The notion that we must keep everlastingly active to justify our existence is not a deep one. Much of what we do has no real value.

32

To this extent, that he provides the requisite time and solitude every day for meditation and study, it may be said that he withdraws himself into a life apart.

33

Withdrawal from the familiar environments, for brief intervals, is good if properly used, that is, if one moves over to the attitude of being a detached observer of that environment and of what has already happened within it.

34

Each aspirant must solve for himself this problem of gaining time and solitude for the mystical phase of the quest. First, he has to gain twenty to thirty minutes every day for a period of meditation. Next, he has to gain a few entire days or weeks every year of retreat from social distractions, business preoccupations, and family gregariousness for study of the wisdom teaching, more frequent efforts after meditation, and surrender to the inspiration of Nature. A small secluded cottage is excellent for this purpose.

35

It is an attempt to unshackle consciousness from the tensions generated by outward activity, a respite from the attachments formed by living incessantly in the personal ego.

36

A man must empty himself in these allotted periods of withdrawal, must then let go of memories of his past and anticipations of his future, of passions and desires in his present.

37

We not only need a bodily bath after we have been too much in the world but also an inner bath, to wash off the negative, mean, and irritable feelings of the day.

38

This dipping into itself on the mind's part is a rare movement. Ordinarily it happens only in sleep.

39

If he is to come to terms with the world and live in it, he must begin to learn the art of doing so out of the world. In times of private retreat, of personal isolation, he must seek intellectual quiet, mental passivity, and emotional impassivity.

40

If he is led by the guidance of intuition or by the prescription of a spiritual director to seek solitude and shun society for a period of time every day, or even for a period of weeks every year, let him do so literally and not submit to the enforced intimacy of a monastery or ashram.

41

The need to withdraw is the need to accumulate reserves of inner life, light, and power.

42

It is true that, since we carry the ego with us wherever we go, the notion that in some other place, the more remote the better, we might find tranquillity is an illusory one. Yet it is not always a foolish one. A mere change of scene has not only helped physical invalids but also mentally agitated persons.

43

There is a mysterious moment or moments on the frontier between sleeping and waking which offers opportunity better than at other times for awareness of the higher consciousness.

44

These who are so over-active and under-meditative may be incredulous of the suggestion that they might go farther by going slower. But it is a fact.

45

It is good to withdraw for a while to bathe in the pool of profounder thought—not to escape life but to gain stronger faith for living, clearer vision for action, and a true impetus in all things.

46

Withdraw for a while, not necessarily for moral inventory and personal stock-taking, although it could well include them, but essentially for deep realization.

47

The critics of those who practise withdrawal talk of "escape" in derogatory tones, as of some cowardly and shameful act. But why is it so meritorious to stay chained forever to burdens, problems, anxieties, and crosses? Why may a sufferer not take refuge from their weight and pressure, seek relief from their tension, forget and let them fade into abeyance for an hour? This too is worthwhile even if, unlike the monk proficient in meditation exercise, he feels no positive peace. For the instinct which leads him into it is a sure one, however dim and unformulated it be. It is a far-off recognition of a profoundest fact—the connection with a Higher Power.

48

If he seeks to avoid the cares of life and the burdens of reponsibility by retreating into rural solitude, cutting ties and curbing ambition, he is entitled to do so. But he will be much better entitled if his desertion of the business and tumult of the city is only for a time, and only to learn what the Overself alone can teach.

49

The return to ordinary conditions from these withdrawals may find him somewhat relaxed, perhaps with some feeling of well-being, even if he did not succeed in touching any higher state.

50

Prepare for the day's life by a period of complete stillness.

51

Open yourself in these silent periods to new intuitive feeling, and if it directs you to any new course of action, it will give you the power needed for that course.

52

He is entitled to turn away from social existence from time to time if that existence stands in the way of his aspiration and growth, if it obstructs the light producing his vision of life's infinite greatness.

53

Each person has the right to a certain privacy for these few minutes of meditation, or half hour, or even longer. He has the right to secure solitude for this purpose, to withdraw from those who claim him and from duties which never end. On this matter he may meet with opposition or derision from other members of his household, but by careful, patient, tactful, yet unyielding handling, he must try to live it down.

54

Those who give too few minutes during the day to thought about, remembrance of, or meditation on the higher self cannot justly demand a spiritual return out of all proportion to what they have given.

55

Retreat from the world is as necessary for a healthy inner life as return to it.

56

From these contemplative ponderings he may take back truth and strength for his day-to-day living, solutions for his personal problems.

57

A man who does not give himself the leisure for study, reflection, and meditation does not give himself enough chance to grow mentally and develop spiritually. Such a man will not be able to bring to his life the best preparation and must not expect the best results.

58

The worst troubles fall into better perspective when we enter into these withdrawn periods, when we look at them from the deeper self's poise.

59

Stop doing what you usually do, cease your daily toil for a while, and be still! Thus you die daily to self.

60

By inserting these periods of withdrawal into the business of everyday living, that very business will itself take on clearer meaning.

61

It is essential to set aside a part of his morning for this important purpose. It need only be a tiny part, if he feels that is all he can spare.

62

Japanese proverb: In the buzz of the marketplace there is money, but under the cherry tree there is content.

63

"Be still and know that I am God." Here is a direct command, a counsel, even a revelation which can be carried out only by deserting the everyday activities and bringing both body and mind into stillness.

64

Pushing oneself to the limit may help a man at a certain time, but there is also a different time when letting go may help him more.

65

There are times when the heart's need to feel peace becomes imperative and when the mind's need of long-range perspectives becomes overwhelming. To yield to these needs is not a cowardly escapism but a sensible re-adjustment.

66

Surrounded by the distractions of society though it may be, the mind must retire and concentrate in itself. Seated in the midst of a numerous assembly as he may be, a man can yet dwell in mental solitude, as abstracted as a lonely hermit.

67

Escape from worldly life and big cities for suitable periods and on the proper occasions can be used to promote spiritual advancement and to perfect spiritual capacity.

68

It is paradoxical that a man's quietest moments reveal the most to him, and bestow the best upon him.

69

Let him escape from these busy routines for a few hours or days, perhaps even a few fortunate weeks, not to seek new activity in entertainment and sport but to seek solitude in meditation and study, reflection and prayer.

70

The amusements and entertainments which modern civilization has provided for itself are many and fascinating. But we have only twenty-four hours in a day, and if we give a disproportionate amount of our available time to them we rob ourselves and waste life.

71

If he remains too engrossed in work or pleasure to remember, or to be willing, to fulfil this duty, he remains on the banal level where most others are content to remain.

72

Take these beautiful moments, which Nature's rhythm has provided or man's art has fabricated, as a grace and benefit by them on a deeper level. But to do this there must be a pause in the oscillations of active life, a deliberate stilling of the self, be it short or long.

73

Those are the moments when one returns from such absences with a mind become quite lucid, evocative of many ideas stumbling over each other.

74

If you can achieve enough freedom from the disturbances, the noise, and the bustle of city life, you can use your room, your house, or your garden for the purpose. There will be no need to take flight to a hill, cave, monastery, or forest.

75

Those who are too busy to go into the silence and who have no time for its daily practice, usually have plenty of time to hold negative thoughts and undesirable moods.

76

If men live in the flesh alone, if they have no spiritual core within which to retreat from time to time, they must endure, unsustained by anything from within, the sufferings and infirmities of the flesh.

77

If he finds it necessary to isolate and segregate himself from the rest of society for certain periods—whether short or long—its justification must lie in the loftiness of his purpose.

78

There is much in the outer world to abrase feeling, inflame passion, or weigh down mind. It is then that retreat into the inner world can be made into a healing, helping, or calming one.

Balance inner and outer

79

This antagonism between the meditative life and the practical life is only a supposed one, not a real one. If it exists at all it exists only between their extreme and therefore abnormal forms, between the wholly inactive trance state—which is temporary—and the wholly active extrovert state—which is diseased. The proper human life is not only practical but also meditative. There is necessarily a contrast between the two qualities but there need not be an antagonism.

80

Man's trail leads all the way from the primitive who dwelt in a cave because he never saw a city to the yogi who dwells in a lonely cave because he has seen too much of crowded cities! But it will not stop there. The philosopher will seek an environment where he can unite the quietude and solitude and beauty of Nature with the comfort and stimulation and appeal of the town. He will be partly in the world yet partly out of it. He will commune with his divine spirit yet also with his better neighbour.

81

Philosophy advocates neither the permanent association with society nor the permanent retirement into solitude. It does not vaunt the home at the expense of the monastery or the monastery at the expense of the home. It takes no side in any absolute manner, but it makes use of both in the fullness of its own discretion. It says that at one time or at a certain stage, society will be helpful or even necessary to a man, whereas at another stage or at another time, solitude will be not less necessary and not less helpful. It says that to remain in society when the inner prompting is to go into solitude is to turn society into an evil thing; but on the other hand, to remain in solitude when the inner bidding is to go forth among one's fellows again is equally wrong. A man's need in these matters must be dictated by his personal circumstances on the outside, and by his intuitive feeling on the inside; and if he is in any doubt as to where his duty lies he has to find and consult a competent spiritual director, who will quickly put him on the right track. But, we repeat, philosophy cannot be tied down to any disciplinary formula which is to be prescribed freely to all men and at all times. It is hostile neither to retirement from the world nor to activity in the world, but includes both as being, at different times, part of the philosophic life and needful to a well-balanced temperament.

82

The secret of achieving successful balance between the contemplative life and the active life is to go slowly, inch by inch, and not to jump.

83

What is needed is a daily alternation of meditational retreat and practical action, a swinging to and fro between these two necessities of a balanced life.

84

We must act in society the thoughts and dreams of our solitude. It is difficult to adjust the life of the Soul to the life of the world today and keep a fine balance—but we must *try*.

85

Ought we to flee the world and live in ascetic disdain of its attractions? Or ought we to inlay a mystic-philosophic pattern into the picture of everyday duty? The answer is that both courses are correct. We must build sufficient strength to detach our hearts from enslavement to desire, and we must make practical the insights conferred by this quest of the Overself. We must learn how to do the first without shutting ourselves in monastic seclusion, and how to do the second without losing the proper balance between the universal and personal outlook, a balance which marks the sage. We must mingle with mankind to show them that a nobler existence *is* possible and to share with them whatever they can absorb of insights and experiences which only the elect usually have.

86

It is needful to achieve a kind of rhythm in the day's living, a withdrawnness now and then punctuating the outwardness of the active hours. This is needed whether the activity be mental or physical.

87

The message of Krishna in the *Gita* may be summarized as: "This calm evenness of mind is known as Yoga. He who wins it by solitary meditation in the cave gains nothing higher than he who wins it by ego-detached work in the marketplace."

88

The longing to remove himself from the worldly society around and find some retreat may come upon him from time to time. He should neither resist nor yield to it but try to understand why it arises, what it involves, and strike a debit balance about it. Then only can he see more clearly how best to deal with it.

89

The need of rest periods is not limited only to times after work or any other activity—it is also needed after a number of meetings with other persons. Isolation is needed to balance society. The divine presence is company enough.

90

A life starved of periods of being, that is, a life extroverted into thoughts and actions, is unbalanced.

91

To live in the equilibrium of the spirit while living at the same time in the turmoil of the world—this is the philosopher's practical but glorious task. The monk whose inner voice directs him to seek the cloistered life of a monastic institution must be honoured for obeying it. That is his special way. Some may even envy his sheltered peace while others may shudder at his somber asceticism. But the philosopher, who seeks the One in the Many and finds the Many in the One, sees no undue superiority either in the girdled robe or the trousered suit. He is ready and willing to be a monk or to be a worldling, whichever way the wisdom of destiny, the pressure of circumstances, the guidance of conscience, and the inclination of temperament indicate. However, he will generally prefer to keep his independence by keeping to himself, rather than become prisoner to other people's fanaticism. Nor does his view of life separate the universe from God, activity in it from a godly life.

92

It will be wise to restrict social contacts and activities but not carry the restrictions to extremes. He must use his common sense to judge how far to engage in these activities to keep a proper degree of balance.

93

It is not that he is coldly insensitive to the world tragedy around him but that he needs time to equilibrize himself to deal with it.

94

If he is worried about the lack of money to the extent that he cannot keep the inner peace gained during the periods of such relaxation, that is to compel him to become better balanced, more practical, and rightly adjusted to the physical world. He should treat it not as something to worry about, but as a problem to be quietly faced and sensibly mastered.

95

Philosophy does not advocate outward separation from the life of the world although it encourages occasional and temporary retreats. A total separation is not justifiable and, what is more, not necessary.

96

If he retires to enjoy the tranquillity of rural retreats, he does so only to emerge later for the activity of city ways. He does so only to bring more wisdom and more strength, more nobility and more spirituality into his external life.

97

Although it is extremely helpful for most beginners to cultivate a quieter life, meeting fewer people and keeping less busy, retiring into the temporary solitude each day of a study-meditation period, the aspirant need not reject society altogether or totally retire from everything worldly. Some do, of course, and join ashrams or monasteries. But such a drastic move is difficult for most persons in modern life. Nor is it recommended by philosophy. The opposition encountered in that life, its materialistic unpleasantness, may be treated as a challenge. The exercise of keeping the emotional self peaceful, or making the mind calm, despite provocation, is of the utmost value in such circumstances.

98

The difficulty of carrying on with the mystical Quest in the midst of domestic cares and the duties of a household is admittedly great. Nevertheless, karma has put us where we are in order for us to learn certain lessons. These lessons can only be learned there, amongst children, husbands and wives, and relatives. The need of solitude and of retreat to Nature is genuine, but this can be satisfied by taking occasional vacation trips.

99

To believe that one *must* live in a monastic ashram if progress is to be made and to despise the world outside as being spiritually unprofitable, is a mistake. This has been amply verified by experience, observation, and reflection. A life wholly spent within the walls of an ashram without lengthy periodic returns to the world, is an unbalanced one. On the other hand, it is equally true that a life wholly spent in the world's activities without periodical retreats into solitude or Nature is also an unbalanced one. Therefore, philosophy, in the true sense, places balance as one of its foremost practical aims. This reference to ashrams is used only by way of illustration.

100

The prudent and sensible way, which is also the philosophic way, is to retire from the world as and when such a course is needed, as and if one can, and then to turn one's back on retirement itself.

101

We gain our victory over the lower nature both by struggling with it and by flight from it. That is, we need the world-arena because of the temptations and oppositions which it provides to test our strength, try our character, and reveal the real measure of our attainment. But we also need places of solitary retreat where we can detach ourselves from the outward struggle occasionally, examine its nature analytically and survey ourselves coolly. Only by playing this double role of activist and hermit, householder and monk, only by practising this double movement of entering the fight and withdrawing from it, can we achieve that properly balanced progress which is solid to the core and is as substantial as it appears to be. Let it be added, however, that whereas the world's business must necessarily take a large share of our time and energy, the recess and quietude need take only a small one.

102

A balanced way of life requires a person to hold determinedly to this regular retreat while yet working actively in the world most of the time. In this way the world's destructive effect will be countered, the spiritual vitality will be renewed, and the inner tranquillity regained.

103

Jesus showed men what to do, for although he often went apart to commune with God, he always returned to live with his fellows.

104

It is not solitude nor society that must be universally prescribed but rather the rhythm of both together. It is their alternation, not their cancellation, that fosters true spiritual development.

105

Too much solitude is unnatural; too much society, unbearable.

106

Although the highest end of life cannot be to spend it idly in an ivory tower, this is only complementary to the other truth that occasional and temporary retreat to the tower for contemplation will help us to achieve that end.

107

It advocates a life of action punctuated by shorter periods of retreat to maintain spiritual balance. Then, amid the jar and jangle of city streets, he may yet keep an inward peace whilst he goes star-gazing. He doesn't despise the earth on which he stands.

108

We have looked outward long enough; it is now time to look inward as well.

109

Religion is for the gregarious many, mysticism for the solitary few, and philosophy for the very few who are above both gregariousness and solitude, who can embrace or dispense with either as necessary.

110

Although an obscure and peaceful life may be his desire, karma may will otherwise and bring fame and action, with their concomitant troubles, into his existence.

111

We need this rhythm of activity and retreat because we need time to deepen faith and freshen understanding, to recuperate spiritual forces and clarify inner vision.

112

It is true that the would-be mystic needs leisure and needs quiet but he does not need them all the time, only some of the time.

113

He moves in a different world of thought from that of the persons— and they are many—who are incapable of response to higher promptings, and he knows it. Therefore he must keep some part of his day—however small—for himself, some place where he can be by himself. Much non-sense is talked or preached in religious circles about "love," "community," and so on. It evaporates when the truth about it is sought. A man can start to give love when he has it to give, but he can give nothing when he has none of it. The ordinary man lives very much in his ego and can only give his egotism. If he seems to give love, there is an egoistic thought or motive behind it. The aspirant who immerses himself in somebody else's ego may make the latter feel happier but both are wallowing in the same element. Real service, real charity in the world are admirable things but rarely pure. The daily retreat from the world, if for higher purposes, may in the end be better for others, too. If a man uses these periods to get away from all other influences and seek only the divine presence, he may in time have something of it, even if only atmosphere, to bring others. His enjoyment of that presence cannot help but put really sincere goodwill into his attitude to them. The sharing of what he feels becomes a natural activity. This is love in a deeper more enduring sense, and more productive, too.

114

Just as philosophy advocates the rule of occasional and temporary retreats as being helpful to practise meditation, pursue study, and clarify the mind, so it advocates the rule of temporary asceticism as being helpful to purify desire, fortify will, and discipline the body. This is a component of its moral message to the present age just as total retreat and total asceticism was the right rule for former ages. Such a difference is of vast magnitude to the individual concerned and of vital importance to the society in whose midst he dwells. It is often a personal convenience to combine the two—the retreat with the asceticism—and thus keep any disturbance of social life to a minimum.

115

It is needful to correct mistaken impressions that it is wrong to try to escape from daily activity, and its troubles, into the silence. On the highest level, there actually are no problems, for the great work of evolution is then known to be all-inclusive and always effectual, and the world-experience is seen for what it is. The ultimate purpose of living itself is, of course, to attain this state. On the relative level, there coexists the necessity of accepting everyday life, together with its difficulties and problems, if we are to develop the resources needed in order to progress. The philosophic attitude reconciles both these viewpoints as being complementary and necessary to each other.

116

Those who seek closer conscious relationship with the Overself must pay the price, part of which is resistance to the allurements of using leisure only for pleasure.

Shorter pauses

117

Throughout the day he is to take advantage of odd moments to lift his mind to a higher level. The practice reveals positive qualities of strength and serenity not ordinarily known to be possessed by the person.

118

These reserved periods, these minutes scratched for his own best self, may be given to reflective thought or to silenced thought. The day's particular need or the hour's intuitive urge is to be the guiding finger to his decision.

119

It is not only in the special periods given over to the practice that mental quiet may be striven for, but also in the quite ordinary occupations of routine existence. But here a very short time—perhaps even a minute or two—will have to suffice. Nor can it go very deep. And it may have to be disguised or hidden to avoid drawing attention. Yet if it is repeated at every opportunity during the day some spiritual profit must emerge.

120

The method of recalling oneself, at the time the clock strikes the new hour, to the practice of an exercise in relaxation or to dwelling on a Declaration—and this only for a couple of minutes—is a valuable one.

121

He should cultivate the power to disengage himself mentally and emotionally, when busy with affairs or worldly occupations, and turn quickly towards prayer or meditation.

122

The shift from activity to repose should be sharply done, immediate, almost automatic.

123

Man's need to isolate himself temporarily but regularly from the world's turmoil is more urgent in this century than in any previous one. The intent should not be to escape but to rally the spiritual forces and recuperate from personal stresses, to take a proper look at the kind of life-pattern he is weaving and to note defects and plan amendments. No one would be worse and everyone would be better for taking a little time out of his day, for suspending his daily activities for perhaps a half hour every day, to "go into the silence." Life becomes spacious and unstrained, its horizon of daily living enlarged, when a still timelessness creeps into a man's make-up. He will become less hurried but not less active. He knows that his future is assured because his present conduct is serene and that it is safe because his present understanding is right.

124

The divine part of our being is always there; why then is it not available to us? We have to practise making ourselves available to It. We have to pause, listen inwardly, feel for Its blessed presence. For this purpose meditation is a valuable help, a real need.

125

He can practise for a single minute or for five minutes whenever opportunity shows itself. This may happen in his office during a pause between two interviews, in a railroad waiting room during the brief period before his train arrives, or in some other place.

126

His earthly business will not suffer *in the end* but he himself will gain much profit if he detaches himself from it once or twice a day to turn his attention toward celestial business for which he was really put on earth.

127

In whatever way he uses this period, whether to pray, to relax physically emotionally and mentally, or to meditate, the first need is to drop his affairs of the moment abruptly and let go of them completely during this short pause. No matter how tightly bound to a timed schedule his business has made him, here at least he enters a timeless world.

128

The meditation may be short but must be frequent, so that there is not enough room in one's life or mind for the world to swamp one completely.

129

It is more than a short respite from personal troubles, more than a white magic which leads him away from a hard and crazy world: it is a return to the source of Life.

130

The familiar routine of ordinary prosaic life should be broken into short periods of pause. In this way it may be possible sometimes to encounter the unfamiliar hidden background of all our thoughts.

131

By withdrawing his attention into himself, by becoming conscious of Consciousness, he rebuts the world.

132

He is asked to pause at least once a day in these worldly pursuits that are hindering him from hearing what the intuition can tell him. He is asked to centre himself, to draw his thoughts together on this single and supreme theme.

133

To introduce these calm moments quite deliberately and quite regularly is to introduce strength and depth into one's life.

134

If he cannot find a few minutes of his day to rest in the higher ideas and sacred aspirations, his life is indeed a failure, however successful it may be by other standards. What are all these other things in comparison with a divine visitation?

135

From these brief daily retreats he can gather enough strength to withstand the pressures of conformity and preserve his independence.

136

It is much more prudent to set the regular hour for this practice than to leave it to be set by caprice, for then he will not be able to find time for it at all.

137

There is so much power and light in these quiet periods that the public ignorance of meditation is more than regrettable.

138

He puts aside the world's problems and his own worldly problems so that in this cleared space within his mind, the divine peace may enter.

139

The capacity for contemplation rarely exists today among Western peoples. It is a new one for them to develop.

140

At the Lone Star Steel plant in Texas, there was erected at the company's expense in 1954 an interdenominational chapel for the use of their 3500 employees. The handsome building bears a large bronze plaque as a cornerstone, inscribed with the words: "For prayer and meditation, where men shall find light for darkness, assurance for confusion, and faith for doubt and despair."

141

Solitude is as necessary at certain times to the quester as society is to the chatterer. The man whose object in life is to find himself must provide these vacations of pause every day, if possible, every week if not, when he can be alone and meditate.

142

The man who cannot free himself for half an hour every day from overactivity whether in work or in entertainment is a self-made slave. To what better use could he put this small fraction of time than to withdraw for such a high purpose as seeking himself?

143

He is soon distracted by the routines, the duties, the cares, and the activities of life, however petty they are, so that the great eternal truths recede from his vision. This is why such periods of temporary withdrawal are absolutely necessary every day.

144

If he will take the time to withdraw for a short period from the continuous physical and mental activity that goes on from the moment of waking in the morning to the moment of falling asleep at night; if he will use this period to observe within himself certain delicate nuances of feeling and subtle changes of thought, he will begin to cultivate his awareness of soul, his own link with God.

145

The pause between the discharged breath and the intaken one is similar to the greater pause which takes place in nature between night and day at sunrise and between day and night at sunset. All these three points are important to man's inner life. But if he is ignorant and uninstructed he misses the opportunity to take the fullest advantage of them. Just as this can be done by meditating either at sunrise or at sunset, so it can be done by spiritual remembrance between the fall and the rise of two breaths.

146

Whenever one has the opportunity during the day, while not interrupting other duties, one should recall his aspiration for spiritual realization and rekindle it anew. It is equally necessary to pay strict attention to one's conduct and to work in the direction of achieving greater moral elevation, controlling the passions, subjecting the emotions. Good thoughts lead to good results.

147

Is it too much to ask a man to pause in each of his busy days long enough to cultivate the one faculty—intuition—which offers him an utterly disproportionate return for the investment of time and attention?

148

The modern man, who spends his working hours in a densely peopled factory or office building and his pleasure hours in just as densely peopled playhouses, needs more than his forebears ever did this short daily period of solitude, relaxation, and silence.

149

Those who are willing to look beyond the day's familiar routines into wider spaces, willing to bring routines, activities, and engagements to a complete halt for a while, put themselves in a better position to discover the transcendental self.

150

Men who are so extroverted that they can live only in external scenes and external activities need some counterpoise to redress the balance. This is well provided by a short daily period of meditation. They would still be a long distance from those pure introverts, the mystics, and they would still have their feet on earth.

151

Some city workers who feel it would be too trying to attempt the early morning practice, welcome the brief break of half their lunch hour which they spend in a quiet church. This is made possible, of course, only if they eat a simpler meal and if the church is near enough to their place of work. After the morning's stress, they are glad to have their minds calmed and nerves soothed by this brief retreat, even if no spiritual experience comes to them.

152

He is to give his mind the chance, at set intervals, to withdraw from the endless activity of filling itself with worldly, petty, or narrowly personal thoughts. He is to replace them all by the central thought of the Overself.

153

For all things a price must be paid. For this treasure of peace he must isolate a certain period daily, withdrawing it from personal affairs and devoting it to the search for inner stillness.

154

If you are not willing to interrupt your affairs to the extent of devoting a quarter or half hour, once or twice a day, to this practice, you are revealing what sense of values actuates you.

155

The perplexed men who work and walk in our larger cities seldom take time to consider metaphysical or mystical topics. Yet since these deal with the purposes of living and the fulfilment of human existence, they are worth a little thought every day.

156

Without belittling the practical values of daily living which the Western world shares everywhere, it must be said that a better-balanced use of its time would bring it a better realization of our spiritual possibilities. A period—however short—of physical isolation from its restless routine of bustle, work, and pleasure, repeated every day and used for meditation, would be well repaid. Nothing would be lost by playing the recluse for a few minutes or, better, for a fraction of an hour; but much would be gained.

157

Is it not worthwhile to shut out the busy world for a little while, with its turmoil and troubles, and withdraw into the grand silence and great peace which are to be found at a certain deep level within ourselves?

158

This period of withdrawal needed to disengage himself from the routine rounds of everyday living should be limited to circumstances.

159

What he finds emerging from these daily withdrawals enables him to support more calmly and more courageously the difficulties which offset the satisfactions of worldly life.

160

His hope lies in detaching himself for a short time daily from his normal routine, in brief separations from all that constitutes his personal life, or in impartial examinations of that life.

161

He must draw aside from the day's restless life and sit down for a while with himself and by himself.

162

The Overself asks to be alone with him for certain periods every day. This is not too much to ask, yet it seems too much to give for most people.

163

These isolated periods are to be devoted to another kind of mental life altogether, far away from that which preoccupies him during the rest of the day.

164

It is a practice which helps to transform character. The shallow-minded become deeper; the sharp-tongued become kinder.

165

If men were inwardly passive to the thought of the spiritual self for some minutes each day, they would be more wisely active the rest of each day.

166

A day may come when builders and architects will make a small room for silence and meditation a part of every structure—be it residential or business.

167

He may have quite valid reasons for living apart from the world and should therefore do so, but can he? Few in this modern era can find the freedom required, the place suitable, the circumstances permitting it. Nearly everyone and everything is hostile to such an intention. Total removal is almost impossible but partial removal may be attainable. What is within easier access for most persons is a temporary and partial removal. That is, in the privacy of home, to arrange a time and corner where he can hope to be left undisturbed for a half hour or longer to put his mind on something more uplifting than that which the worldly environment customarily demands from him. This recess over, this daily retreat ended, the confrontation with the kind of life he has established in the world to satisfy its requirements and his own personal needs for survival will have to be repeated.

168

It needs only a brief interval now and then to practise this self-recollection during the day; it is only a matter of two or three minutes.

169

A few minutes every day for relaxing the thoughts and feelings will help one to endure the harassments of time and activity. A little study now and then will reveal the Higher Purpose behind it all—and there is one!

170

No man is so busy that he cannot take a few minutes from his day or night for this purpose.

171

We dread the mysterious calm of Nature; we fear to break our own chains of activity and plunge into the still lagoon of meditation, and we dare not pause to question ourselves as to the meaning of it all.

Longer pauses

172

Sometimes it is high wisdom to desert the world for awhile, resting in a hermitage or reposing with Nature. For a fresh point of view may be found there, what is happening within oneself may be better understood, the tired mind may gain some concentration, and the fringe of inner peace may be touched.

173

The opposition, struggle, and difficulty of life in the world provide the needed experience which teaches the man to control his grosser nature, leads him to discipline his animal self, and compels him to cultivate his intelligence. But it does not teach him about his higher nature or lead him to his mystical development. For this he must remove himself to solitary places from time to time where the forest, sea, or mountain can provide the necessary conditions for that.

174

He will come to look upon these seasons of private retreat as among the most valuable of his life. He will learn to regard these periods of self-recollection as oases in the contemporary desert. What he gains from them must not be put in the same category as the artificial spirituality which may be got from the public retreat of ashrams. For he comes into intimate realization of the living power within his own soul.

175

All men who refuse to engage perpetually in the struggles of worldly life are not necessarily insecure escapists, hesitant before problems, dangers, and difficulties they feel unable to cope with. Some are "old souls" who have had more than enough of such experiences and who feel the need to stand still for a proper evaluation of them rather than to continue a blind participation in them.

176

Let him take to rest and seclusion for a period of days or weeks, somewhere away from city noise and interruption. To those who say that circumstances make it impossible to do so it must be asked: what would you do if you were ordered to a hospital?

177

He will greatly profit if he retires from the world to be alone with Nature and his soul. But he should do that only occasionally and temporarily. In this way he makes use of the method of the retreat to refresh his aspiration, to purify his heart, and to intensify his mystical life.

178

The period of a retreat may be only a half-day, a weekend, or a whole month. It may even be a half-year. But it should not be longer.

179

If it is objected that this attention to self-discovery does not help the world or solve its problems, the answer is, first, that it is part of the way to help the world, second, it puts one nearer the source of inspiration, of creativity, so that one sees better how to solve those problems, and third, the isolation is temporary anyway and with each return to society one is a better person.

180

Those who escape from the world do not thereby escape from their worldly thoughts. The advantages of occasional temporary retreat from the world for study, reflection, or meditation are many; the advantages of permanently hiding from the world are few.

181

Philosophy asks no one to turn away from the world, for in its view the divine spirit is not absent from the world. But it counsels all aspirants to get away from the world from time to time, and especially at certain phases of their inner life.

182

When he is weary of his own ego, of the futility and frustration it leads him into, he can turn with relief to this precious retreat.

183

To retire and do nothing while others work and do something is not necessarily a sin. It may be so in the case of the young, the healthy, or of those with obligations: it is certainly not so in the case of the aspirant who has reached a crisis where he needs to get away for a time to give all his thought, all his energy, to the inner search for God.

184

Not all those persons whom our modern psychiatrists pronounce maladjusted to their environment, or escapists from it, are blameworthy. Why should they adjust tamely, or conform timidly, to the world as it is, to its many evils and spiritual ignorance? Why should they compromise and come to terms with something which can only degrade them? Who are the real cowards, the many who smugly accept such a world or the few who faithfully stick to the Ideal? It calls for courage to break with a familiar environment and to seek a new one that offers the chance to rise higher or, if remaining, to try to change it for the better.

185

If such retreat is to be most useful, it should be spent alone and with Nature.

186

When we walk under the groined arches of a cathedral we do not usually feel the same emotions as when we step out of the lift into the bargain basement of a department store. This is what I mean when I say that every place has its mental atmosphere, formed from thousands of thoughts bred in it; and this is why I suggest that retreat now and then into a secluded place for spiritual self-development is something worthwhile for the aspirant who is compelled to live amid the tumults of a modern city.

187

It was a good practice, that which was formerly done and is still having a fitful changeful existence in some places of Burma, China, Japan, Korea, and Vietnam, whereby for a day or two any layman could go to a monastery and live there like the monks during the short period, and could repeat his visit every week or every month or every few months just as he wished. There would always be a place for him where he could practise meditation or study or consult or merely associate with the monks. This gave him a useful change of atmosphere.

188

Life in a monastery can never constitute a satisfactory or honourable end in itself. We may use these retreats for temporary refreshment of heart and renewal of mind, only to throw ourselves more powerfully into the world-struggle again.

189

An individual who has worked very hard all his life and feels an inner need to take some time off should do so. A rest of this sort lets the contemplative side of his nature come to the surface. He must keep worry and anxiety out of his thoughts during this time. Experience and observation have shown that nothing is lost in the end by such temporary retirement. Later on, if it becomes necessary to look for a new position, his own intuition and more philosophic outlook will be invaluable aids both in finding work and in carrying it out.

190

Most aspirants have to go through a period of withdrawal in order to devote some time to study and meditation. However, if they are to benefit from it, and not become idle dreamers, they must not commit the error of doing what is right at the wrong time. There is a definite time to attend to outer affairs and another, different time to withdraw from them. The two approaches can and should occur at certain periods of the same individual's life, at different times. Only fanatical extremists, or those who are utterly one-sided, say that we should live for ambition alone or for renunciation alone. Philosophy does not limit itself to such narrow attitudes.

191

Only after one has been away from civilization for long stretches at a time, can one truly appreciate its physical and intellectual delights as well as really penetrate its hypocritical shams and outworn relics, its stupid snobbishness and frivolous aimlessness. Then it is that one realizes that to lead an independent existence is the only way.

192

If an annual short retreat is difficult to arrange, or of insufficient value, a retreat every two years for a longer period—say some months—may be more easily arranged and is certainly of superior value.

193

The goodness and wisdom that are within us may be tremendous, but if we are not intuitively receptive to them, they might as well not be there. Retreat helps to make this receptivity.

194

The strife and opposition of the world give you the opportunity of testing progress, an opportunity which the monk does not get. Retreat, retirement, and solitude are certainly necessary, but only temporarily and not for a lifetime. Retreat for a limited time, for a week, for a day or for an hour, and then go, return to the deserted arena. Retreat for a month, or for six months or a year, if you feel the necessity of it, but go back and ascertain what you have really attained. Moreover, hold the rhythm of solitude in the midst of activity.

195

Thus retreat becomes occasional rather than permanent, a means to an end rather than an alternative end in itself. It is valuable to those who have become impatient with, and refuse to lose themselves completely in, the surface life of our frustrating, tumultuous times.

196

Each renewal of inner quiet during these short retreats not only endorses the value of meditation practice but makes life again worthwhile.

197

Is it not significant that Lord Byron found a strange peace of mind during the couple of months he spent daily visiting the Armenian Monastery on the Venetian island of San Lazzaro? His life had been tempestuous, his emotions elated and depressed by turns, but here he was, in his own words " contented . . . the most difficult attainment."

198

The risk of being carried away by the world is always present for those who try to spiritualize their life in the world rather than in a monastery or ashram. It is a risk which calls for watchfulness, management, and occasional periods of retreat.

199

A respected leader of one of the psychoanalytic movements criticized yoga because it was allied with retreat from the world, and so became a form of escapism which prevented the escapee from facing unpleasant personal problems. I answered that it could become such but it need not necessarily do so. So many criticisms—whether shallow or serious—have denounced "escapism" that the practices of retreat, solitude, and withdrawal, however brief and temporary, are regarded as things to be ashamed of. This is often wrong. They may be quite honourable.

200

It is practical wisdom to surrender the annual holiday to go to a summer school or periodic retreat for the purpose of intensive study, meditation, and, if possible, contact with those who are spiritually more advanced. If a competent teacher is there too, it will be better fortune.

201

There are times when he must live a withdrawn life for a while if the slender young plant beginning to grow within him is to survive.

202

The period of withdrawal is to be given over to intensified study and, more especially, to intensified practice of meditation exercises. They are to be days of recollection.

203

Anything that gives a man such uncommon power for living cannot rightly be labelled as an escape. Everything depends on the aim of the retreat, or the purpose for which it was made.

204

They are playing the truant from the world, true, but this does not necessarily mean that they are playing the truant from life.

205

We may not like the thought but it will bear the deepest analysis: a man has the right to withdraw himself from society, if he chooses to.

206

He does not come here to escape responsibility but to reexamine it, to see whether it be worthwhile and to what extent.

207

In these quiet solitary retreats he may gain a solid basis and a serene balance for all his future life. But this will be true only if he uses them wisely.

208

More and more a place is being found for spiritual retreats within oneself, whether it be practised at home or in a religious community house, whether in the city or the rural countryside, whether for an hour or a day.

2

WITHDRAW FROM TENSION AND PRESSURE

Civilization has carried us far away from the sources of life. We have no first-hand contact with the Mother Earth. The problem for those of us who are disquieted by this unhealthy condition—though every sort of malfunction and evil happening must eventually force awareness of its existence upon the others—is how to go back some of the distance to our origins without abandoning our machines or discarding our material comforts.

2

It is a fact that millions of people are being stimulated to seek what they do not already possess, are kept insatiably discontented with what they do possess, and are thus kept out of inner peace.

3

The need to relax from the burden of worldly duties, to renew contact with the Unearthly at least now and then, is left unsatisfied. If prolonged over the years, this leads to personal imbalance, to psychosomatic illness, to vague discontent.

4

In the end he has to seek refuge from the world's stresses. This he can try to do in external withdrawal, or in a cultivation of inward detachment, or in both.

5

We must let the others rush on their frenetic course and hasten in their neurotic way since that is their acceptance. We hear quieter and gentler suggestions which must be valued more because their source is high.

6

The practice of these meditational exercises and the study of these metaphysical doctrines formerly required a withdrawal into solitude where, in an atmosphere of unhurried leisure and unworldly purity, they could be patiently and safely pursued.

7

If the struggle to earn a livelihood, or to support a family, or to realize an ambition is not to overwhelm his thought and energy and leave him bereft of spiritual aspiration, he should detach himself from time to time and take note of what it is doing to him. If the gathering of necessary possessions is turned into the gathering of superfluous ones, he will harass himself with new desires and seduce his spiritual pursuits in consequence.

8

There is a calm which falls upon the harassed mind when it succeeds in shutting off the world's cares, the world's noise, the world's strains and pressures.

9

The worse the world's pressure, tension, conflict, or violence increases, the greater is the need of some kind of retreat from it.

10

If, being a modern, he *must* be tense, he can guide himself into a better state by letting the tension stretch toward his ideal self.

11

It is a noticeable fact that so many men and women of our time have more highly strung nerves, and consequently find living more difficult than those of earlier times. This is obviously because the clatter and vibration of machines fills their days or the pressure and quickening of time fills their hours. In the case of more evolved and more sensitive individuals, neither the movements of the human body nor the workings of the human mind could successfully adapt themselves to the movements and workings of the power-driven machine. In their case the result is fatigue, nervousness, irritability, and sickness. If their sanity is not lost, their poise is.

12

If passion and wrath are two great destroyers of man's inner peace, worry and hurry are two great disturbers of it.

13

Unless a man firmly and stubbornly and repeatedly asserts himself against these materialistic surroundings, they will tend to overwhelm him. He must bring to his self-defense qualities abnormally developed if they are to be successfully used.

14

When energy—mental and physical—is excessively consumed by business or profession, it leads to nervous and spiritual penalties.

15

The dominant habits, regimes, and practices of the regular routine which modern Western man follows show in themselves how far he has lost the true purposes of living, how disproportionate is the emphasis he has put on the things of this world.

16

The time and strength spent in taking care of one's own or one's family's needs, have to be reduced if more time and strength have to be given, as they ought to be given, to taking care of spiritual needs.

17

Is he to become one of the many who are submerged beneath the dictatorial pressures of society and who have consequently lost their sincerity, faithfulness, and intuitive guidance?

18

When he is charged with nervous tension, a man more easily commits errors of judgement.

19

The mental longing for inner quiet as a refuge from agitated emotions or tired nerves, is often felt first as a physical longing for outer quiet as a refuge from excessive noise and incessant bustle and continual hurry.

20

If a man is to be free in the modern Western world, he must be able to earn his living in the way that he likes, or else he must have a sufficiency of money to save him from that necessity, yet not enough to tempt him daily.

21

Life can be better valued in the quiet of the study than in the tumult of the street.

22

It becomes more and more difficult for a man of inner development to express himself in modern civilization without adulterating, diluting, or dropping his spiritual integrity. The dreamers in their ivory towers—few and rapidly diminishing as they are—will one day have to awaken brusquely to the harsh facts.

23

For a man of the highest ideals there is hardly a place in the world of today. The food that will be offered him, the business, work, or profession that he must follow, the taxes he will have to pay in contribution for war preparations or defense, the vivisectionative cost he must contribute to cannot possibly be fully consistent with those ideals.

24

He finds it less trouble to get out of the way of people for whom he does not care than to endure the irritating friction of meeting them. "Whom God has put asunder, let no man join together."

25

Some leisure and a little training are certainly desirable advantages for metaphysical study, but they are not absolutely essential advantages. Again, if city life denies the first it offers the second, whilst if country life denies the second it offers the first. The moral is that we must make the best of what equipment and what conditions we already have. To the extent that we do this, we invite help from the Overself's Grace.

26

It is no more turning his back on life for a city dweller to take to rural quietude than it is for a country dweller to take to the city.

27

Action is right, needful, and inevitable, but if it is overdone, if we become excessive extroverts, if it drives us like a tormenting demon, then no inward peace is ever possible for us.

28

We grip so strongly on the timed life, with its pressures and turmoils, that we do not find the secret way to utter peace of mind—perhaps do not even know of its existence.

29

He must not only learn to relax, but also learn to relax in the very midst of this intensely stimulated working life which America thrusts upon him. Whenever in the morning or the afternoon it seems that he must pack an overwhelming amount of work into a short time and must feverishly try to complete it, the very moment this is realized, he should get up and leave both office and work. He should walk slowly and leisurely outdoors, amid the bushes and trees or out in the open spaces until this foolishness, this needless anxiety to get finished something that by its very nature can never be finished, is forgotten. Then, and only then, may he return to the office desk and continue calmly at his task. It is idling, yes, but who shall say that idling, too, has not its value?—at least as much value as overdoing oneself? Is it not rather a kind of receptive serenity?

30

The irritability of temperament and the rushing attack at activities are connected together. A quieter, less hasty approach to them will lead in the end to a relaxed, less irritable temperament.

31

Tensions will disappear if you refuse to rush with the multitude, if you walk and work in a leisurely manner.

32

The opposition to deeper spiritual aspiration and to wiser everyday living habits has grown stronger with each decade. The evils and difficulties are too formidable, too plentiful, too overwhelming to be overcome successfully. The battle against them can have no other ending than failure. The helpless individual who can do nothing for the salvation of humanity under these circumstances can at least look to his own salvation and make some headway in achieving it. This involves retreat, withdrawal, and perhaps even flight. But it is better than abject surrender to an environment which renders the practice of spiritual exercises a matter of formidable difficulty and in most cases almost impossible. It is better than wasting time and life in futile struggles and foredoomed endeavours.

33

When the pressures of modern living become intolerable he has to make a choice. Either fall into physical-nervous breakdown, make a physical escape, or learn some art of relaxation, such as hatha yoga.

34

The stress impulses which bombard the body must be stopped in their activity at regular periodic times.

35

Most aspirants have to spend their working days in an atmosphere that has little use for their ideas and ideals, that is harshly discrepant or completely incompatible with the one that they seek to cultivate or find during meditation and study. What exists in the latter vanishes when the former is entered.

36

Too many people feel that they are too tired in the evening after a day's hard work, and by reaction too keen on using their leisure for social purposes or for light entertainment.

37

In the circumstances of modern life, it becomes increasingly difficult to find a place where he may withdraw into silence from the noise which accompanies modern civilization, or obtain a time when he may withdraw into stillness from its pressures.

38

The insistent demands, the ever-multiplying duties of the world come pressing down on us. How seldom do we retire into ourselves to search or to listen or to understand or to draw on unused resources!

39

We complain of the lack of time in modern life. Yet it was an ancient Greek who said that when men are free from the stress of affairs, they have time to think and discover mind.

40

Crowds of people live in the illusion that they are getting somewhere when in fact they are really getting nowhere.

41

It is not only beneficial to stand back at times from the furor and pressure, but also quite necessary if nerves, feelings, and ideas are to be kept sound.

42

A malady of the nerves can block his onward progress to the same extent that a fault of character can block it.

43

Is it cowardly to withdraw from a world where so many evils are rampant, and to abandon its duties and responsibilities? What is the yearning which prompts such thoughts but a homesickness of the inner man, an intuitive recognition that he was born for a higher purpose in life than a merely earthly one?

44

There comes a time when integrally developed persons find this artificial way of living so obnoxious to their instincts and so contrary to their principles, that they are forced to consider totally withdrawing from it. This is a statement, not a complaint.

45

Are we not suffering from too much civilization, too much science, too much loss of contact with Nature, too much restlessness? For when excess is leading to destruction is it not more prudent to call a halt, and adjust the unfair balance? Has not the time come to look the other way for a while, meanwhile keeping our gains?

46

Mind turns itself more readily and more easily to these devotional and meditational exercises of the inner life where there is quiet, peace, and beauty in the outer scene.

47

The turmoil which goes on everywhere in the world and which is being daily recorded in newspapers throughout the world is not conducive to the inward search for truth and for peace of mind. It gives too many personal shocks, creates too many vague apprehensions, and provides too many disturbing mental excitements.

48

The civilized mode of living is not conducive to the birth and growth of spiritually intuitive feelings; it generally obstructs and stifles them.

49

The tension of modern living is such that a truly balanced and spiritually integrated pattern of inward being and outward conduct is almost impossible to achieve.

50

Prolonged immersion in worldly matters and ceaseless interest in them may dull the mind to the impetus of finer thoughts and to the promptings of finer emotions.

51

Where tumult and clamour prevail, do not expect to hear the Overself's whisper as easily as where silence prevails.

52

My plaint is that all these modern complexities hamper the free outlet of spiritual forces.

53

All this over-emphasis on doing, which is such a feature of our time, leads to under-emphasis on being.

54

This nervous rush and speed, this flight from boredom into diversion, defeats its own purpose in the end. It brings satisfactions that must be repeated and multiplied because they are too ephemeral. The correct way out is to learn to relax, to seek inner repose.

55

When the divine is utterly forgotten in the press of daily activity, the negative, the foolish, and the self-weakening will be easily remembered.

56

Such is the very nature of twentieth-century civilization that it robs him of tranquillity, of seclusion, of quietude, and of calmness. It seems to give him so much yet it fails to give him the one thing which his harassed nerves demand—inner peace.

57

Today the average American city dweller tries to do ten times more than the average European city dweller of a hundred years ago did. He is overactive in a physical and mental sense.

58

Some tension in life there must be, but when it becomes continual, as in modern life, it becomes reprehensible.

59

The hurried life of the West is all shell and little kernel. Our bodies are overactive but our souls fall into disuse.

60

Time tightens around modern man today. He is urged, pressed, invited, persuaded, and ordered to do more than he can fit into his schedule.

61

We have made a cult of activity and a virtue of gregariousness.

62

We who live in the world's fastest moving epoch have to keep hold of our inner still centre all the more.

63

They can find no room for the one activity which is the most worthwhile of all activities. All the trivia of life are included in the day's programme but the holy communion which can bring us into contact with the essence of Life itself is excluded. They are blind, yet the only remedy which can make them see is crowded out.

64

The modern man, hustled by the timetable of an industrialized age, harried by the cares of accumulating wants, is hardly ever happy. Hence he seeks to find in fleeting pleasures what he has not found in daily life. His life rides on a set of iron rails, the unseen locomotive being the steely system into which he was born.

65

We moderns live too quickly to live happily. If it yields pleasure, it must inevitably yield pain also.

66

To find an oasis of peace in a noise-ridden world becomes more and more a rarity. This is the quester's problem for he needs to study and meditate, but it is also a growing problem for general humanity.

67

We moderns live so restlessly, or work so hard, or pursue business and pleasure so intensely, that our attention is continually drawn outwards, rarely inwards. We do not live at peace with ourselves. Under such conditions, the development of intuition and the cultivation of mystical states is quite hard.

68

The haste of modern times quickens the body's movements but irritates the nerves. The itch of modern times to be always doing something leads to a complete lack of repose.

69

In today's hectic life the gaining of inward peace becomes a necessity. It is no longer a luxury for monks and nuns only.

70

We do not find encouragement for calm thinking in the intense tempo of modern life, much less for calming all thoughts into stillness. The rate at which we work, the haste with which we move through our days, blurs our keener perceptions of what we really are and what our higher purpose really should be.

71

The ordinary frantic activities of modern living keep our faculties, mental and physical, at an unnatural stretch for long periods. Although habit has made it seem natural, it is in fact dangerous to sanity peace and health.

72

Too many persons feel that they must keep busy all day and every day. Some are so overwhelmed by this feeling that it becomes an obsession.

73

Their souls find no resting-place in the modern world, wilt before its harsh noise and finally wither in its tough materialism.

74

The pace today is beyond the nerves of some persons and a torture to the nerves of others. The philosophically minded person who seeks to preserve his balance will refuse to be rushed while coming to terms with it if he can. If he can not, then he will have to seek a new and different set of circumstances.

75

The scenes of boyhood are fast vanishing—wooded, winding lanes, sheltering relaxed village refuges—and with them the quietude and dignity of a bygone era.

76

The tendencies to outward action are much stronger than the tendencies to inward rest.

77

All this busyness and activity is not his real life but only marginal to it.

78

The great capitals of the world are civilized, they say, and it is true. There you may find the intellectual and the aesthetic arts flourish most; you may observe more elegance in the manners, speech, clothes and homes than elsewhere. But the work and wealth centered there indirectly breed slums, multiply sins, and degrade men morally.

79

A simple man, unspoiled by city influences, close to earth and Nature, is more likely to listen to a religious message than a brain-sharpened, politics-excited, and ambitious urban dweller. Yet the latter needs it more than the former!

80

If we must escape to some rural retreat in the country whenever we can, to shut out the world's turmoil and turbulence, its din and clamour, and to shut ourselves in with peace and calm, let us do so. But if we are captives of the monstrous city and cannot even do that, let us do the next best thing. There are churches where we may sit in quietude for prayer and meditation. There are the early morning and late night hours when the world is quieter.

81

The conditions of city life are such that periods of withdrawal from it are absolutely necessary. We need these periods for going into silence, for tranquil concentration, for self-examination, and for self-detachment.

82

If you want to practise meditation or study scriptures, a tumultuous city will disturb and hinder you. But if you want to test your practice and live the truth you so far have, the city is as good a place as any other.

83

The massing together of millions of people in one vast city is unhealthy in a psychic as well as a physical sense.

84

Let him be openly unashamed of this inspired casualness, quite unabashed before others about this deliberate evasion of fixed schedules and endless programmes, routines, or itineraries.

85

Those early men who left the crowds which pushed and shoved their way in city streets and who took to the desert, cave, forest, or mountain— anywhere to escape their neighbours—must have had good reasons for doing so. They did. They found that if they were to achieve the kind of peace which comes through meditation, they would have to achieve it in the country, not in the city. Withdrawal from the competition, struggle, friction, strife, and temptation of worldly life became to them a necessity for which they were willing to pay the price.

86

Let it go, this bustle and hurry of the cities, and seek another way of life where the mind can come to some measure of peace instead of losing what little it has.

87

To move one's residence and work from city to country is not escape from the world but revaluation of the world. To take social contacts in small doses is not wilful moroseness but wiser management of time and energy. To bring leisure, beauty, reflection, and repose into the day is not to run away from life but to seek it more fully.

88

The serious worker in the arts, like the serious mystics, must have his periods of solitude. If he lives in a city he must be on his guard against being trapped in a network of appointments and invitations, entertainments and extraneous business.

89

This feeling of a need to get away from crowds into solitude, to escape from city tumult into rural quietude, may be the intuitive warning from the higher self of an impending deterioration unless this change be made. It may be a guidance toward better nervous and even physical health. To denounce it, as a materialistic section of psychiatrists denounce it, as morbid and psychotic escapism is a grave error.

90

When the city job becomes a source of ulcers and the city apartment becomes a straitjacket, it is time to remember that woodlands, beaches, rivers, hills, meadows, and wide open spaces also exist and that the man who makes up his mind that he wants to live among them for part, most, or all of the year can find some way to do so if he is really determined enough. If it involves taking some risks and making some sacrifices at the beginning, he will take them only if his desire to escape is ardent and strong.

91

What is the ideal solution of this problem of withdrawal? That which really attracts us to monastic life but which cannot be satisfied by its rigidity would better be satisfied in country-cottage life. We will have retreat, freedom, inspiration, and peace there.

92

Some people are happier in the country with its solitary activities, but others—and they are the most numerous—are happier in the city with its social activities. A well-balanced life would incorporate both sides as far as possible.

93

Country life is more conducive to prayer and spiritual development, besides being less trouble socially.

94

The glorification of countryside and village life, the denigration of urban and city life, making the former conducive to spirituality, if not paradisical, and the latter satanical, a breeder of evils, is an oversimplification and an exaggeration which does not chime with the facts. There is no Yin without its opposing Yang: to ignore this basic principle of Nature and man is to ignore truth.

95

It is unadventurous and unexciting to live in a quiet backwater of life. Nevertheless, if the mind is sufficiently reflective and the intuitive or aesthetic feelings are sufficiently active, such an existence can be pleasant, contented, and peaceful.

96

The modern idea that such a quiet country life is also a dull one, is both right and wrong. It is right where inner resources and intuitive appreciation are lacking but wrong where they are present.

97

The high-pressure American civilization, its swarming cities packed with frowning buildings and hustling people, need not hinder a man's mystical growth if only he will resolutely remain in inner harmony with Nature and regularly keep an appointment with his Overself.

98

To take the modern city's life into his mind and not be affected by its materialistic narrowness and avaricious triviality, he would need to be a superman.

99

What was the name of that Greek colony in Southen Italy or Sicily which barred all street noises from their city? Surely it must have been Pythagoras' foundation, Crotona? Only he and his disciples could have had so much sense and sensitivity.

100

The din of modern traffic increases, brutalizing even more the already semi-materialistic people in the streets.

101

The restless hum and noisy bustle of city life work insidiously upon the nerves, creating a state of tension.

102

These tensions hold the mind resistant to the entry of intuitive promptings.

103

The roaring swirl of city life would be unbearable to a sensitive person if he had not this secret place of inner retreat.

104

Why blame the man who tires of the scurry and worry of city life, or the one who turns away in disgust from its crime and greed, its sickness and madness, its hate and lust? If, withdrawing from it all, either man finds a happier existence in seclusion, is it really any worse than the existence he has left behind?

105

The general habit of modern city civilization obstructs and opposes the disciplinary habit of mystical seeking. The two go ill together.

106

The city life where people talk too much and congregate too closely continually distracts the mind which seeks to become meditative.

107

Those who stay in the towns when they need not do so impede the intuitive working.

108

They are tired of the economic treadmills associated with the task of earning a livelihood, weary of the high pressures associated with large modern cities, and anxious about the shadowed future of a crumbling regimented civilization. They despise the complicated insincerity of seeking to meet, cultivate, and "cash in" on the "right" people, as well as the absurdity of creating financial strains by "trying to keep up with the Joneses." They feel that life ought to be simpler, happier, serener, securer, and truer than that.

109

The desire for the countryside's adorable quietness springs from a deep need. After he has endured the city's noisy sounds and fretful busyness for a long period, a haven of rest is really balm and medicine for a man.

110

How soothing to pass from the feverish activity of our cities to quiet unhurried existence in the meandering lanes of a country village! Here piety is not yet dead, although the assault will doubtless come with the large events yet to appear.

111

The immense concentration of evil thinking which is to be found in vast metropolitan cities makes the sensitive and the aspiring feel the imperative need of escape at frequent intervals.

112

He is more likely to learn these truths in lonely places than in the noisy throngs which press around the city streets.

Price of excessive extroversion

113

The extroversions of the ego block the communication of the Overself.

114

Men absorbed in the ceaseless activity of their five senses can have no comprehension of mysticism's meaning, no sympathy with mysticism's practice, no real contact with mysticism's exponents. For their hidden failure to know themselves underlies their obvious failure to know mysticism.

115

With thoughts and the body living their own egoistic life, the world must needs be regarded as obstructive to spiritual development.

116

This continuous attraction to outer embroilment is fatal to inner life. It exists only because they abandon the real self for it. It exhausts them, so that neither the desire nor the energy to search for this self are able to arise.

117

The good man or the religious man will take the trouble to weed out bad habits but never dream that his excessive extroversion is not the least of them.

118

Too much absorption with outward things, too little with inner life, creates the unbalance we see everywhere today. The attention given by people to their outer circumstances amounts almost to obsession.

119

Most men are so smugly content to do their own ego's will all the time that it never enters their minds to pause and enquire what the Overself's will for them is.

120

We listen to so many outer voices that we do not have time, or give place, to listen directly to the Inner Voice, the Overself's.

121

The mass of outer activities becomes a heavy burden. Whether trivial or important, casual or essential, they keep us from looking within for the real self just as much as preoccupation with the mass of superfluous possessions.

122

Our anxiety to keep active constantly is in relation with our restlessness of mind.

123

The soul speaks to us in moments of peaceful realization and in times of quiet thought. Nay, it is always speaking, but in the fret and fever of active existence its voice remains unheard, its face unrecognized.

124

Are these people in the charmed circle so fortunate as they think they are? Only by comparison with those who have less money, inferior positions, or no talent. But by comparison with the mystics who live quietly and serenely, who use their leisure in deep pondering or religious devotion in silent contemplation of God, they are life-wasters and infinitely poorer.

125

Those who are insensitive to spiritual nuances are mostly those who are obsessed by their immediate activities and local surroundings.

126

Our attention is now so fully absorbed by externals that we never have the leisure to cultivate inwardness or the inwardness to make a spiritual use of leisure. We are enslaved by attachments and distractions. We pursue the mirage of life, never life itself.

127

If man insists on keeping so busy with the affairs of ordinary life that he has no time to give for the affairs of the life that transcends it; if he insists, with various excuses, in staying outside the central area of wisdom and peace that lies within, he himself is largely to blame for his darkness and ignorance, his agitation and misery, his vexation and fear.

128

They never hear the inner call because they never listen for it. The setting aside of special times for meditation is like lifting a telephone receiver to hear a voice at the other end of the wire. If the receiver is left always on its hook, that is, if the mind is kept active with other matters, no connection can be made.

129

Many of these compulsive actions are the result of nervous tensions, either due to specific situations or to general personal characteristics.

130

They live too much on the outside of themselves, too little inside themselves.

131

The more activities that receive his attention, the more is he apt to be distracted from his higher purpose.

132

While men are caught in a tangle of work or overwork, with the worries that often accompany it, they are unable to give their concentrated thought to abstract questions and spiritual issues.

133

If worldly business and external pleasures occupy modern man's mind to such an extent that they have virtually crowded out all thoughts of the higher meaning and spiritual duties of life, then that business and these pleasures will lead him not to a happier earthly existence, as they could, but to bitter disappointment and painful catastrophe.

134

We cannot get to ourselves because the world is in the way.

135

If people keep too busy to entertain any thoughts of a higher value or to rest altogether from thought itself, they have only themselves to blame if the next great crisis in their lives finds them with weak defenses.

The true place of peace

136

The true place of peace amid the bustle of modern life must be found within self, by external moderation and internal meditation.

137

Modern life, with its pressure and pollutions, is bringing the need for relaxation from anxieties and the worth of meditation to modern Western man's attention. It is no longer the monk's privilege, no longer the unconcern of practical men.

138

After he has exhausted all worldly means and hopes, in any particular direction, where else can a man turn except backward—back to his own divine source?

139

Meditation must become a daily rite, a part of the regime which is, like lunch or dinner, not to be missed, but regarded with a sacredness the body's feeding does not have.

140

Another hindrance provided by our modern way of living is that it breeds haste, tension, pressure, and strain. These attitudes he carries from his daily routines into his meditation and thus spoils the practice or dooms it to failure. It is useless to approach such a delicate exercise with a demanding spirit which wants all the results all at once, with a haste which is better suited to the racetrack or the busy store. Success in meditation can only be had by discarding such attitudes and by sitting down to it with a willingness to give steadfast patient reverent effort which is not disappointed if the goal is not quickly reached.

141

Those people who object that their lives are too problem-filled, their minds too agitated by pressures, their days too busy with demands to find time or inclination to sit down and meditate are the very people who need meditation most.

142

Those who let a civilization which has lost balance rob them of both the time and capacity to meditate, must not only blame that civilization but also themselves.

143

The more activities you need to deal with, the more preparation you need to make, in meditation, for them.

144

Extreme fatigue may be one obstacle to the practice, the want of leisure may be another, and unsympathetic or crowded surroundings a third obstacle to it.

145

When the very nature of modern living is set for a totally different tempo and utterly alien atmosphere, it is somewhat astonishing that techniques of meditation can not only find an audience to listen to their description, but also find some practitioners.

146

How valuable are those few minutes deliberately removed from the daily routine for this practice of mental quiet! The world is so busy with its business that the profit to be gained from inner contact with the Source is quite unperceived, even unknown.

147

The businessman who moves through his days at top speed need not therefore be bereft of these serene consolations. Let him find twenty to thirty minutes wherein to open himself up to the Overself and if he uses them aright, they will suffice to keep open his line of sacred communication throughout the day.

148

Most forms of occupying leisure periods ease either the pace or stress of life by relaxing a part of the brain, the instrument of thought; or a part of the body, those muscles and organs most used; or the emotions and passional nature; but the deeper kind of meditation brings peace to a man's whole being.

149

Ascetic withdrawal from the world is one thing, but withdrawal from involuntary mental images of the world is another.

150

There is also the factor of the desperate overcrowding of their leisure with trivialities and frivolities. If they complain of the lack of time for meditation, let them ask themselves whether there is a lack of time for going to parties, cinemas, and theatres. These offer them an amusing form of relaxation. Both will relax their minds and nerves and body. But whereas the one leaves no benefits behind, the other will leave valuable benefits as its legacy. If they would organize their leisure by the light of spiritual values, instead of haphazardly drifting through it, they might find some time for both amusement and meditation too.

151

Most persons who are willing to grant a place theoretically for meditative practices are still unwilling to grant them a place practically. They complain of being prevented by too many distractions.

152

We have become so extroverted that it is thought queer for a man to sit immovable, inactive, without stirring a muscle or fidgeting a limb, sunk completely in rapt contemplation!

153

All that we can find in the world without us cannot be beyond in range or quality what we have already found in the world within us. "Man, know thyself" is a practical rule.

3

RELAX BODY, BREATH, MIND

The most important propaganda campaign the Western world needs is that which will teach it the wonder and worth of true relaxing—its power as an emotional detoxicant and its beneficence as a bodily healer.

2

We keep ourselves too occupied and then wonder why our nerves are taut, our minds without ease, our nights without sleep. The man who knows the art of perfectly relaxing his body, breath, and mind has a better chance to find health, poise, and peace.

3

Tension may be eased by the simple exercise of total relaxation. At least twice a day, the student should stretch out and lie perfectly still. He must endeavour to consciously relax every part of the body. Breathing should be slowed down and kept at an even pace, the intake matching the outflow. The exercise need only take a few minutes—or until all signs of tension are gone.

4

The unrelaxed person has tight muscles or taut nerves. Mentally he is too self-centered: a few simple exercises will relieve his tensions. The body is to loosen its muscles working from the feet first and then by degrees to the head. The mind is slowly and repeatedly to make affirmations of universal healing and restorative truths. The breath is to lengthen and deepen itself for a few minutes with inhalation and exhalation following a certain rhythm. Within a few minutes the person will become refreshed and relaxed.

5

If he can take a few minutes of concentrated rest at odd times, or even only one to three minutes at a time when he can get no more, he will benefit out of all proportion. The nerves will be soothed, the mind relaxed from its cares, the body-battery recharged, and the emotions calmed.

6

Too many modern men are expert in deceiving themselves with the justifying of their lives by showing results, getting things done, or catching up with work and studies. They do not know how to let go nor understand the need of relaxing quietly, so as to hear the voice of their deepest soul.

7

Sleep exercise: Roll your head around in a circle until the neck muscles are well relaxed and the chin easily touches the chest. Rest. Repeat the cycle of exercise and rest a number of times. Its effect is to increase the capacity to fall asleep more quickly.

8

"Let not the sun go down upon your wrath," is surely one of the choicely phrased, immensely practical pieces of biblical counsel. But perhaps it is not less commendable to take out and change the last word and make the sentence read: "Let not the sun go down upon your agitation." For when the nervous toil and turmoil of the day, whether coming or begone, and the fret and load of thoughts and emotions have passed and settled down, it becomes possible to search within for hidden peace. The more one relaxes, the quicker it is found.

9

The seated relaxation exercise: (a) Sit upright on a chair of comfortable height, with the knees and legs together, if comfortable, or slightly apart if not. Lean slightly forward, keeping the spine straight, and allow the arms to hang down completely relaxed and full length, like heavy weight.

(b) Lift both hands very slowly at the elbows, almost to shoulder height, taking care not to move the shoulders. Next, abruptly drop them, palms upright, on the upper thighs. Keep the feeling of limpness and heaviness in the arms, and the rest of the body utterly relaxed.

(c) Picture an ethereal aura of pure, white, electrifying Light all around you. Then, imagine this magnificent Light is actually pulling you upright by the top of your head. Its compelling force should, as a result, automatically straighten the spine, and the back of your trunk, neck, and head form a perfectly erect line. Finally, imagine the Light is pervading inside the whole of your body.

This exercise should give a feeling of physical refreshment and complete physical repose. It is also useful when having to sit continuously and listen to lengthy lectures or when reluctantly trying to practise meditation after a fatiguing day.

10

Supine relaxation exercise: The object of this exercise is to learn how to relax the physical body with complete thoroughness, for even when most people think that they have relaxed themselves, they unconsciously still keep some of their muscles taut.

Lie down flat on the back on a couch, the arms parallel to the trunk, palms upright. This supine position is more effective for most persons, especially the middle-aged, than the sitting one for relaxation purposes, because it reduces the heart's work in pumping blood, and this imposes less strain upon it. In the sitting or even squatting yogi position, the heart is forced to raise the blood up to a level higher than itself, whereas this is not required when the body is lying flat on the back.

This exercise is divided into five sequences to tense and relax each different body-part by turns.

(a) Begin with the feet and twist them from right to left, then back to right, a few times. Stop abruptly after each complete twist and relax as much as possible.

(b) Turn the legs and hips as far as you can to the right and left a few times, stop suddenly and relax the muscles affected completely.

(c) Twist the head and neck a few times: first backwards, then to the right, then forward and lastly to the left. Immediately after the last turn let the head fall limply forwards as if it were weighted.

(d) Every part of the body has been progressively and perfectly relaxed in turn. Now the whole body should be left in this limp posture for two to five minutes.

(e) Double up the fists loosely and place them on the upper chest. Take a deep breath, *slowly* and *easily*. As you breathe in, gradually tense every part of the body, from head to feet, tightening up as much as possible without strain. Hold this for as long as is easily possible. Then gradually and slowly untense while expelling the breath. When normal condition of the body is attained continue to loosen up further free of all tensions. Repeat three or four times.

11

In this exercise pay attention to the state of the knee muscles. If they are not relaxed, then usually the entire length of the legs is not relaxed.

12

The easily excitable person will benefit by the in-and-out breath-watching exercise. This is not only because there is a direct connection between breathing and consciousness but also because the practice calls for patience and self-restraint.

13

Breathing exercise to remove fatigue: Repeat the Supine Relaxation Exercise. Then practise deep breathing exercises for five minutes. Make the intake and the outflow of the breath rhythmic and unlaboured. Hold the thought that fresh energy is entering you with each inhalation.

14

Breathing exercise to calm the mind: (a) Repeat Fatigue-Removing Exercise for two minutes.

(b) Breathe in to the count of four seconds; hold the breath for the count of two seconds; breathe out again to the count of four seconds.

(c) Concentrate attention solely on the breathing process. If this is done perfectly, all other subjects will be kept out and the array of thoughts, which ordinarily run helter-skelter through the mind, will vanish. Later, when this exercise becomes effortless through constant practice, and there is less difficulty in preventing the intervention of outside thoughts, concentration on the breath-count may be dropped.

(d) Imagine a living aura of pure, white Light to be pouring into and through the body. Think of It as the blissful essence of Peace.

15

Addenda: Conceive this light as the healing power in physical Nature but as originating in spiritual being. It is primarily a spiritual force. If and when it comes, and the invocation is successful, the signs whereby we may detect this include a feeling of well-being, a lifting of the whole nature toward a more joyful and less depressed mood, and a sense of increasing vitality.

16

Recuperative meditation: (a) Sit in the position used in the Seated Relaxation Exercise.

(b) Picture and feel the living, white Light flowing, like the blood, all through your body and into your fingertips. Think of It as the vital essence of blood and nerve-cell alike. Distribute Its energy to every part of the body. Next, give each individual organ a rejuvenating treatment by bathing it in the white Light; begin at the bottom of the trunk with the lowest organ and proceed upwards to the head.

(c) Visualize and experience the radiance of this Light as enveloping you and drawing you into It. Offer yourself willingly to Its Perfection and Protection. Since Light is the closest we can come to actually *seeing* the Absolute, think of It, here, as the One Infinite Life-Power.

17

Exercise: Every hour, on the hour, stop whatever you are doing and assume the Corpse hathayoga posture, lying on a couch or a rug, for one to four minutes. This reduces a high blood pressure.

18

Harmony meditation:

(a) Repeat Supine Relaxation Exercise.

(b) Try to feel that the aura of Light has an actual substance which becomes part of you. Then imagine that you are melting into It and becoming one with It. Next, think of It as being the pure essence of Love, whose centre is the region of the heart.

(c) When this Love has been experienced as a sensation of heart-melting happiness, let it then extend outwards to embrace all the world.

This exercise should leave you with a feeling of being in harmony with Nature, with the universe, and with all living beings.

19

Just as farmed earth needs periodic fallow seasons if it is to give forth its best life, so does the human entity need these occasional periods of cessation of all activity if it also is to give its best. This is done for physical result in sleep but for spiritual result in meditation.

20

What do Isaiah's lines mean, "They that wait upon the Lord shall renew their strength," unless they mean this entering into the silent pause of meditation?

21

The continually out-turned attitude of humanity, operating mostly through the body's senses, leads to off-balance functioning. The need—especially important for health, nerves, mind, and heart—is to turn this tension backward in the opposite direction and let it dissolve there.

22

So many unnecessary motions of the trunk waste muscle and nerve force; so much useless fidgeting of the hands, drumming of the fingers, and shaking of the feet imposes extra strain. Such constant tension of the whole man dissipates the mind's attention and depletes the body's energy.

23

Tension of some kind cannot be avoided, for all activity, physical or mental, calls it forth. It becomes harmful when it is not rightly balanced by relaxation, when it alone rules the man.

24

Few know this wonderful pacification of the entire being—body, mind, and feelings—for though so close to everyone's hand, it is, through lack of aspiration and training, out of reach.

25

It may ask a little courage from him to tune his movements and activities to the more leisurely and less hasty tempo indicated by the inner voice. Some risk of loss may seem to be that way. The risk is an illusory one. Nothing that is really worthwhile and really meant for him will be able to miss him. The rest does not matter. The higher forces which he is beginning to invoke will attend to his true welfare as he attends to them.

26

Release from tension is the beginning of release from ego. To relax body, feeling, and mind is to prepare the way for such a desirable consummation. The current propaganda and education of people in relaxation methods is to be welcomed for this reason alone, quite apart from the reasons usually given beyond which the propagandist's vision does not usually extend. But to remove tension is only a first step, not a final one.

27

There is no doubt that the man who has completely mastered relaxation can let it pass into meditation more easily and quickly than the man who has not.

28

The relaxation is not to be inert and languid but alert and alive.

29

A warning: Do not practise relaxation or even meditation to the point of passing into a trance state.

30

Even metals like steel are found in the laboratory tests to suffer from fatigue when over-used. How much more must the delicate elements composing the human body suffer from it? If metals need the rhythm of rest, how much more do we? The living tissue of the flesh shows its wonderful balance in the unconscious action of both diaphragm and heart muscles, where every movement is counterbalanced by a rest. If Nature assigns such an indispensable place to the principle of balance in the human body, it is perfectly logical to believe that she assigns it in the human mind too.

31

This kind of relaxation is not to be confused with mere flaccidity or mental stagnation. It is creative and contributory towards his permanent benefit.

32

How often have businessmen, who have driven themselves relentlessly, enslaved themselves to their work, been driven in turn to a bed of sickness! If they could read the lesson, they would learn to relax and thus to balance their day more wisely. Their illness is often, not less but more, an inner one. Without mental therapy and spiritual change, they would only be temporarily relieved, not permanently cured.

33

He refuses to be forced by his contemporaries into their feverish activity but insists on retaining the dignity of an unharried pace. The body may be fugitive but his own existence is eternal—whether viewed as emerging in other appearances on earth or as pure timeless spirit.

34

Something inside keeps him from being caught and swept along by the world's hasty ways, as he was formerly swept along. This controlling brake substitutes, instead, a regular deliberate slowness. Even if every task or affair or walk now takes longer, as it does, he knows that this leisurely rhythm is ordained for him, and that in the end nothing worthwhile will be lost by being obedient to it.

35

When the great liberation from his ego is attained, his entire physical organism will reflect the experience. All its muscular tautness will vanish; hands, shoulders, neck, facial expression, and legs will relax spontaneously of their own accord as his mind relaxes. He will be transformed.

36

If used in conjunction with the exercises embodied in philosophic techniques, such rests have a constructive effect on the moral nature and even a curative one on the physical body.

37

All of him has to relax—nerve and breath, limb and mind.

38

The period set aside for the purpose of sleeping at night or relaxing by day will best achieve this purpose if the body is stretched out so completely, so loosely, and so free from muscular contractions that every part of its back, like a cat's, touches the bed's surface.

39

It is needful to bring oneself to abstain from all actions for a short time daily, and to let thinking and feeling slip little by little into complete repose. As the movements of the body are suspended and the workings of the mind are reduced, the rest afforded both of them opens a way for the presence of intuition to be detected, recognized, and connected with. The ego begins to get out of the way, giving what is behind it a chance to reveal itself and be heard.

40

The first step is to secure enough mental and emotional rest each day to give the intuition a chance to be felt and recognized. This is done by relaxing mentally and remaining inactive physically for whatever period of time the aspirant can both make available and endure. He has really nothing to do except refrain from all those activities which keep his ego assertive. He has only to *get himself out of the way*. This practice will not only restore depleted nerve energies but also bring poise into the mind.

41

To let the world and its burdens go for at least half an hour every day, whilst relaxing the mind and body in the repose of meditation or in the aspiration of prayer, is absolutely necessary to him. He ought to realize this, for the benefit will be out of all proportion to the time spent.

42

Relaxation exercise: If he chooses to sit in a chair his feet should not be pressed heavily on the floor but allowed to rest lightly. The palms of his hands should not suspend from the arms but should be supported by his lap, where they may rest on one another. His eyes should not be tightly closed, but slowly and gently the lids can be allowed to droop until they shut.

43

Start relaxing the body from the top of the head, then nape of neck, then shoulders.

44

Relaxing exercises which include lying flat on the back should have arms spread out and head thrown back.

45

The relaxed businessman locks his problems away when he locks his desk every evening.

46

That is not true repose where the mind is rushing from thought to thought, even though the body relaxes or sleeps.

47

To relax is to free oneself from undesirable bodily attitudes and to drop undesirable emotional ones.

48

If the exercises given in *The Wisdom of the Overself* are too advanced for him, it is not important that he should do them. It will be enough to relax mentally and emotionally for a few minutes every day, to go into the silence, to cease from striving and to pray silently to his higher self for its grace.

49

In most people their thoughts are normally circling around their personal affairs including their spiritual ones. To get away from them is one purpose of meditation.

50

In these groping efforts to find the Stillness within, he expresses a very modern need—release from tension, freedom from distraction, the need of letting go. And what is this but a contemporary version of the mystic's aspiration to become absorbed in what the pious call God?

51

A useful exercise to induce relaxation in tense nervous persons is to concentrate on the beating of the heart. It is used as a meditation while sitting down or lying down.

52

During this period he should try to separate himself mentally from his personal interests and activities.

53

In Japan, *Mokso* means the art of meditation, in the sense of resting the body and emptying the mind after, and in the midst of, their persistent activity. This may be practised for only five minutes before lunch, as with the children and adolescents of some schools, or for long periods as with monks.

54

Many complain that they feel too tired after a day's work to sit down for the practice. But if they would only lie down, utterly flat on the back, going limp all over the body, they might find that this exhaustion would actually help the emptying of their mind, coming as a welcome relief. And is not this result half the work in meditation?

55

That silence can be instructive, that we can learn lofty truths without a single phrase being sounded out, is beyond ordinary comprehension—certainly beyond the comprehension of those who gabble together by the hour.

56

Feeling utterly relaxed is the first sign that he has slipped out, however briefly, from the ego's tyranny.

57

Relaxation exercise: Stand erect. Place weight on right foot. Then, keeping left leg straight, raise left foot in front as high as it will go, slowly. Lower foot slowly. Repeat exercise for right foot. Then raise each hand, describing arc in front of body, until hand is stretched at arm's length over head, slowly, first with left hand then with right. This exercise relieves body tensions.

58

The leisureliness of the mystic is a thing to envy, and even imitate. He does not hurry through the streets as though a devil were pursuing him; he does not swallow his tea at a single gulp and then rush off to some appointment; he does not pull out his watch with nervous, restless hands every half hour or so. Such physical relaxation is itself an approach to spiritual peace, that peace which our world has all but lost and is now desperately searching for through ways and means that will never lead to it.

59

By becoming mindful of the rise and fall of breath, by transferring consciousness to the respiratory function alone, thought becomes unified, concentrated, rested in a natural easy manner.

60

The breath should be brought in with measured attention, slow spiritual aspiration as the background, until a pleasant high-quality calm is felt.

61

We in the West do not know enough of the effective powers, the practical contributions, and the psychological functions of tranquillity. Hence we do not give it a proper value, and do not usually try to cultivate it systematically, as it is well worth cultivating.

62

There is a correspondence between the state of the mind and the speed of one's walk. A slow, measured, deliberate manner of breath and movement, accompanied by attentive, detached observation of the thoughts and the steps, is a useful exercise.

63

Do not interrupt those wonderful moments, when all is still, by descending to trivial doings, or even necessary ones. Let them wait, let brain and body rest, let the world go, and give this fraction of time to the Timeless.

64

When relaxation is fully felt, physically, mentally, nervously, muscularly, and emotionally, then the ego is released and the practiser is momentarily free. But this will not happen if he is stubbornly negative, if there is no belief in the higher self and hence no wish to transcend the lesser one. Give the faith, surrender, and get the grace.

65

It is worthwhile giving all his attention to any feelings which he may meet unexpectedly within himself and which show an unusual relaxation, a release from tenseness, a freedom from care. They are to be caught on the wing, not allowed to escape and pass away. They are to be nurtured, cherished, and developed. They may be silent voices from the higher self drawing his attention to its own existence.

66

Let go of the thoughts which make so much turmoil in the head, so much stress in the nerves, and enjoy the calm of Mental Quiet. This is more easily said than done. So bring in help—from the body, from profound sayings, from the exercises of both Long and Short Paths, and from the remembrance of God.

67

What happens during these relaxed moods? The focus of the conscious mind is withdrawn from the flesh and the vital centres, leaving the unconscious mind in sole sovereignty over them. What results from this? The destruction of the body's tissue is repaired, the fatigue of its nervous and muscular systems is removed. The fuller the relaxation, and the soul activity within, the fuller the recuperation.

68

It is dismally hard to accept the wisdom of letting go, to learn the art of doing without.

69

The best and fullest way of relaxation is to subside with head, neck, and spine flat on the floor. Put, if needed, a clean covering underneath, such as a rug or sheet.

70

In this total Stillness a man may come to realize his best possibilities, even if only for a few minutes.

71

The time may come when he will truly love this practice, deriving unequalled satisfaction and profound consolation from it.

72

He comes to the point where he is unable to let a single day pass without this renewal of his spiritual energies.

73

If he suffers from that kind of nervousness which shows itself in fidgets, he ought to begin by repressing them and by declaring war on them.

74

The high tension of living tends to reflect itself in the high blood pressure of the body. We should be watchful of ourselves and heed the first warning signals.

75

To be poised and relaxed is not to be petrified: it is activity in repose, ready for use whenever necessary.

76

In that brief moment of relaxed tension, he comes closer to God.

77

The practice will benefit health, too, by increasing resistance and decreasing nervousness.

78

To cast out tensions of body and mind and keep relaxed is to keep free and open and receptive to the higher forces—and especially to the intuitive ones.

79

To render the brain responsive to the spiritual forces, a state of physical relaxation and of mental calm must be induced.

80

"There is one form of art which is superior to all other forms—the art of remaining quiet and silent. . . . All the arts serve a limited purpose and provide only momentary joy. But the art of silence and the resultant peace ensure happiness. . . . That all should cultivate." —*Shankara of Kanchi*, 1958

81

Once allured by the benefits of being free from tensions, some of them will naturally want to taste for themselves the benefits of more advanced techniques, which lead to truth.

82

What a prize to gain this tranquillity of the mind! How greatly one appreciates its daily presence! All events pass and leave only memories but this stays with me, loving and blessing.

83

A sense of humour may help one who is on this quest. Why? Because it may relax him.

84

All tense contractions of the muscles are unnecessary when he is sitting, resting, or sleeping. If sustained too long they may even be harmful.

85

This constant watching of the personal life and this unceasing aspiration to reform it create a tension that would be hard to bear if there were not Grace-given brief releases or momentary relaxations.

86

If some abstain from speech in order not to betray a secret, the mystic does so in order to obtain a secret!—one which lies within his own self.

87

Every symptom of distress is a message to you, uttered in the body's own language, telling of a wrong you have done or are doing. Learn to interpret this language accurately and remedy the wrong.

88

How to relax is one department of bodily training, how to energize is its opposite and necessary complement.

89

Even where he is unable, like most persons, to relax the mind freely, it is not so difficult to relax the muscles of the body. The exercises are easy but must be practised regularly.

90

It is a fact that overactivity creates tensions which contract various muscles and that excessive preoccupation creates anxieties which have the same effect. This has become so habitual with most men and so unconscious that they have to be taught as little children how to relax and the value of it.

91

It is essential to lie as completely recumbent as possible. Make sure that the whole of the spine and not merely a part of it touches the floor, rug, or couch cover.

92

There is real temporary relief from fears and phobias in a single relaxation treatment; how much more if it is persistently given every day?

93

He rises from these sessions feeling inwardly renewed and outwardly rested.

94

If he were to move his body leisurely, he would be able to move his thoughts more peacefully.

4

RETREAT CENTRES

Those who live in this world, must accept its pains with its gains—they cannot have one without the other. And this applies just as much to those who live in the quiet of monasteries or ashrams as to those who live in the turmoil of large cities. But the men and women who have withdrawn do have this advantage: that they give themselves some time to look at the spectacle and study the words of prophets or teachers who understand it, and reflect on how they ought to act in it. Consequently, they are in a better position to forestall avoidable suffering and self-caused trouble. Nevertheless, if their pains are less, their gains in a worldly sense are less too. The inward gain of mental peace will compensate for that, if they find it.

2

The divine power is not less present in the home or the office than in the church or the monastery. If we do not find this so, it is because we are more ready and more willing to give attention to it in the one than in the other.

3

If a spiritual centre—be it ashram, church, or temple—be established, its purpose should be to receive pilgrims doing reverence and students seeking knowledge.

4

The notion that spiritual life must be sought only in the cloisters is a wrong one.

5

Monasteries and ashrams really exist for the sake of spiritual novices who are struggling to attain the life of meditation. When, however, they become spiritually mature they would do well to leave these places of gregarious retreat which have now become hindrances rather than helps just as they left the busy world itself when the latter became a hindrance.

6

Whether we prefer communal life or solitary life is not the essence of the matter, for both become expressions of what we feel at the time.

7

The monk has the advantage of living in an external atmosphere which does not draw out his lower nature by its emphasis on lower things. He has the benefits of an environment which is friendly to his higher aspirations.

8

It is not by renouncing the world like a monk that he fulfils himself but by refinding the world like a philosopher. For the new meanings that he sees in it and the new light by which he looks at it, render flight from it quite unnecessary.

9

The world must be fully understood before it can be fully deserted. Whoever makes a premature renunciation will be subject to tormenting inner conflict.

10

Most mystical creeds say that we *must* leave the world if we want spiritual fulfilment. Philosophy says we may live in it or leave it—that is not the point, not the issue. Understand what you are and what the world is; then only will fulfilment come.

11

Nearly sixty years ago Pierre Lotz predicted that the contemplative life would vanish before long. It almost did—in the onrush of modern "progress"—but the wars and other activities, especially the personal efforts of seers, saved it.

12

Some enlightened souls are to be found inside the walls of cloistered monasteries but others are to be found outside them.

13

Most men and women are engaged in the world's activities: those who retreat and withdraw from such activities are comparatively few. Generally circumstances render it impossible to do so, nor is the desire to abandon them sufficiently strong to materialize in action.

14

Monastic life quells sensual activity, reduces the area of sensual temptation.

15

Since there are not many who are fitted for the life of renunciation, it would be vain and imprudent for many to enter upon such a life.

16

It is not a refuge for escapists, although such refuges have a proper title to exist. It is a deepening of the inner life.

17

The girdled robe remains a constant reminder to the monk of two things: the aspiration to which he is dedicated and of the self-discipline needed to realize it.

18

Man can find spiritual life inside an ashram, if he prefers such a place, or inside a city, if he wants to remain there. God does not only dwell in ashrams but also in busy towns.

19

On balance there are likely to be more good men in monasteries and ashrams, than in the large cities. But this is the very reason why the good men should come out from time to time and help the others.

20

To renounce the world is merely to exchange one kind of residence and one form of activity for another. We live in the consciousness, experience all happenings in it, and cannot renounce it whatever form or appearance it takes. There is in fact a hierarchy of worlds to be passed through.

21

The ideal ashram or centre should be a sanctuary favouring mental quiet and emotional harmony, goodwill and tranquil study.

22

The great religions, with the exception of Islam and Judaism, have found their support and drawn their strength from monastic and conventual institutions. They should be placed in the quiet countryside not too far from a city, so that access to them for visits by those compelled to live in the cities should be possible. They should have pleasant walks in old-world gardens and stone-flagged paths with benches here and there. They should have libraries, meditation halls, and lecture rooms. They need not be bare and ugly, it is good if they are pleasantly ascetic. Instruction should be available there, not only for the few permanent residents, but for the many visitors who come there seeking repose and spiritual knowledge. For the sake of those who find it difficult or impossible to get away from city life, some should be built within a city, preferably on a side street, away from traffic with high thick walls around.

If the rooms are kept spotlessly clean, if the decorations are cheerful and not gloomy, if there is some simple comfort there, if the discipline is gentle and not like that of an army barracks, if there is a measure of individual freedom, it will be possible to get away from the harshly ascetic, prisonlike atmosphere which has too often been associated in the past with such institutions. Much also depends on the management, whether it be tyrannical or humane, cultured or illiterate.

23

Let it not be thought that we would deny all place to monastic retreats in modern existence. On the contrary, we regard them—if well managed and competently instructed, which is seldom—as excellent institutions which are needed in the rush and tumult of such existence. Our objection is only when they claim to afford the sole path to salvation and when they degenerate into permanent escape-mechanisms to avoid facing the realities of human life today.

24

He is indeed a strong man who can willingly, at the height of his worldly achievement, relinquish it.

25

The sadhu who has to live by the traditional rule of keeping only what he needs to live from day to day may be envied for his freedom or pitied for his poverty, but he cannot provide us with a model. Yet he may provide a mental attitude—detachment.

26

What they do not see, what they cannot see, is that the ashram is only a *means* to achieve a certain end. It is not the end itself. For that is entirely an inward affair, leaving the man entirely free to live in or out of ashrams. If a monk says that the spiritual attainment is possible only in a monastery, this proves that—however reputed or revered he may be—his own attainment is a limited one.

27

The true meaning of such a place is hidden in the quiet seclusion it affords.

28

I mentioned in *The Hidden Teaching Beyond Yoga* my admiration for the Japanese method of returning some monks back to the World's life. Those who do not want to go back, who fail to accept the training period as a preparatory one and the monastery as a school *for life*, are regarded as stuck in a cave and unwilling, or unable, to get out of it and progress further.

What is needed today?

29

The modern spirit does not favour monasticism, does not approve the relinquishment of outward occupations for constant contemplation. And modern mysticism endorses this attitude. It says stay in the world, but preserve a half hour daily as a refuge from the world. Hold on to worldly relations but regard them in a new and nobler light. Only the foolish ascetic will despise the senses. They are natural and necessary. A wiser man will despise their being allowed to run away with reason. The ascetic will rail as he has railed since history began at comfort, ease, and luxury. The wiser man will accept them all and rail only at the weakness which would make them essential to his existence.

30

The modern age has less use for the institution of monasticism than the medieval age, and in this matter the modern age is right. Let it not be led astray by those who have committed themselves to an ancient tradition merely because it is ancient. Let them set up the monk as the perfect type if they wish. Let them adopt the holier-than-thou attitude. But the generality of modern men should not imitate them. Who administered and carried out the work of the Inquisition? It was a monastic order, the Dominicans. They practised ferocity and denied charity, all in the name of God. And they did it with a terrible earnestness. Mercy was unknown to their shrivelled hearts. Today's need is not a narrow-minded and unfeeling monasticism, but a broad-headed and large-hearted practical spirituality.

31

It is useless to ignore the fact that something separates most of us from these monks and nuns of today, whether they are found in the exotic Orient or in the prosaic Occident. But it would be just as useless to ignore the fact that they have found more contentment, more peace, and more faith in life than we have. Can we not bring together—nay! ought we not to do so?—the two disevered halves of inward spiritual seeking and outward practical comfort? Then only would we be able to use both of our eyes and see existence as it really is.

32

The ancient medieval and traditional hermit's life, monk's life, contemplative's life, or ascetic's life cannot be usefully offered as a universal example to twentieth-century men, nor regarded as tolerable to their temperament, nor advocated as practicable for more than one person in a thousand. The modern outlook is too broad to find such limited, one-sided existence acceptable.

33

The modern society's general attitude is hostile to renunciation—whether it be renunciation of position or possession, the world or the ego. Therefore it does not provide as many recruits for monastic life as the medieval society did.

34

The Indian yogi can beg his food or find support from a patron but here in Euramerica begging and vagrancy are offenses against the law. The higher life in these Western civilized lands, it seems, is open only to those who have accumulated some wealth, if such a life requires withdrawal from the world without attaching oneself to a monastic institution. For money alone will give a seeker the freedom and mobility required for the inner life. This is why young men with spiritual aspirations ought to be ambitious enough to make enough of it as quickly as they can and then retire to live on their savings, devoting the rest of their life to the study and meditation needed.

35

Where is the modern Euro-American who is lucky enough to be able to withdraw from the game, unless he withdraws into a monastery? An expedient like this may be practical enough for an Indian, but not so for him.

36

It seemingly would be futile and irrelevant to indulge in controversy against the upholders of mysticism and asceticism. These are not live problems for modern man. But the spread of Hindu cults in the West advocating them may make them so before long.

37

The old methods of segregating a special class into ashrams and monasteries is unsuited to twentieth-century conditions.

38

The need today is for Christ militant, for the spiritualization of life in the world and not for flight from the world.

39

Those who seriously suggest that we should return to the ways of the desert fathers of antiquity and copy the outer lives of medieval ascetics are not doing what is best for us.

40

The monastic solution is not congenial to the modern temperament, which is unwilling to endure the associated hardship and discomfort. Then why is it that more new monasteries and convents are being built in the United States and England to accommodate applicants whereas existing ones in Mount Athos and the Greek mainland are becoming emptier and emptier as new recruits fail to appear?

41

The new age demands new methods. The day of monasteries is over but the training which men received in them is not over. Institutions must arise where men can receive a monastic discipline, a spiritual training which may last three weeks at a stretch or even three years but which will end. Then they will return to the world, but they will work with clear eyes, lofty ideals, and clean hands.

42

If, in those centuries when life was simpler and environments more religious, men found it necessary to desert the world, how much more are they likely to do so in this century, when life is complicated and environments more materialistic!

43

What is needed in the West today are houses of retreat, quiet places in the country, free from the noises of a city, where persons who are mentally and temperamentally ready and who are prepared to live with some measure of ascetic restraint may pass a short or long time in study and meditation without entering a monastic order and without submitting to old dogmatic religions. In these retreats men can work at cleansing themselves from the stains, and healing themselves from the wounds, with which existence in the world has marked them. In these protective nests they can nurture ideals whose height and ethereality would seem impossible to the manacled denizens of that world. Any wealthy person who devotes some part of his fortune to founding such establishments will certainly make some favourable destiny for himself.

44

These houses of retreat ought to be of a semi-monastic character, and used only for spiritual purposes.

45

Retreats should exist as places of temporary refuge for the mentally distressed seeking peace, as places of temporary refreshment for the spiritually aspiring in need of fellowship, and as places of temporary instruction for the students of mysticism in need of a master.

46

Modern civilization renders it harder and harder to find a quiet locale in any city. And, now, the invasion of countryside regions is bringing about the same condition there. The noise-lovers are well-served: the silence-seekers are ignored. Whoever wants contact with inner stillness must be either a millionaire, who can surround himself with plenty of space, or a monk, who can hide himself in a monastery. Is there no solution to this problem for the non-millionaire and non-monk? I know of none that is complete; but a partial one is offered by the Retreat-Plan. If this is to be independent, involved in no creed, cult, dogma, or organization, even this would need financial support for its creation, but could keep itself thereafter by charges to those who use it.

47

In this wide cultural approach which philosophy recommends, there is no room for prejudice, bias, fanaticism. Places of spiritual retreat are beginning to appear in ordinary lay society, and they are very much needed and can perform a useful service; but the less they are linked with traditional or untraditional religions, organizations, or movements, the more useful will be that service. There are enough places for those who wish to attach themselves to organizations. Let there be places for those who wish to remain uncommitted but who seek silence in a noisy world, high knowledge in an ignorant world, and inner peace in a tense world.

48

The modern world rushes on with its work and pleasure, with its mere existence. Where is the time in all this tension for inner stillness? It suffers from spiritual malnutrition: and it is living only half a life. But an equally bad result of this is the spread of mental sickness, which is filling hospitals and institutions with patients and creating intractable social problems. A beginning must be made with providing quiet places where a change of atmosphere can be had, where the world can be let go for a few minutes, where a person can meditate on higher concerns. Churches ought, of course, be the first to offer such retreats, but other places, non-denominational in character, will still be needed.

49

What is needed by the West is an institution to supplement, co-operate with, churches, chapels, synagogues, where people could go into creative retreat, into stillness, for short periods.

50

We need such sanitariums to restore us to true sanity.

51

Places are needed where aspirants can visit for periods of study and meditation, free from *distractions*, *interferences*, and *oppositions*.

52

A mystical ivory tower into which one can retreat when the world's burdens become too nerve-wracking is not a luxury in these times but a necessity.

Motives for entering

53

What motives draw men to bury themselves in retreats, caves, and hermitages? The longing for a peaceful atmosphere after the world's turmoil and materialism must be a frequent cause. The aspiration to make something of themselves spiritually and morally must be another motive. The state of surfeit following pleasures, passions, and desires may turn them toward asceticism. The death of wife, child, a beloved, creates real loneliness for others and the old familiar social circles become uncongenial in the need of a new scene. And then there are those who look at the international scene darkly, gloomily, with forebodings, and withdraw from it in hopelessness. There are the misfits who simply cannot cope with the difficulties of living in organized society as it is outside the monasteries and so retire inside them. Lastly, many a flight arises from a guilt complex.

54

If the hardships and difficulties of existence drive some into renouncing the world, true devotion toward the spiritual goal drives others. If some seek a carefree calm, others seek more time for meditation, prayer, and study.

55

If some shut themselves up in a monastery out of disgust with the world, a few do so out of disgust with themselves. They hope a new way of life related to God may change them, may bring them farther from themselves and nearer to God.

56

There are two classes of men who withdraw from the world: those who seek to escape personal problems and those who seek to confront themselves. And the latter know that they can do this better in the solitude or privacy of retirement. They are well justified. But the first class are not, for they do *not* want to face themselves.

57

Those who regard the struggle of civilized life as not worthwhile, sound the bugle of retreat and go backwards to the comfort of inertia.

58

Monasteries offer an easy escape from the harshness of life's difficulties for fragile personalities, ashrams a convenient alibi for those who can find neither place nor pleasure in it.

59

He will be called an egoist who runs away from problems and hides from the world. But is he any more egoistic than those who stay in the world either because they are chained to it, powerless to escape, or because they have personal ambitions to satisfy?

60

Whether a man renounces the world for a monastic life is sometimes a matter of expediency, of what is most convenient to him at the time. If he has spent many years already in busy activity, he will naturally find it more helpful to withdraw from it for study and meditation. But if his obligations and responsibilities are such that he cannot desert them without the question of right and wrong arising, then it is not a matter of expediency. He must then consider well the ethical view of his situation.

61

The medieval Chinese system did not allow anyone and everyone who felt so inclined to enter and dwell in Buddhist monasteries. That was a privilege granted only to learned scholars, who were first examined and certificated to show their competence. Such eager seekers after knowledge could be trusted to use solitude and quietude for their proper purposes of study and meditation, whereas others were likely to use them for improper purposes, for indolence and parasitism. When the system lapsed, the general deterioration of the monks proved the need of such precautionary measures.

62

The man who has never been tempted to rise above himself, never yearned for more rays of light to penetrate the dark room of his life, will not be able to understand why other men and women have forsaken themselves or fled the world in search of God.

63

If the purpose of shutting himself in a monastic ivory tower is self-training in meditating, self-improvement in character, study, and reflection, only that he might emerge later to apply and test and give what he has gained to the world, then it is a right purpose. If he takes to retirement not only for its own sake, but also that he may exhibit its results in activity, then none can blame him.

64

The retreat into the personal solitude of desert or mountain and the retirement into the fraternal monastery of a holy order are outstanding social features of an asceticism which frowns upon the world as Satan's haunt. India has not had a monopoly of them nor was she needed to teach other countries how to practise them. The first years of Christianity witnessed the arisal of hundreds of thousands of hermits or monks in the land of the Nile, on the rocks of the Thebaid, and among the deserts of Libya. In the fifth century, the social dissolution and economic miseries which preceded, accompanied, and followed the break-up of the Roman

Empire spread millions of Christian monks and nuns throughout Europe, North Africa, and Asia Minor. For it is pre-eminently during times of earthly despair that men turn most away to celestial hope, as it is during periods of social disintegration that they seek solace in ascetic peace. They feel the futility of human undertakings or disgust with human sins. The reaction is natural and pardonable. But it may also be an attempt to reject the heavy problems of life by running away from them altogether.

65

Renouncing the world in an endeavour to rule the self, forgetting the world in a search for memoryless peace, this is the correct basis for hermit or monkish life.

66

Wherever he goes, he will find that he cannot really leave his old self behind. It insistently pursues, or accompanies him. If he goes into an ashram to escape from personal problems, he is entitled to do so. But he will find that the same search for peace which led him into the ashram may one day lead him out of it again. That man alone can successfully give up the world who no longer wants the world, not he who is disappointed in what he wants from it.

67

It is possible to perform the same act for two very different reasons. One may withdraw from the world because he finds its situations unendurable and its goals unrealizable—in short, because he is a failure. If he then takes an escapist path, he has the right to do so. The retreat will certainly comfort him and may refresh his energies for a further and later attempt. But it still leaves his central problem unsolved. The deficiencies or weaknesses within himself which led to his defeat are still there. Another man may retire because he is well on the way to fulfilling ambitions and satisfying desires—in short, because he is a success. But he is not deceived by all this. He has taken a proper measure of earthly values, and found them wanting. Both men had the right to withdraw into a life of meditation. But the first one did so prematurely.

68

They come to these ashrams and convents either in embittered contempt as refugees from the world, or else in naïve expectation as aspirants desiring mystical ecstasies.

69

There seems, in the eyes of a certain mentality, both intellectual safety and emotional security in withdrawing to an ashram or monastery.

70

There are two kinds of passivity and escapism. The wrong one arises from a lack of the energy, knowledge, or courage wherewith to cope with life or from a sense of defeatism after a series of failures or from the inertia of a dreamy temperament.

71

It is ironic that the emotion of pessimism and disillusionment which drives so many persons into monasteries drives others out of monasteries!

72

The corruption and iniquity of the world may lead a man by reaction to philosophy, but the latter need not remove him from the world.

73

The meditative life may encourage laziness and discourage service in some temperaments, but it cannot do so in those who have understood, accepted, and guided themselves by the principles of Philosophy.

74

Observations in these monasteries and ashrams showed that although most of the members came there out of their spiritual need, some came hoping to find a kind of insurance and security for the rest of their lives, while a few came to find an easier way of life than struggling in and with the world.

75

Once a young man leapt on the train which was carrying me out of Singapore and insisted on travelling with me all the way to Penang. He was somewhat excited and declared that he felt a strong urge to renounce the world and that he wanted to attach himself to my service forthwith as the inauguration of such a new life of retreat and meditation. I gave him what good counsel I could but, being defeated in his purpose with me, he ignored it and emigrated to South India where he joined a certain monastic Ashram. A year later he was home again in Singapore, disappointed in his expectations of it and still far from the peace he sought. In chastened mood, he wrote me a letter belatedly promising to follow the counsel I had originally given him—to do some necessary preparatory work on himself while in the world before he tried to leave the world.

76

Non-cooperative escapism is empty, a refuge for the indolent.

77

What is a hard way for one man, retiring from the world to seek God, and incurring greater suffering than remaining in it, is an easier way for another man. Some find the world's troubles and struggles too much to cope with, others find the monastic regimes too harsh to endure. But whether an individual stays in the world, rightly performing his human spiritual duties while learning inward detachment, or whether he renounces it altogether, each path can contribute to his development and lead him farther on the road to the Goal.

78

If the cloister becomes a seeding-ground which yields its fruits later in the productive life of the world, it justifies itself.

79

It is easy to turn to asceticism when one lacks the means of satisfying the senses and has little prospect of ever obtaining them. It is natural to renounce the world's struggles and enter a monastic retreat when one has failed to cope with those struggles. If ineffective persons prefer the comparative peace of an ashram to the miseries and frustrations of society, why should they not do so?

80

Those who are unable to meet the responsibilities, afraid to tackle the difficulties of ordinary living may find a transient peace in retreating from it.

81

Those who practise contemplation for its own sake are entitled to do so, but those who practise it for the inspiring and enriching of their outside active life are equally justified.

82

Is it necessary to forsake the world, withdraw from its struggles, cease to grapple with its problems and abstain from its affairs? For most men in the West the answer is already preordained by compulsive circumstances: they cannot even if they want to. But for a few men, who may well have endured their share in earlier lives on earth, the way may open out to become monks or hermits.

83

The beginnings of this inner life require him to be alone and to keep them secret. It is best to have only a spiritual guide who is understanding and sympathetic around. He needs protection against those whose violence, materialism, or scepticism would thwart, obstruct, or stifle the tender growth. It is because such conditions are hard to secure in the world's ordinary life that convents, ashrams, and monasteries were established.

84

Those who have been forced by circumstances, and especially by the necessity of earning a livelihood, to spend their whole life in materialistic surroundings, to fall in with the excessively extroverted attitudes of today, will naturally desire to take advantage of the first opportunity to reverse this trend and give themselves up to an interlude of solitude, meditation, study, and spiritual companionship. For such, the monastic retreat has a justified existence and a definite value.

85

Some withdraw from society as the only way to preserve their individuality and protect their independence in a search for truth.

86

The deeply bereaved, the sorely afflicted, and the emotionally exhausted need this monastic escape from the world as much as the religiously aspiring and the innately ascetic. And if they choose to remain in after the original pressure has faded out of mind or heart, rather than return to the world, that is their freedom of choice. If only as a symbol, as a reminder, there is a definite place for the monastery, convent, and ashram.

87

To withdraw from the community of worldly society into the community of monastic society, or into the solitude of one's own society, may be an act of progress or an act of retrogression. But to most men at some time it is, for a limited period, an act of necessity if they are to find themselves.

88

It is true that personal contact with the world brings salutary instruction and enforced facing of facts. It is also true that deliberately to ensconce oneself in an ashram or monastery brings another kind of equally needed instruction and other kinds of facts to be regarded.

89

It is right, natural, and pardonable for a young man to be ambitious, to make a successful career for himself in his chosen field. But it is equally right and pardonable, if he finds himself to be one of the few who feel a call to higher things, who are more attracted to and admire the life of meditation, study, and self-mastery, to withdraw from the struggle of worldly life.

90

The call for total withdrawal from the world into monastery or ashram, convent or nunnery comes very definitely to some persons and they must respect it to the point of full obedience. But let them not seek to impose their own response upon others who have not heard this call.

91

There are some who, by reason of circumstances, by their inability to endure the harsh competition or incapacity to cope with the great stresses of modern existence, would find relief, hope, and home in a monastery. They belong inside such a sheltered community and nothing said here should deter them for it does not apply to them.

92

The values of a monk's robe include the one which announces to others that here is a man who is seeking from them no profit-making trade, no paid position or honoured office, no sex: in short, no personal advantage. It is also a protective emblem for himself.

93

Any criticism I have made in the past of monastic institutions and ashrams is not to be taken as a refusal to see their positive value. Of course they fill a needed place in the religious scheme. They suit those who need to be guided and led in all details of thought and deed—who appreciate rules and regulations to which they can give unquestioning obedience. I am by temperament unsuited or unable to adjust to such institutions, an independent needing freedom, unfitted for community life, unwilling to stop thinking for myself. But most persons are not like that and should certainly follow their way.

94

Without inner strength the temptations of the world may prove too much for him, or at least for his thoughts. Without outer kindness his life in the world may prove too abrasive. The withdrawn way may seem more practical and prudent. But it is so only for a time.

95

If the world's activity is too strenuous for them, if they are not capable of participating in its fierce competitiveness without suffering the shame of inferiority or the misery of defeat, why should they not withdraw from it into the sheltering walls of a cloistral retreat? Those who say this is a backward movement must first prove whether the assumed going-forward of the world's activity is a reality: it may equally be an illusion.

96

Earnest monks and brown-robed ascetics should not become angry with our candid examination of their claim, but rather should try to understand another point of view which does not accept unreal antinomies. We honour and respect those who, through deep sincerity, are faithful to their renunciatory ideals, but we ask them not to be intolerant of a different road to self-discipline and not to lose their sense of proportion by making monkish prejudice an obsession.

97

There are other ways of life than our own and we ought to be large enough in mind and heart to allow for them. There is, for instance, the monastic way. It is more charitable to accept it for others as a vocation if they want it. But the monks and nuns should practise an equal tolerance and not seek to impose theirs on ours. They have good reasons for not being willing to get embroiled in the family life but we laymen have equally valid reasons for remaining what we are. But these statements are true only on the philosophic level. For those who cannot rise to it, then withdrawal—whether into the religious community or the hermit's solitude—is still the superior way.

98

Why should he not be free to withdraw from all other preoccupations so as to be free to devote his whole time to the inner life?

99

It can lead in the end only to chaos if rules intended for those living the withdrawn life are imposed on those who are not.

100

If a man wants to try the monkish way of life there ought to exist the material and social possibilities allowing him to make the experiment.

101

The traditional view in India especially, and in sections of the Christian world, has been that taking monastic vows or renouncing the world to become a celibate recluse, a praying and meditating monk *is* actually to apply the higher phase and doctrine of the religion. It is regarded as the next step for anyone who is really serious about his quest for God, and deeply earnest about his faith. It is practised religion on the highest level.

102

Has he not the right to give up the endless struggle against the world, which keeps everyone down to his lowest levels?

103

It is not likely to be easy in this harsh yet tempting world, so they may be excused for moving into monasteries if they are men, into convents if they are women, or into communes if they prefer to mix the sexes.

104

On the positive side a monastery will not only shelter him against the materialistic world but also support him in his endeavours. This is the theory. What happens in practice is another matter sometimes.

105

Despite all the theorizing in Zen Buddhism about its resentment of regulations imposed from outside and its rebellion against forms which hamper freedom, in the practical needs of everyday living every inhabitant of a Zen monastery has to submit to disciplinary regulations to conform his conduct to set patterns and to shape his activities to specified patterns.

106

Communal life attracts beginners but to say that it is necessary is to reject the lessons recorded in history and biography. A community is good or helpful to those who like it, who feel helped by its useful features, but it is not so good for the more advanced persons. After spending seven years in monastic life Thomas Merton called out silently but vehemently to God for solitude.

107

If the return to nature and the simple life means nothing better than living as savages live—a primitive animal existence, uncivilized, uncultured, unaesthetic—then its denial of intellect, art, and comfort is mere retrogression. When the spiritual forces overwhelmed the young lad of seventeen who later became Ramana Maharshi of South India, he fled his village and eventually finished up in a cave on a mountainside. People today admire this spirituality. But he himself once remarked to me: "Had I then known what I knew in later years I would not have left home!"

108

In the Tibetan records of the Buddha, it is expressly mentioned that he sent out apostles "to spread the doctrine that would help all creation." Thus, even Gautama, the founder of monasteries, did not intend them to become places wholly given over to self-centered spiritual development alone. He knew that the truth is really for all, because it can benefit all; it is not merely for hermits and monks. Even where he turned numbers of men into monks, he did not wholly withdraw them from society but laid down a rule that they should serve the useful purpose of being spiritual teachers.

109

Father Theocletos, secretary of the Monastery of Dionysiou on Mount Athos, shrewdly observed that the communal monasteries are suited to spiritual children, where the preliminary work of instruction and purification enabled novices to get rid of bad thoughts and passions to an extent sufficient to enable them to pass on to the higher stage of recluses living alone or in pairs in cottages or huts and enjoying mystical experiences.

110

Terese, the Saint of Lisieux, confessed on her deathbed: "What I have most suffered from in my religious life, physically, is the cold. I suffered from it till I thought I should die." What need did this poor girl have of such torments, when her sole longing was for the divine, non-physical, union? How unnecessary and how cruel the regime to which she was subjected.

111

I recently visited a convent in Spain where the structure was much the same as it had been when built in the medieval period, except perhaps for the addition of electric light, where the nuns still wore the same heavy, coarse, and ugly dress which was prescribed at the time, and where the daily program of services, prayers, contemplation, and work was still much the same as then. They were a very poor Order, and lived in strict seclusion, so that I had to speak to them through a special grille. When I asked, "Are you happy?" all thirty-six of them exclaimed as with one voice, "YES!" and laughed and giggled among themselves.

112

Homage to the greatness of the Contemplative Orders, especially the Enclosed Orders within the Catholic Church, including nuns and monks. This is not to be confused with appraisal of the Catholic faith and dogma. I find that in meditation practice and in personal holiness some of their members have touched levels not less high than those touched by Hindu and Buddhist monks, nuns, and hermits.

113

Shankaracharya laid down a three-day maximum period for visits to his ashram.

114

When one remembers the long stretches of practice in the Carmelite monastery at Roquebrun or the Lendo hall at Kamadura, where hour slips into hour but the monks remain persistent in their meditation, the few minutes that most Western beginners manage to find for their own endeavours seem ridiculous.

115

It is true that there are many escapists who live in a dream world of their own who have taken refuge in mysticism, but it is also true that there are some spiritual realists who have found in mysticism inspiration and encouragement for their struggling activities in the world. The celebrated Spanish mystic, Saint Theresa, was one example of this. She understood this technique of divinized work thoroughly. She did not become a futile dreamer or a pious imbecile. On the contrary, she established foundations in a manner that testified to her practical ability and executive capacity.

116

Mixing two castes together may put both ill at ease. Father Maurus told the story of a monk at a Scottish monastery who one suppertime suddenly rose to his feet and smashed his platter over the head of the monk next to him. "He'd reached the breaking point. For twenty years he put up with the sound his neighbor made by sucking his soup."

117

Monasteries began to appear throughout the European and Near Eastern world as a result of the crumbling of civilization, of the disgust with conditions in the world, and of the feeling that the only way to a modicum of happiness was through the inner life.

118

The conventual life, though usually providing only for the bare necessities of nuns, was sometimes managed with more humane consideration and shrewder understanding. In the new seventeenth-century convent of Anacapri the recruits came from well-born families so they were thoughtfully provided with suites of rooms each with its own servant.

Problems, limitations

119

When monasticism conquered those who took their spiritual aspiration seriously, it drew the inner life away from the outer one, made it seem an entirely separate and unconnected thing. This error was disastrous for those left behind in the world's life and activity. It cut men off from their best source of wisdom and strength.

120

The more secluded, less active, and above all highly introspective life which the would-be mystic leads in monastery, ashram, or private retreat may tend to turn him into an ill-balanced dreamer. It is useful for him to descend into the cities at times and take his place among their varied dwellers and doings. For his inner world will have a chance of being examined and brought to the test by hard contact with the outer world. Such experience will expose futile dreams and shatter wishful thinking just as it will endorse imaginings that do correspond to realities.

121

It is just as much after he returns from a retreat to the society of his own kind that its results will show themselves, as during the retreat itself. In his outward acts, deeds, and speech he will reveal whether the retreat was only a spiritual narcotic or whether it was a spiritual stimulant.

122

In the sphere of action, he will find tests of his will or motive, useful exercises which he can practise to draw out latent resources. For this sphere will present him with problems from which he cannot run away or with temptations which will show him as he really is. The intervals of retirement are good and helpful, but the stretches of active existence are no less helpful to his development.

123

When there are temptations to be overcome by will and trials to be met by fortitude, character has a chance to test itself and thus develop itself. The secluded monk misses this chance.

124

The world is there; it cannot be ignored. It may be side-stepped for a time, but in the end it reinserts its claim to be noticed, dealt with, and understood. He must come to recognize its place in the Divine World-Idea—that it *must* have such a place. He cannot do otherwise.

125

It is one thing to feel spiritually minded or even spiritually aware only under the special conditions of a monastery, a retreat, rural quiet, or mountain top but quite another to do so under the everyday living conditions of a city, a factory, a hotel, or an inharmonious home.

126

The world gives him a chance to apply what he has learnt in retreat. If the new values which manifested themselves as the fruits of his meditation can endure the searching tests of society and activity, then they are truly his. If not, then he will know that he has still to strive more fully for them.

127

He who can find the divine presence only in a monastery, an ashram, or a cave, has still to finish his quest. If he does this, he will discover the monastery to be no better than the world, activity no worse than contemplation.

128

There is a danger that the atmosphere of goodness evoked and cultivated in monastic institutions may become artificial and studied. Goodness becomes more natural when it is lived out and tested in the busy haunts of men.

129

The peace which depends on taking refuge in monastery or cave is questionable, for it may not be peace but escapism. The peace which remains adamantine in busy towns and unshattered by constant work is unquestionably the true peace. It will have this advantage over the other kind, that it will be so strong and stable that it can neither be shaken by unexpected attack nor overthrown by unexpected temptation.

130

It is open to question as to who gains a better perspective on life and a truer proportion of its experiences—the man who takes flight and surveys it from a distance or the man who remains active and breathes with its pulsations.

131
Philosophy is against monasticism as a general path, because it is against separating people from the tests of this world. If the monastic path may give peace, it may also give delusions.

132
Thus what we develop mentally in solitude we must work out physically in society. What we achieve quietly in the heart's stillness must be expressed and tested in external activities. What we learn in peaceful rural retreat must be appraised for its soundness by bustling city work and pleasure. This integral approach must be the twentieth-century way, not the permanent indulgence in escape which was the way of antique and medieval monasticism.

133
The consequence of the monk's misinterpretation of his own position as being the highest is a natural but deplorable one. For having turned away on principle from active participation in the worldly life, he turns away also from the realities of particular situations within that life.

134
They cannot spend all their time in formal meditation or in prayer because they need to be reminded of the higher existence when they leave those sacred sessions behind, when they leave their precious peace behind, to find themselves again among selfishness and ignorance, materialism and brutishness.

135
These noble feelings, these lofty thoughts, these grand intuitions are welcome testimonies of the change that is happening. But until they—and we—are brought to the test of everyday living, their correct measure and ours will not really be known.

136
Mysticism thrives better in isolation from practical life but philosophy can stand up to it. The mystic is shielded by conventual or ashram life.

137
The monastery, the nunnery, and the ashram may be helpful to begin spiritual progress but they will not prove so helpful to advance or complete it. That can best be done in the world outside, where alone moral virtue or mystical attainment can be thoroughly tested down to their last foundations.

138
Those who flee the world do not thereby flee from the intellect's working. They merely change its field. Thought's wheel continues to rotate whether they live in forest hermitages or in cities as crowded as beehives.

139

In the apparently safe seclusion of Eastern ashram or Western monastery, he may console himself with a superiority complex for the inferiority complex which the world gave him.

140

It might be useful for him to ask from what is he escaping: certainly not from his own ego. He cannot change his individuality or cut himself off from his past entirely, nor isolate himself from his ego.

141

In these retreats men are protected from outward temptation. This has a certain value. But they are not protected from the inward temptations by memory, imagination, and personal tendency.

142

Egos thrive in ashrams just as they do in the world beyond their borders. This is inevitable because they are hot-houses where each inhabitant is as busy thinking of his *own* development as the worldling outside, who is engrossed in his material fortunes. The insulation is only physical: Self is still the constant preoccupation of both groups of human beings.

143

Even when he withdraws from the world and gives up its work and rewards, its activities and pleasures, it is the ego which leaves them and the ego which hopes to gain something as a result. Whatever he accomplishes will in the end still be inside its enclosure, however "spiritual" a form it assumes.

144

The petty feuds which mar mystic and ashram society also reveal the sad fact that egos are carried into these institutions, live and thrive there just as they do in the outer world.

145

Whether he shall separate himself from the world or, remaining, bring a holier influence into the world, is not really the essence of the matter. He may isolate himself from other men's affairs but that does not isolate him at all from his own ego. Or he may meddle with them, compelled by destiny or willed by choice, and be captive to this same ego in every transaction.

146

Whenever men and women are brought together in frequent contact for a length of time, whether in established institution or organized group, frictions often appear, envies are felt, and complaints are made. This is true even of ashrams and monasteries. The egos rear their heads.

147

There is of course some danger of the growth of spiritual pride when a small group isolates itself from the rest of society for the purpose of spiritual development.

148

It is not so easy to escape from oneself by the mere act of becoming a monk. Said Kaisarios Daponte in the eighteenth century: "I changed my clothes and my situation, but not my character." He had been a well-educated diplomat but became world-weary.

149

The petty fault-finding, destructive gossip, and biting criticism which so many worldly people practise among themselves is also found in professedly spiritual people. It is also directed towards those who teach or espouse doctrines unacceptable to them. The faults in character which lead to these sins in speech are poisoned arrows shot at the good and bad alike.

150

Misdirected idealism sets traps for the young, the naïve, the inexperienced, and the ill-informed in political circles as much as for the aspirants or the seekers in spiritual circles, takes pleasant sounding, attractively suggestive words like "harmony" and "unity" or phrases like the "brotherhood of man" and uses them as if they could become realities. This is just not possible in human relations, not in any full, adequate, or lasting sense. Not only so, but it has never been possible in the past— despite the myth of an imagined golden age—nor clearly is it possible in the present. Everywhere we see that even where such idealism seems to be successfully realized, it is only on the surface and vanishes as soon as we probe beneath the surface. We see religions, old and new, well-known and hardly known, divided into sects, groups, or factions which oppose each other. Nor are the ashrams and monasteries very much better, as they are supposed to be. In the world at large, where little wars and rebellions are being fought with savage ferocity, where political success is achieved by attacking, denigrating, or besmirching others, a semantic analysis of present conditions shows up the self-deception of the idealists and utopians. The lesson has not been learned that because egoism rules men, brotherhood is not possible, and that because no two minds are alike, unity is not possible. Harmony can be found only inside man himself, not in his relations with other men, and then only if insight is developed enough to track the ego down to its lair, expose it for what it is, and live in the peace of the Overself. But other men will continue to live in and from egoism.

151

Monastic life brings its monks into continual contact with one another, keeps them always in one another's company. It gets on the nerves of some and fosters petty intrigue among others.

152

Should he shut himself up in a monastery, or in a room, or in a cave, the problem of his ego-centered thoughts remains the same.

153

A change of scene may prove helpful, or it may merely prove that he has transferred the ego, with all its troubles, from one place to another.

154

To shift the centre of interest from worldly to spiritual affairs but to magnify the ego as a consequence of doing so, is something that happens just as readily to dwellers in ashrams as to those outside them.

155

The monastic cloister and the mystical ashram are not necessarily the homes of spirituality. They may be the homes of a disguised or unconscious worldliness.

156

Jealousy and fault-finding exist inside these ashrams just as they exist outside them. The seeker after noble-mindedness will be forced in the end to look for it amid the solitudes of Nature.

157

I remembered the words and marked the truth of a conversation I had once with Yogi Pranavananda, himself an advanced ascetic, amid the solitudes of the Himalaya mountains on the Indo-Tibetan border. He said: "My master does not favour ashrams. He has not established one and does not want to do so. We disciples visit him at intervals according to our degree of development and to our needs, and follow the path in which he has instructed us. He even regards ashrams as likely to be deleterious both to his own work and to our self-reliant progress."

158

If people wish to practise philosophical ethics and apply philosophical ideals, they need not and ought not live together in little colonies or congregate in little monasteries to do so. They can and should do it just where they happen to be. Such colonies always disintegrate in the end, such monasteries always deteriorate. It is a common misconception amongst many mystically minded persons that they have externally to separate themselves from society to live by themselves in a fenced-in community or in a contemplative ashram. The actual experience of these places shows how foolish is the notion that they really promote the spiritual advancement of their members. This is where the vital difference between philosophy and mysticism shows itself. Philosophy is a teaching which can be applied to any and every situation in life. It is not something which can endure only in artificial hothouses.

159

We find in these ashrams that what should be retreat is actually mere non-cooperative idleness, just as in the world outside them we find that what should be work is actually sheer neurotic overstrain.

160

The ascetic character easily becomes a self-righteous one. The monastic character easily falls into depreciation of those who live in the world whilst praising itself as following a higher way of life. All this is not necessarily true.

161

No handful of dreamers hiding themselves in an abode away from the world and fearful of its common everyday existence is likely to affect or elevate the world.

162

Another danger of these monastic retreats is the danger of falling into a pious lethargy of supposed renunciation which is as futile for the mystic as it is sterile for mankind.

163

If one could buy spiritual self-realization for the price of a ticket from any Euramerican city to any Oriental ashram, it would not be worth having. The fact is that a man carries himself about wherever he goes, that the real work to be done must be done inside his own heart and mind, not inside an ashram, and that no such geographical transplantation has even half the value admirers believe it has. Going to live in an ashram to get inner peace is like taking drugs to help one sleep. The longer you take them the harder will it be to regain natural sleep. The petty squabbles and ignoble jealousies of ashram life bore the intelligent travelled man.

164

Environment alone does not give spiritual enlightenment. You may squat in an ashram till Doomsday and emerge as much in the dark as when you entered it. Unless the proper *inner* conditions have been established, unless the mentality and character have been prepared and purified, travelling to the East or sitting at the feet of the gurus can lead only to the *hallucination* of enlightenment.

165

An ashram should be a place where one could go to get the benefits of a spiritual atmosphere, metaphysical discussion, mystical meditation, and exemplary living; but the gap between what should be and what is, is often unfortunately too wide to be ignored. Those who look for little utopias in little ashrams may find them. But it will be only at the price of substituting imagination for reality. Unfortunately, wishful thinking finds this easy. Cozily huddled, half-asleep, or fully a-dream in their ashrams, what did the war mean to them? It meant nothing where its thunder did not actually break in upon their complacent lives.

166

A mind that is continually turned inward upon itself tends in time to exaggerate its own importance. This is why ascetics and monks are often mildly unbalanced or unduly self-obsessed.

167

The failure to produce moral uplift in the world outside their retreat is paralleled by the failure of moral striving in the smaller world inside the retreats.

168

The law of compensation is everywhere operative. If the disciple smirks complacently about his residence in a holy retreat or his connection with a holy master, the danger is that he may fall into the delusion of rapid progress where in fact there is none. For in the emotional stimulation provided by such retreat or such master, he may naturally feel that he is now at levels of character, spirituality, and even consciousness which are far superior to those he formerly possessed. And in a sense there is some truth in his feeling. What he overlooks, however, is that the stimulation will one day be withdrawn (it is not necessary to go into the how or why of this here), that his condition is only a temporary one, and that he is really like a man basking in warm sunshine who imagines that the warmth and light are radiating from himself instead of from an outside source.

169

The recluses who segregate their sympathies along with their bodies, develop a view of human life which is as narrow as the door of the ashrams in which they dwell.

170

It fulfils a great function for those who are tired of the world and who need rest: they would be happy there indeed. But those who have to press forward on the path to Truth or those who have to do real service to mankind, may lose precious years if they settle permanently in an ashram, for they will be drugged by the relative peace, which will be delusive because temporary. Permanent peace must be worked for and there is no complete work possible without the complete discipline of the Quest.

171

The European recluses in their monasteries, the Indian monks in their ashrams, easily lose themselves in the most fanciful or most futile beliefs, the most hallucinatory, mystic experiences, suggested to them by the institution. The oppositions of the hard world and the tests of practical experience are lacking.

172

The belief that the mere cessation of external activity is an avenue to holiness is another of those curious superstitions which have fastened themselves on the human mind since the earliest times. And the related belief that if a number of such persons who have adopted a do-nothing existence segregate themselves from the world and live together in a communal institution such as an ashram or a monastery, they will become wiser better and holier than those they have left behind, is likewise a superstition.

173

Those who lead outwardly unproductive lives because they lead inwardly vigorous ones are within their rights. We must respect their choice. But they do not represent the philosophic ideal.

174

The antipathies and frictions of group, institutional, monastic, or ashram life are inevitable. If one is not to withdraw from the association, acceptance and tolerance are necessary. If he feels called upon to improve the others, it is better to do so in silence, by intercessory prayer or benedictory meditation.

175

It is true that being removed from worldly temptations does help; but the battle is either simply transferred to the imaginative plane or a truce is called *for a time*, or a new defect, that of hypocrisy, will be added.

176

Those who live in ashrams or monasteries, whether outer or inner, and who despise the ordinary concerns of ordinary people as vulgar, materialistic, and worldly, are extremists or fanatics.

177

The notion that life in the world is necessarily worse for the aspirant than life in the monastery is not a correct one. It might be but it need not be. If it is beset by dangers, so is the other. If it has vices and struggles, so has the other. Ambition, sensuality, pride, covetousness, envy, cruelty, and intrigue are weeds to be found in both gardens.

178

The monks who drop the selfishness of worldly desire, adopt the selfishness of worldly desertion.

179

But the atmosphere of an ashram is rather a special one, something like that of a hothouse where tropical plants are reared in a northern clime—just slightly artificial. How will an inmate behave if he has to come out and pass the remainder of his years in the ordinary world, in an actual situation like earning his daily bread, his livelihood?

180

The temptations of monastic life are different from those of the outside world, but they are just as present and exigent. The weak disposition which yields to the one may just as easily yield to the other. The constant inner battle against oneself can only change its form, not its necessity.

181

These ashrams and monasteries are communities where the individual is submerged, where he is supposed to abandon his own will in favour of God's will, or rather, and actually, in favour of God's representative—the guru of the ashram, the abbot of the monastery.

182

If they imagine that renunciation of the world and flight to an ashram will take them out of the world, they will have to undergo the actual experience itself before passing into the scepticism which is founded on disillusionment. For in ashram or monastery, in East or West, the preoccupation with finance and the quest for power enters into the administration and brings in a worldliness of a special kind.

183

It is easy enough from the safe distance in space of an ashram to talk about the vanity of all things, or in time from the safe distance of old age. But it is unfair to leave it at that. For many of the things in the actual world have been, and are to be, enjoyed.

184

There may come a time when the ashram's usefulness will be limited to supplying his physical and, sometimes, his intellectual needs, when instead of leading him to the Overself's freedom it becomes a prison.

185

We like to believe that Oriental ashrams and Western monasteries are havens of refuge from the evils and sins of worldly life. But we find in actuality that even in such sacred and dedicated precincts, human beings are still weak, petty, mean, selfish, envious, and hostile. The embodied nobility and goodness we would like to meet are met only in single occasional individuals, who may be met in the world just as likely as in these places.

186

"May our studies be fruitful. May we not quarrel," says the *Keno Upanishad*. So even in those days, and even in the forest ashrams, the dissensions which mar modern communal retreats also existed!

187

It is unlikely that new ideas can penetrate such cloistral fortresses as these ashrams.

188

Undisciplined or intriguing members of the ashram soon make trouble appear; jealous or ambitious ones drive away the more independent, less tractable, more advanced seekers.

189

A man should continue his work in the world and not use his spiritual aspiration as an excuse for idleness that corrupts. He will find peace not by joining the ill-mannered squabbling bickering self-centered inmates of an ashram but by keeping out of it!

190

We hear of those who find the world too much for them and flee to the shelter of ashram or monastery. But what of those—doubtless a much smaller number—who find the cloistered communal life too much for them and flee to the freedom of the world?

191

Those who have sojourned in ashram or monastery, Eastern or Western, with open eyes and hearing ears, will know that tensions and frictions exist here, too, but they will be mainly petty ones.

192

It is not enough to surround ourselves with possessions that human skill, taste, and invention have made if we are to become truly human beings, and not fractional ones. But it is equally insufficient and certainly unhelpful to sit in a monastic corner and decry them.

193

The yogi who looks out upon the world from his sheltered retreat often cannot see the world at all.

194

The surrender of personal freedom and the submergence of personal individuality are the cost to them of whatever relief and peace the ashram gives them.

195

I have seen too much time dawdled away in monasteries by their inhabitants to overvalue these institutions. But neither do I want to undervalue them.

196

Rabelais held up to ridicule the inner emptiness of so many monks who were his contemporaries. Yet Rabelais was not a layman criticizing from the outside: he was himself a monk and knew from the inside what he was writing about.

197

It is men who are suffering and toiling in the world who have a heavier burden to carry than the monks in the ashrams. And it is the depth of suffering which in the end measures the extent of aspiration to be liberated from it.

198

The man who keeps his eyes open will not find any spiritual community, monastery, retreat, or ashram that is absolutely good. Romantic Utopianism, whether of the mystic or the Marxist type, belongs to the world of dreams, not realities. "I do not believe in perfectability," remarked Keats, and because he was thinking of our earthly existence at the time, he was right. The absolutely good community does not exist simply because absolute goodness must be wrought within our own spirit and can be found only there. Both the logic of a true metaphysical world-view and the experience of a widespread search will confirm this.

199

They begin by making the mistake of seeking, or of expecting to find, an ideal community. It does not exist here and consequently cannot be found. It would be better to limit their search, or their expectation, to a congenial community.

200

The belief that paradise is to be found among the monastic retreats of the West and the ashram communities of India is a romantic fallacy that sustained contact from inside will expose. There is as much nobility of character to be found outside them as among the inhabitants of these retreats and the members of these communities. The excessive attention which is too often given to the inner condition of their own egos almost amounts to an unhealthy and unbalanced obsession. This does not tend to paradisaic conditions.

201

Always these utopias exist either in the far past, as with religious myth, or around the future's corner, as with materialistic economics.

202

If his experiences are sufficiently numerous and sufficiently varied, this rosy-coloured optimism about human nature will be drained out of him. He will slowly lose the naïve belief in the possibility of creating a *social* kingdom of heaven on earth, in the utility of organizing an association of spiritually minded people, in the dream of achieving unity and harmony amongst them, let alone amongst humanity in general. He will see that innate psychic attractions and repulsions are implanted in us by Nature, that uncrossable differences of mentality and outlook are fashioned in us by development and that although misunderstanding, friction, and hostility may be kept out in the beginning, they cannot be kept out in the end. He will decide that heaven can only be internal and that the quest can only be individual.

5

SOLITUDE

One needs a place where the only noise is that which one makes oneself. Then, the lovely stillness without helps to induce the lovely stillness within.

2

The solitude which accompanies or is necessary to these first periods of stillness should be accepted and gloried in to preserve the experience from being broken into. Do not run and leave it prematurely. For although at the end of this quest the mind's silence can be found anywhere within the bustle and activity, the turmoil and the noise of modern city life, the first faint tender ventures must be guarded, protected: solitude, outward solitude, is the best way.

3

We go apart into solitude or take a walk alone to think over a personal problem which has suddenly come up. How much more is solitude desirable to think over the larger problem of life and to meditate deeply on oneself?

4

It is harder to find solitude in this mid-twentieth century than it was in the mid-eighteenth century. We have gained more neighbours, easier communications with them and transport to them. But we have lost much of our chance of just being alone, just being with our own self and getting acquainted with its deeper aspects. Yet the pressures of civilization have increased, so that this need of finding inner strength and gaining inner poise has also increased proportionately.

5

This need of communing with our own soul expresses itself as a need of solitude, as a disgust with society, or as a nervous hypersensitivity.

6

When his commerce with God becomes his most important activity and remembrance of God the most habitual one, solitariness grows deeply on a man. His need for friends grows less.

7

If he grows in real spirituality, and not in the emotional imitation of it, he will grow to love solitude as much as most people dread it.

8

He will come to enjoy solitude as much as formerly he enjoyed society. For when alone, he is alone with the beauty and serenity of the Soul but when with people, he is also with their greedy natures, their bad tempers, and their ugly insincerities.

9

We are least troubled and most content when we are in solitude and silence with the Overself. It is when we are with others that these states are harder to feel.

10

Whoever is willing to take up the inner work of quietening the activity of thoughts and add the disciplining of feelings will find with time that solitude is a valuable help. If the possibility of country rather than town life can also be realized, his way will be easier.

11

If you want to know why so many hermits have sought their solitude, the answer awaits you in the character of man.

12

We must find ourselves, our spiritual centre. We know that the discovery comes only in solitude, but make no mistake: Yogic cave, nun's convent and ascetic's monastery are only for the few. Withdrawal from the affairs of life is not for the many. Theirs is to be the solitude of the inner life, the keeping of a reserved spot in the heart while busy in society.

13

Everything depends on the point of view. To most people this experience is a retreat from reality but to a few people it is a return to it.

14

It is not that he shuts himself up in his own life because he has no interest in society's but rather that the fulfilment of the purpose which, he believes, God has implanted in his being, is paramount.

15

In the end and perhaps after many years he finds that he cannot get away from man's innate loneliness.

16

There is a vast difference between an idle morbidly-introspective solitude and the inwardly-active creative solitude advocated here.

17

Sufi idea: To be worldly or to be in the world is to forget God. You may go to caves and mountains but that is not to leave the world. Live a normal life and remember God. That's all. Don't live outwardly but inwardly.

18

He will learn to appreciate and even become tough enough to like this aloneness. He will realize that he has enough in himself, as well as in the inspired writings that he will keep around him, to last a lifetime. He will come to see how soft, how weak are all those who cannot live without craving for, and constantly having at least one other human being near at hand.

19

Aloneness is good for a man, but when it is felt as too overpowering, it is not. Then the balance must be redressed by society.

20

The decision by unmarried persons to live alone rather than to share an apartment or a house with other adults is not necessarily a misanthropic one: it may be a nervous necessity. There is too much strain and pressure involved in such sharing, too much confinement and limitation, too much lack of freedom.

21

When *in meditation* a man faces God, or his own higher self, he arrives at a complete solitude in the sense that no other person is present to his consciousness. It is a curious fact that on his way to this unique experience, he tends to live more and more within himself, less and less in the *mental* sphere of society.

22

Even Paul did not straightway start on his mission to the Gentiles after the vision of Jesus, but lived for three years of solitude in Arabia to prepare himself. What did he do there? What else could he do other than pray, learn, meditate, purify himself, and strengthen himself?

23

It is enough at the beginning to make these occasional excursions into the quieter and lonelier places. If they can be absolutely quiet and utterly lonely, his purpose will be best achieved.

24

One may take a warm interest in what is happening in the world, be thrilled or saddened by dramatic events, and yet refuse to join in the scramble to get on, the fight between opposing parties, the denigrating gossip or foolish movements. One may live as a hermit, while living in the world, and thus live with oneself.

25

There are times in the career of an advanced meditator when he needs to avoid contact with humanity and live entirely alone.

26

If he refuses to give himself to the demands of society, that is not because of disdain for it, but because of a felt need to give his highest aim his whole attention. By isolating himself from worldly contacts he can develop with less hindrance those qualities which the worldly do not possess, and even discourage.

27

To the man with sufficient and active cultural interests, solitude may be quite tolerable but to the man without them it may be unbearable. To the man who has learnt the secret of entering inner stillness, it can be an exquisite pleasurable experience.

28

The mystic who dissociates himself from the affairs of his era and shuts himself up in seclusion may still contribute some influence on that era. But it will be necessarily limited to the plane nearest to the one on which his meditation operates. He will affect the minds of sensitive persons.

29

This need of solitude and privacy as being not merely a temperamental but also a vitally spiritual one, is recognized by some monastic orders. In Catholicism, the Carthusians live shut in their individual cells.

30

The criticism is heard that this idea if put into practice today seduces the intelligent individual to try to strengthen himself by weakening society at a time when society itself is most in need of being strengthened, and that it withdraws the unselfish man from the common effort at a time when his services could be most fruitful.

31

When a man enters this phase, he begins to feel a great weariness with life. He loses his interest in many things which may have absorbed him before. He becomes emotionally indifferent to activities and persons formerly attractive to him. He withdraws more and more from people and society. When this fatigue with all existence descends upon him, then he will be more ready and more willing to lose the personal ego in the universal ocean of being.

32

So far as the rest of mankind live for aims directly contrary to his own, he himself must live inwardly apart from them.

33

For a sensitive person privacy is a need. And if he also happens to be both a scholar and a writer—without mentioning a meditator—then it becomes a very real need. The irony is that, the modern world being as it is, his possession of it depends on material things, that the only way to assure it is to have money; the more money the more is privacy possible—and such a person is the least likely to accumulate money.

34

The desert has given mankind some of its greatest prophets. Out of its solitude there appeared a wild-looking man, dressed in a rough camel's hair girdle. He came living on locusts and wild honey, but fasting often. He went among the cities of Judea, praying, calling for repentance, denouncing wickedness, and proclaiming the Coming. This man was John the Baptist.

Immediately after illumination came to him on the road to Damascus, Saul went to the desert. He stayed for three years, engaged in self-training and inner development. When he emerged from it, he was Paul the Initiate.

Islam was born in the desert wastes of Arabia.

It was not for nothing that the early Christian mystics of lower Egypt fled from populous cities to the open spaces of the desert. Their instinct was right.

35

He will find the Path leads him away from the crowd into solitude; and, later, away from the thoughts of the crowd that people solitude into himself.

36

It is hard to get this privacy, harder still to get solitude in the full sense. Other people will not let him alone. If they cannot intrude physically, they do it by letter. If not that way, then by thoughts about him.

37

Most of those who have attained this pure philosophic truth not only revolted against and deliberately lived apart from worldly communities, but also from monkish communities. This was not only because they were entirely free from religious sectarian bias (with which religious organizations tend to become identified) since they usually acknowledge no ties—but also because the physical habits of living among worldly people were repellent to them.

38

He may have goodwill to all mankind but this does not make him sociably inclined to all mankind.

39

People misunderstand his motives, resent his keeping to himself, reject his need of solitude, and prove totally unable to understand his reasons for staying on his own lone path rather than society's beaten path. So they descend to injustice, call him haughty or self-centered or poseur. His refusal to get involved in relationships which will sap time and energy needed for higher things or in situations whose troubled outcome he can foresee quite clearly, will be denounced with anger as inhuman.

40

Without moving from one's home, without any experiences in the world outside it, a man may form character and acquire wisdom, but only if he correctly understood and faithfully followed the philosophic meditations.

41

Total independence is impossible to attain in this or any other society. But what may not be found outwardly may still be found inwardly.

42

I have known quite a number of hermits, ascetics, and monks in my time and travels, but I have never known one who was so totally withdrawn from the world that he was not, in some small or large way, dependent on the world. Complete isolation is theoretically possible but practically it is not permanently possible. Even the millionaire who seeks it needs those who will help create it for him, and to that extent he depends on them.

43

But the essential thing is what we do with the mind. Socrates nurtured his philosophy in what was for that time a large city; he did not need, like Thoreau, to withdraw into Nature's solitudes.

44

It is important to his success or failure that this temporary isolation be protected against unwanted intrusion.

45

The old yogi, sitting under the shade of a neem tree, unconcerned with the bustling world, is entitled to his withdrawal and justified in his view. But those who follow another way, who stay in the world without being "of it" are not less deserving of tolerance and respect.

46

The more he can find a place, a time, and a circumstance when he is least likely to be distracted by any cause whatever, the better will his meditation be. In this connection it is needful to remember that to help achieve this purpose of solitude, seclusion is better than society—even than the society of one person and that a member of the family or a close friend. This is because the other's thoughts and feelings may penetrate his consciousness in a vague way and disturb it since he is sitting receptively and passively.

47

He must resist the interruptions of his privacy whether they be boorish or well-meant if they lead to interruptions of his peace.

48

It would be interesting to count the men of your acquaintance who are able to stand on their own solitary opinion, who refuse to be strapped down in the straitjackets of conventional public opinion. You will usually find that such men, by taste or by circumstance, are accustomed to pass somewhat lonely lives. They like to sequester themselves; they prefer to live in quiet places. If destiny grants them the choice, they choose the place of quiet mountains rather than the prattle of little men. Such men develop their bent for independent thought precisely because they prefer with-drawn lives. Society and company could only assist to smother their best ideas, their native originality, and so they avoid them. Thoreau, that powerful advocate for solitude, could never be intimidated by anyone.

49

In the still hours of the evening, when the activities of the world drop from its tired hands, the mind can find anew its olden peace. But in solitude there can be comfort and healing. Genius fleeing the multitude, as Wordsworth did, knows this to be true.

50

So few know either the meaning or the delight of inner silence; so many know only the depressive associations of outer silence, such as ancient ruins and peopled cemeteries.

51

Privacy is a great privilege—almost, in these noisy days, a luxury. To be able to live without being interrupted by others, to be able to converge all one's thoughts, without being disturbed, upon the highest of all thoughts, the discovery of the Overself, is a satisfaction indeed!

52

Not many persons are suited for solitude. To get the best it has to give requires a special sensitivity of temperament, a fine appreciation of Nature, and a little knowledge of the mind's possibilities.

53

A time must come to every sensitive person when he tires of the multiple distractions activities and tensions of twentieth-century civilized living, when he yearns for a simpler, less exhausting, less complicated existence.

54

The higher creative works are best developed in isolation. Those to whom they are offered later would, if present, disturb the concentration needed or obstruct the blowing wind of inspiration.

55

A hermit sitting in a sequestered retreat may eventually draw to himself by the mind's mysterious power, as some Oriental sages have done, certain spiritual seekers, those who were then benefited by the contact.

56

The man who cannot be as happy in his own society as in that of others will never attain true happiness at all.

57

Not all persons leave the world because they cannot cope with it: some do so for the very opposite reason. They can handle its affairs only too well, they know its human weaknesses and deformities from personal experience and can counter them. But enough is enough: their scale of values is now on a new higher level.

58

The mind germinates with great truths after these lonely sessions.

59

The demands made by acquaintances, and even by friends, ought not be permitted to supersede those of the inner life.

60

The enforced cessation from external activity which imprisonment may bring could be a help to spiritual awakening. A few months before he died Oscar Wilde said, "I have lived all there was to live. I found the sweet bitter and the bitter sweet. I was happy in prison because there I found my soul."

61

Why should he contend with a society that is dominated by materialism, motivated by egoism, and saturated with sensualism?

62

A man who is spiritually minded often has moods when he sickens of frequent contact with his more sordid fellows, when he prefers to withdraw and become a mere commentator on life.

63

The theory of breaking all connection with the world in order to make connection with the Eternal Spirit, is sound enough.

64

They withdraw from experiences because they want to withdraw from the senses.

65

It does not need much thought to understand why it is easier to find the presence of God in the absence of people.

66

For a month every year Muhammed withdrew from the world and from Mecca into complete solitude, and thus balanced activity with contemplation.

67

He deliberately isolates himself from the crowd at these regular intervals because he believes that only in loneliness can he approach the Ideal. Not that he ever really achieves such a condition, for God alone is alone.

68

The man who is frightened by loneliness is not yet ready for philosophy.

69

If solitude is filled with growing knowledge and deepening peace, one never wearies of it.

70

I am too enamoured of this tranquillity which solitude gives me to accept the overtures of those who have no connection with me except a geographical one. If there is no spiritual propinquity it is better to stay alone.

71

The creator in art and the thinker in philosophy need privacy for their work. Those who break into it without being invited—whether in person or by letter or, worse, by telephone—deprive others, rob humanity.

72

It is his inner apartness that enables him to keep his freedom and pursue his quest. Whether it has to be translated into outer terms is another matter, and one dependent on his circumstances: it is not inexorable and essential.

73

Solitude becomes intolerable to those without inner resources. The time passes too slowly for them, too boringly. Unless they have some outer activity to keep them busy all the day, the inactive hours become unendurable.

74

Whether a bodily withdrawal should follow the inner one at the same time, or at some later date, or is not necessary at all, must be determined by each person for himself in accord with his outer circumstances and personal strength.

75

To be always among other human beings, be they in a city or a village, is suffocating to the growth of awareness of one's own higher individuality. There are times when even the involvement of family or the cloistered life of a monastic institution have saturated one's aura and occasional liberations are needed.

76

The hermit who tries to improve himself, to deepen himself, to purify himself, and to enlighten himself is, indirectly, also contributing to the improvement of mankind generally.

77

To put it plainly he has less time for society because he wants more time for God.

78

Loneliness he is thankful for and comes to regard as a blessing, not as the misfortune it is so widely supposed to be. If choice and destiny have brought him seclusion, he would not give it up easily.

79

The recluse who finds his spiritual and cultural resources sufficient company is as happy—in a different way—as the householder enjoying his family.

80

Loneliness is cold to those who know only the self which gives them a personal existence, but very warm, very friendly, to those who know their other self.

81

It is a matter of temperament and circumstance whether he shall bury himself in a solitary existence or not. The inner life is always available, whether he is active or passive, for in both cases it is available *only as he turns toward it*, retreats into it, or draws upon it.

82

He finds that his solitude is inhabited by another being than his familiar own, that a higher presence has entered the area of consciousness.

83

By communing with his deeper self in quietude and solitude, he can renew his battered ideals and fortify his aspirations.

84

There are a few periods of his inner life when complete isolation is greatly needed and greatly advantageous.

85

The law which completes every thing and every movement in Nature by its opposite or contrary acts here, too. If a period of self-sought isolation is prolonged enough, a man inevitably gets tired of it and desires a change.

86

Read the Book of Genesis and note how Joseph's inward liberation came during his outward imprisonment. Read the biography of Sri Aurobindo and note how his spiritual awakening came during the year spent in jail. Read the poems written by Sir Walter Raleigh during his last confinement in the Tower of London and note the depth of religious feeling they reached.

87

Periodic retreats into solitude are a necessity to the advanced soul if he is to fulfil his purpose in attaining true, free, and inspired Individuality.

88

Although few will have troubled to perceive the fact, or may even be able to perceive it, we all have to live in inner solitude anyway.

89

The need of withdrawing at certain times from outer contact with other human beings will be felt and if so should be obeyed. If he disregards it, he misses an opportunity to progress to a higher stage.

90

Swami Ramdas: "You should not take refuge in any ashram for the purpose of realizing the supreme state. What you need is solitude and suitable environments."

91

The difference between seeking holiness in a corporate monastic life and seeking it in a solitary one is wide.

92

Man's long search to find himself may begin with a crowd but must end in complete loneliness.

93

He will have to endure at times the solitude of the man who finds himself on a summit.

94

He will tend to become more and more solitary in his social habits, less and less disposed to carry on with external work, for he will grudge the time and feel that it belongs by right to the prayers and meditations which are leading him inwards. The same solitude which may lead others to despair or madness must lead him to calmness and wisdom.

95

Because he has to find a balance between the wordly life and the inner life, he discovers and develops a portable solitude. This he takes with him to work or social leisure.

96

The same mental isolation which may lead to illusion in the mad may lead to truth in the well balanced.

97

When the disadvantages of fame are severely felt, the advantages of flight into obscurity become attractive.

98

It is not so much that he, as an individual, has come into conflict with society as that he finds the goals offered him by society to be unsatisfactory, sometimes even frightening. So he withdraws from it.

99

The love of solitude will not be felt by those who are still enthralled by the love of gregariousness.

100

His sensitivity to the world's evil currents may become unbearable, forcing him to withdraw into isolation or else to suffer enormously.

101

The world thinks it could hardly wish one a worse fate than to be cast away like Crusoe on an uninhabited isle, and the mystic could hardly wish himself a better one, for then he might come to complete grips with himself and follow Ariadne's thread till he finds the Soul.

102

If for a while and in certain ways the student has to learn to live unto himself alone, this is only that he may later and in other ways better carry out his responsibilities towards his fellow creatures. He has not washed his hands of this responsibility but he has decided to equip himself better for it.

103

A princess once told me about a friend of hers who had been an officer high in the Russian Army and a popular member of the Russian aristocracy. After the Bolshevik Revolution he escaped to Greece, renounced the world, and made his home in Mount Athos. There, in the hermit settlement perched on the windswept cliff-face of Karoulia, he occupies a kind of half-cave, half-hut, perched high above the sea and reached by perilously steep unprotected steps. He sleeps on the floor with his head on a stone pillow and with the bony skulls of former monkish inhabitants of the cell lined up on a shelf. Father Nikon, as he is called, is one of the very few educated and mannered men to be found in the peasant-stock illiterate community of Mount Athos. In a message he sent the princess after many years of this solitary existence and in response to her enquiry, he said that he had found great peace and had never before known such happiness. The visitor who carried the message was struck by the contentment which radiated from him and the serene self-mastery with which he bore himself.

104

The wider his experience of the world, the more he is tempted to become a recluse.

105

The impingement of other people's auras, if they be inferior and if he be sensitive, causes him a kind of suffering. Can he be blamed for preferring solitude to sociability?

106

The man who seeks to defend his solitude and protect his privacy for spiritual purposes is not the type that the public admires. Yet why should he present his sacred treasures before scoffers? Why should he cast the divulgements which come to him in quiet meditation before a sneering world?

107

The man who prefers his solitude to listening to the silly chatter of those who talk endlessly but say nothing worth saying, has at least done no worse.

108

When a man becomes disgusted with the world's ways, he may decide to leave it to its own fate, retreat into solitude, and seek out his own progress.

109

He is not afraid of being alone, nor even of living alone. It is in such solitude, he knows, that he can become acquainted with his real self. But neither is he afraid of sharing his solitude with someone else's. The Spirit is large enough to be findable in one or the other, despite all monkish or ascetic claims to the contrary.

110

People blame him for being a recluse, but then he will rarely meet a beautiful soul whereas he can always meet a beautiful bit of Nature. Do they blame him for preferring Nature? Besides, he is so taken up with this task of getting to know himself that he has little inclination left to get to know others.

111

If he is to be away from outer temptations which stimulate afresh and keep alive thoughts that he is desirous of subduing, then it is better he should be away from society. If he is to avoid the semblance of situations which may outwardly compromise him even though he is inwardly guiltless, it is again better that he should be away from society.

112

There are times when a man needs to be alone, apart from others, to be wholly himself and think his own thoughts.

113

It is hard for such a man to stay in society without compromise, without playing the hypocrite, without becoming half-insincere. It is understandable if, disgusted, he would rather retire from the world and be a recluse.

114

His revulsion against this materialism is understandable. Its denial of the finer culture which he is beginning to find is reprehensible. Shall he follow the Indian example and withdraw from the world, repudiate its values, and disengage himself from all relationships? It may not be the easiest way to live but it is certainly the sincerest.

115

Hearing some nearby worshipper singing out of tune, say quite flat, does not promote the feeling of reverential worship, let alone of brotherly love. Yes, the argument for privacy in worship is a strong one!

116

Left alone, with no intrusion of other people's auras to create tensions, a beautiful placidity takes over the mind of a philosophically developed man.

117

"I regard my last eight months in prison as the happiest period in my life. It was then that I was initiated into that new world . . . which enabled my soul . . . to establish communion with the Lord of all Being. This would never have happened if I had not had such solitude as enabled me to recognize my real self. Although I did not study mysticism, the mystics I read in prison appealed to me tremendously." —Anwar el Sadat, former president of Egypt

118

No matter how many other persons anyone surrounds himself with, he is and remains fundamentally alone. He may not recognize it, or may refuse to recognize it, but an hour comes when the hidden truth is forced upon him.

119
He must use a shield against intrusive society, against aggressive egos ever ready to desecrate what he holds most holy. That shield is concealment.

120
The lonelier he is the likelier is meditation to appeal to him.

121
Solitude is not a necessity of the meditative existence. A man may go his own way in the midst of a society inwardly detached, calm while outwardly busy and alert, weary of the witless talk that imposes upon their dementia a pomposity which provokes right and proper ridicule.

122
This is not my own discovery. The ancients and the medievals knew it, too. Richard Rolle, the fourteenth-century English mystic, states, "In ancient days many of the more perfect went out from the monasteries to dwell alone." I myself witnessed the procession of the more advanced of Ramana Maharshi's disciples exiling themselves, one by one, from his ashram during his lifetime.

123
At such times, when he is alone with the best in himself, he will come to appreciate the worth of solitude.

124
The recluse who rejects society is entitled to do so and to find his own spiritual path in his own way; but it is neither just nor wise for him to impose his way upon the others who have to live in society, who can not reject it.

125
To the man of thought, feeling, and meditation, privacy is a treasure—a necessity of his way of life, a creative and fruitful period.

126
Solitude is the best way of life, Nature is the best company, God is the best presence. Those who are wealthy surround themselves with servants, so that they never have solitude, but always other presences, other auras around them. Privacy is the accompaniment of solitude and where there is no solitude there is no privacy.

127
It is pleasant to live ignored and unknown. The world then lets you alone and keeps its negative thoughts off you, directing them to someone else. To be regarded as a nobody and let others find out after you have passed from their physical ken or moved elsewhere that you are a somebody prevents unwanted intrusions.

128

He is a prudent man who does not much encumber himself with commitments to other persons upon the journey of life but retains some measure of the freedom which is found in aloneness and independence.

129

Who has full freedom and complete independence? Who is walled against the actions, the influence, the suggestions, and the presence of others? Even the recluse who withdraws from society will find it difficult to live or be alone. He prefers to be inconspicuous among others, to live quietly in society, to have a humbler rather than a grander position, and to hide himself in anonymity or obscurity. But these are his own preferences. If, however, the Higher Power wills or instructs him intuitively to come into the public eye, to be publicly active, he will reluctantly have to obey the call.

130

This mental solitude will seem to be enchanted, almost magical, outside the working of time itself.

131

He must not be afraid to hide himself if that is the only way he can avoid being disturbed.

132

Many people look upon living alone and staying alone as often as possible with something like horror and to be avoided. The philosopher has no such attitude, for on the contrary he is able then really and truly to be himself—and not what the pressures of others force him to try to appear to be.

133

The large spread of vulgarity in the world makes a fastidious person find more enjoyment in solitude.

134

The better part of his character revolts against much that he finds in the world but which others have long since received into their concept of an acceptable and respectable society.

135

The mystical temperament covets solitude and quietude, detests multitude and noise. The mystical way of life renounces the limited ego, battles against the lower instincts, and abjures personal strife. Consequently, the mystic is inevitably repelled by much that belongs to the active life. His breadth and depth of outlook find little attractive in it. He wants to save the time and energy it absorbs so as to make his life inwardly profitable.

136

If he seeks to live apart from others for long periods, he is entitled to do so. Society and community may do much for a man but they do not give him inner peace. For that he must fight alone in the full sense of the word.

137

A sensitive man is entitled to protective shelter from intrusions to his private tent in the wilderness of this world. Aloneness with the Overself may be his particular way of life. Solitude may be his necessity, but someone else's curse.

138

Has he obligations to society which remain unfulfilled if he chooses solitude whilst he remains in it, or withdrawal into a retreat when he does not? Is he acting dishonourably? The answer is that he is entitled to his decision: it is personal. His own future life is at stake, not society's.

139

The criticism that the man who withdraws and excludes himself from the turmoil and agitation of ordinary life for spiritual reasons is antisocial and selfish is a narrow, one-sided, and superficial one. If he uses the hermit-like retreat to improve his character and to foster resolves to amend his conduct when he returns to society, he will surely be a better member than before. Since society is composed of individuals, that which leads to their moral elevation cannot fairly be called antisocial. And since everyone benefits by it in the end, it cannot be called selfish.

140

Is the man who has gone aside for a while to collect his forces, to quieten his mind and to study the ancient wisdom, to be labelled a deserter of civilization? How false such a label, how foolish the critic who affixes it! All that is best in civilization has come from men who for a time went aside to gain the inspiration or the vision out of which their contributions or creations were born.

141

The disgust with the world which Shankara regards as one of the four essential qualities for the Quest, or dispassion as it is sometimes translated, must also include disgust with humanity. Therefore, if it leads a man to seek a solitary existence in order to find what the world's influences obstruct, he ought not to be blamed.

142

If the hermit is busy with quietening his thoughts, penetrating his consciousness, deepening his attention and uplifting his emotion, his unsocial behaviour is quite justified. He knows now that he must fulfill his duty to himself and that it takes time and strength. If he leaves other persons alone, does not intrude into their lives, it is because he is trying to make his own life so much more valuable, and this in the end will make him so much more valuable to society. Thus, not only is his own patience called for, but also the patience of society, to bear with his solitary ways.

143

Experience will instruct him that until he attains a certain inner status, the more he moves with others, the less often he finds the inner light. The more he is alone the easier it is to commune with Nature. It needs courage to practise solitariness at the proper times, for too many meetings and too much chattering deprives.

144

When he sees how much malignancy there is in the world, a man may be excused if, without turning misanthrope and for the purpose of higher development, he cuts himself off from his fellow men and withdraws into seclusion.

145

The hermit who isolates himself from neighbours in order to enter a deeper intercourse with himself, is entitled to do so. It is the spiritual motive which justifies the antisocial act.

146

To leave the worldly life, out of clear perception of its insufficiency and unsatisfactoriness, or out of disgust and fatigue, is not necessarily a cowardly act. It may well be the only proper and prudent act.

Dangers of solitude

147

The benefit which can be got from solitude, is had only by properly balanced minds. The others will be still more unbalanced by it.

148

The hermits who go, self-banished, into their rural retreats have as much right to their solitude as we to our society. But if they avoid all contact with others for too long a period, they fall into fresh danger of monomania, hallucination, or illusory progress. Here, as in all things, a balance must be kept.

149

The tendency to withdraw into oneself in disgust with the world is useful so long as it does not end in a withdrawal to some other part of the ego. The result is likely to be that one shuts oneself up in sulkiness, if not morbidity—a sterile move.

150

If he loses interest in the world to the extent that he is quite willing to let it go hang, for all he cares, where is the evidence of spiritual unselfishness in this? Is it not rather a complete obsession with personal development?

151

So long as he does not go into action, the hermit is in no danger of being shocked into discovering all the truth about himself and about his theories. His meditation may reveal some or much of it but so far as this practice is swayed by his imaginings or permeated by his ego, it may lead him only to false results. But in the world he will meet with events, rocks, oppositions, temptations, that force him to bring up to the surface what is really in him or test the advances he has made to measure whether they be real or imaginary.

152

Hermits who dwell overlong in mountain eyries get out of touch with common life. Their outlook becomes narrow and confined; their thoughts become unable to take wide generous and balanced views. They fall into a fatal complacency.

153

There is a dangerous side to excessive solitude spent in efforts at meditation. It may lead to a dried-up, holier-than-thou sanctity which hides and protects the very egoism he sets out to kill. It may breed hallucinatory visions and pseudo-revelations, in which he gradually becomes lost to the truth and sanity of real vision and authentic revelation.

154

An excess of solitude may lead to a degeneration of manners. The man who lives too much in himself may forget how to live with others. Living alone, unsociable, having no companions, much less confidants, a hermit may lose polish, graciousness.

155

The dangers of introspection exist mostly if he is to revel in egoistic thoughts. But the philosophic aim is the very contrary—to cut a passage-way through all such thoughts and escape entirely from them.

156

The mere indifference towards other men and the self-sought blindness to events which characterize such a recluse are not necessarily the highest kind of detachment.

157

There is something outwardly ironic in asking such a man to love his neighbour as himself. Having secluded himself from all normal contacts with his neighbours, how can he find the chance to love them?

158

Isolation from all culture may either breed insanity or foster wisdom.

159

Prolonged isolation from his fellows can fill his mind with unreal imaginings about his own experiences and wrong ideas about other people's.

160

He becomes too withdrawn into himself in a negative way, ending in a lethargic apathetic self. This is not at all a philosophic result but quite the reverse.

161

The solitary man may or may not have a better chance to attain stillness, not enlightenment. This is because he is likely to have less distractions of certain kinds. But in that case he is likely to have other kinds instead.

162

Solitude may help a man immensely in his spiritual life during certain periods which may be quite long or quite short. But just as any good that is overdone becomes a bad or turns to a folly, so it is with solitude. Too much of it may cause a man to go astray and lose himself in chimeras and illusions. For if he has no other human contact he has no one with whom to check his ideas, from whom to receive constructive criticism, and by whom he may be warned about deviations from the correct path.

6

NATURE APPRECIATION

The beauty we see in a single flower points to a MIND capable of thinking such beauty. In the end Nature and Art point to God.

2

The most spectacular of all full moons in the western hemisphere and the one which lingers longest is the harvest moon which ends the summer and precedes the autumn. This provides a special chance for meditations.

3

Even if we take the Buddhistic view that all is transient, all is subject to change, and all is doomed to decay, we need not deny that the beauty and the pleasure to be found in physical life, however momentarily, still have their value. Is a field of flowers utterly worthless? Is the loveliness of a sunset to be utterly rejected?

4

Nature produces new or nobler feelings in the more sensitive wanderers into her domain. The sunset's peace, the dawn's promise of hope, and the pleasure of beauty's presence are always worthwhile and should fill us with gratitude.

5

His true father or mother is Nature.

6

Even the huge anthropoid apes—so near to man—have been observed to bow their heads solemnly and respectfully before the brightness of the rising moon.

7

It is a mysterious fact that high aspirations and good resolutions born between Christmas and Easter will be more successful during the subsequent twelve months than those born later in the year.

8

It is an error to confuse the inert simplicity and animal naturalness of the peasant with the dynamic simplicity and spiritual naturalness of the sophisticated philosopher.

9

The wisdom of the Overself is the wisdom of Nature. When the new spring leaves arrive birds build their nests the better to hide them.

10

He will accomplish this disciplinary work best if he retires to the quietude and contemplation of Nature, to a country seclusion where he can be least distracted and most uplifted. Here is the temple where aspiration for the Higher Self can find its best outlet; here is the monastery where discipline of the lower self can be easiest undertaken.

11

The beauty in a bird's song, the peace in a sage's face, the intelligence in Nature's actions, these offer hints and clues, as well as topics for meditation, to truth-seeking, ideal-aspiring men.

12

Let him stand at some busy corner, musing quietly and philosophically upon the unquiet metropolitan scene of great crowds of people swarming in and out of the subways, like rabbits swarming in and out of their burrows. Then let him stand on some mountain top and look down upon a scene of tranquil beauty. As he stands in wonder before the panorama of Nature, where spring bluebells dot the grey-green valleys while buttercups and cowslips grow profusely in the wide meadows, something of its serenity may touch his heart. Lulled by this sweet landscape, he will feel pleased at the thought that there is so much distance between him and the world.

13

To look steadily at Nature's own artwork for a while—be it mountain, valley, or moving waves—with growing deep feeling until the self is forgotten, is also a yoga practice.

14

There is a limiting effect upon the mind in the rooms of houses that have no view, in the narrow street of an old town, if a man has to live there. Great ideas do not lodge comfortably in bodies whose outlook is shut-in, restricted. But by the seashore the mind expands with the spaciousness and openness.

15

The strong emotional impression of beauty which a Nature-painted scene can evoke will—if he stays with it and does not too quickly hurry off to other thoughts—take him away from self-consciousness, its narrow confines and severely limited interests. He forgets them, and in the forgetting is released for the time from his ego.

16

When a man is in deep trouble, for which no human voice can bring consolation, it is then the turn of Nature. In the quiet woods, the winding riverside, the view from a mountain, he may gather some crumbs, at least, of that which he cannot find elsewhere.

17

There is not only a poetic or aesthetic value in appreciating the beauty of a mountain stream, the companionship of a group of trees. There is also a still higher value which is findable only if a man looks upward and away from his little personal affairs.

18

Nature is my guru.

19

It is true that God dwells in no particular Nature-made place, no special kind of man-made buildings, being everywhere yet nowhere. But it is also true that in certain places and buildings one can retire more deeply into one's own heart, and thus feel more closely God's ever-presence there.

20

In Nature's solitary places, in its forests, mountains, and grasslands, it is easier to cultivate the philosopher's trinity of goodness, truth, and beauty than in the crowded quarters of towns.

21

We need quiet places where the earth is left in its natural state and where men can seek in leisure and freedom to recover their independence of thought and to restore awareness of their inner selves—so hard to gain and so easy to lose in the modern world.

22

Those who seek inspiration and revelation withdraw into solitude and Nature, for there they may best achieve their purpose. Jesus departed into the desert, Buddha into the forest, Zoroaster, Muhammed, and Moses into the mountains.

23

If the tranquillity of a grove of trees or a grassy meadow, with all its sweetness and healing virtue, percolates into him, why let it go after a few moments? Why not stay with it, leave it to itself, and keep still for a while? Only look at it more closely.

24

Alone with Nature, in places like the lakes and forests of America's Adirondack Mountains, India's Himalayas, Switzerland's less-frequented valleys, it is still possible to find remoteness and feel external peace on this crowded planet.

25

Contact with Nature will, with sensitivity and appreciation, develop into communion with Nature—a purifying experience.

26

In those long, leisured silences while taking in the beauty of Nature, feeling its unstirred peace and unhurried whisper, seek to open up all the sensitivity of your heart to its Presence as a living, friendly, conscious thing.

27

Thoughtful seekers among the ancients and Orientals found fitter temples in Nature, in open desert spaces with the sky overhead and the sand underneath, than in elaborate structures resounding to the chants of professional men who had exhausted their divine mandate.

28

The mountains stand up all around me but the lakes give enough wide space to avoid producing any feelings of being hemmed in by them. They help my meditations, rest my eyes, keep a measure of tranquillity around me. At the threshold of life I was fascinated by Switzerland: at the end of travels, I come home.

29

A convoy of swans comes sailing gracefully toward the Lake Leman shore when they see me arrive with bread for them. But they get only a half of the bag's contents for I must move on later to the eighteenth-century building where a tribe of pigeons dwell on the pediment and eaves.

30

How valuable are those moments when a man finds time "to stand and stare" at some bit of Nature's floral beauty or arboreal colour, or to listen in the right way to music. Much beauty that he did not notice before will now be discovered and severe tensions will vanish.

31

Those who strongly feel the call of rural areas and hilly dales, shady woods and lakeside shores may be drawn not only by beauty, tranquillity, colour and freshness but also, *in a percentage of cases* by the mystical presence with which Nature invests such places.

32

That time is not wasted which a man spends amid the silence of a great forest to ponder on his duty and reflect on his destiny.

33

To come to rest on the summit of a hill, content, alone with Nature and space, is a time to turn thought to God.

34

The sensitive man can freshen his trust in the ultimate goodness of things from a glowing sunset, can renew his inward peace with a forest walk. Nature lovingly speaks to him, all wordless though she be.

35

It is a soothing experience to sit in the grass high on the top of a cliff, to look out at the vast spread of sea, and then to let the mind empty itself of accumulated problems. As the minutes pass, equanimity is restored and repose laps one about.

36

What he learns in a wordless way from such contacts with Nature will not be less precious than what he learns in uttered sentences or written paragraphs from human teachers.

37

The admiration of Nature is a step toward the understanding of Nature's secret, but it is still only a step.

38

In the beauty of a rose and the loveliness of a sunset the man of aesthetic feeling or poetic temperament may unconsciously find a reminder of the grander beauty of the Overself.

39

To the sensitive person, an unspoiled scenery of lakeland or woodland, sea or mountain, brings with its silent contemplation a nostalgic longing for return to his true spiritual home.

40

Those who are responsive to Nature, and more especially to the beautiful colours released at the sun's rise and fall, to the silences of woods and forests, or to the ocean's vast spaciousness, may use such contacts for attempts to get spiritual glimpses.

41

If he is sensitive to refined feelings within and Nature's beauty without and if he conjoins both to mystical ideas, he may come into such experiences as Jean Jacques Rousseau once described in his *Promenades of a Solitary Dreamer*.

42

There is one quality which re-enters man when the spring season re-enters the yearly cycle. It is hope.

43

What a striking sight is that of Sirius gleaming in a tropic sky on a calm mild night!

44

It is a common experience that in shady woodland walks there is an effluence of peace in the atmosphere. We need not wonder that in such and kindred places it is easier to find the quietness within. It is true that men have found their way to the Overself in almost every kind of environment, but there was more help and less conflict when they were alone with primeval Nature.

45

As the axis of the earth heaves itself over, we reach the end of one season and the beginning of another. The calendar points which mark this change mark also the movement of an inner cycle. Each equinox is a time when man may profitably try not only to change and cleanse himself but also to put himself in harmony with Nature, God. It is a time for extra effort in prayer, meditation, and purification. Physically, it is a time for a twenty-four hour fast or semi-fast.

46

Autumn is the time for spiritual planting, winter for spiritual growth, summer for spiritual rest, spring for spiritual harvest. In short, the seasons of nature have a reverse effect on man spiritually to that which they have on him physically. The spring equinox falls annually on March 20/21, the autumn equinox on September 23, the winter solstice on December 22, and the summer solstice on June 21.

47

The awakening of dawn, when every little bird bursts into song or recites a threnody, should bring new hope to a man. But it can do so only if he lets it. And for this he must put his own person aside, open his mind, make passive his heart, and slow his breathing.

48

There is a mysteriousness in the atmosphere at dawn which is paralleled at no other time of the day. It is brief but intense.

49

Just as sunrise and sunset are especially auspicious moments for prayer and meditation, so there are special times of the year, special seasons when the aspirant has opportunities for easier communion and quicker advancement than he has at other times. These seasons were known to the ancient religions of America, of Europe, of Africa, and of Asia. Hence they are universal dates and universally kept in the annals of mysticism. It is because of this knowledge, although somewhat obscure, that the religious festivals and sacred seasons like Christmas and Easter have been made part of various religions, both pagan and modern. Jewish and Greek mystics, as well as those of Egypt and Rome, observed them. These mystically auspicious times were the new moon days following the opening of each of the seasonal equinoxes or solstices. That is, the first new moon after March 21st, June 21st, September 21st, and December 21st. At such times the disciple should make a special effort to purify himself, to fast, pray, worship, and meditate because it is easier then to achieve the result sought.

50

The mysterious sustenance we get from Nature when she smiles, the misery she kindles when she frowns, both point to the closeness of our relation to her.

51

From the hill on whose side I dwell, at the very edge of Montreux, my window looks across sloping vineyards. It has a long view. This means much when one has to live closed in a small apartment every day, every year, with fifty families in the same building. I like the freedom of solitude, the view through unobstructed space. To let the green scenery take my thoughts away into a pleasant harmony with Nature for a few minutes at least, is a daily need, not a luxury. To sit even longer and go far away in consciousness until an unworldly quiescence is reached, is my evening bread.

52

The Hindus carry this admiration for a mountain even farther than we Europeans and Americans do—they revere it. Gods live on or within it in non-physical bodies; yogis find it the proper place for their meditations; it is indeed holy territory.

53

If while lost in admiration of a beautiful land or seascape we are stricken into silence, we get a closer inner relationship with Nature than if we immediately make it into a conversation piece.

54

The gardener who waters his flowers and shrubs with loving patience receives love from them in return. It is not like the human kind, but is the exact correspondence to it on the plant level.

55

The flower's beauty is simply a pointer, reminding us to think, speak, and behave beautifully.

56

Nature herself tries to bring about a correct attitude, but our ingrained habits thwart her and warp the instinct she plants in us.

57

They call it artistic appreciation or poetic feeling, this leisurely taking-in of a rippling brook and its grassy banks, but it is really close, very close to a mystical moment.

58

The silent empty desert may bore one man utterly, but bring another man close to infinite peace.

59

It is at such wonderful times that we pass from admiring Nature's attractive beauty to adoring Nature's divine source.

60

Sit in reverence before the setting or rising sun.

61

Winter marks the opening of that period from just before Christmas and culminating with Easter when the inner forces of Nature make it possible for man to make quicker progress than during the rest of the year. It is a suitable period to intensify aspiration, increase study, and meditate more.

62

If he falls into a kind of loving admiration of the landscape stretched out before him, and stays in it as long as he can, dropping all other thoughts, it will be a meditation as holy as if done in a church.

63

The passage from wonder to worship may be short or long, depending on the kind of man he is; it may need just a few more reincarnations or quite a lot: but it is a logical one, for Nature is a body of God, in time and space.

64

The closer I come to Nature the farther I go from evil. I move towards her because I feel drawn by her beauty and healed by her peace, yet I find that virtue follows them not long after.

65

To the extent that human beings have disturbed the proper equilibrium of Nature, they have brought upon themselves not only the bodily penalties of polluted environment but also the inner consequences of mental disturbance and emotional disequilibrium.

66

The dispension of culture and the democratization of art inevitably lead to lowering standards of taste. The tragedy of vast forests being depleted or destroyed to feed papermills for newspapers catering to low tastes, mental vacuity, moral degeneration and hunger for reports on commercialized pseudo-sport is one sign.

67

The birth of spring was celebrated by most ancient cults and religions. Its culmination in the Christian year with Easter offers a fresh chance for each man to awaken spiritually; but it is for him to take advantage of this inner event and respond to the World-Mind. Those who can respond only with and in their flesh bodies materialistically benefit, too, but link themselves with the animals.

68

When a sensitive man is in distress he will often, if circumstances allow, turn to nature, go to a wood, a forest, a meadow, a park, or even a small garden, either for a changed scene or to muse upon his situation. Why? It is an instinctive act. He needs help, hope, comforting, guidance, or peace. The instinct is a true one, a response to a lead from his higher self.

69

We take nature's beauty for granted and do not adequately understand our good fortune.

70

The lake shore is bright and sunlit; moreover it stretches far away to the other side where steep snow-covered mountains slope abruptly down into the water. Thus the view is cheerful, beautiful, spacious—superb. But here, in this small wood where old broad trees alternate with green turf, the sun does not enter, although the distance to the lake is only about fifty yards. Here the scene is shadowy, a darker tint, and enclosed. The first picture is happier, offers more beauty to the aesthetic mind. But this second one carries a deeper message: one feels a stillness which verges on the mystical. If the first charms, the second calms. The first lightens the heart, arouses hopes, gives enjoyment. The second quietens desires, kindles reverence, lessens anxiety and, above all, bequeaths a more lasting remembrance.

71

Nature, which produces such great beauty in flowers and birds, on fields and mountains, does not hesitate to destroy it, too.

72

In looking for the beauty in Nature, a man is looking for his soul. In adoring this Beauty when he finds it, he is recognizing that he not only owns an animal body, but is himself owned by a higher Power.

73

There are men who may appear to be materialistic but the admiration for Nature's beauty or the inspiration from noble music is their way of showing spiritual sensitivity. It is possibly the only way, given their past history and present character.

74

These truly lovely sights and scenes in Nature suggest to a sensitive or spiritually aesthetic person the invisible but felt and thought beauty.

75

The unbelievably intricate and immensely complicated nature of both microcosm and macrocosm should leave scientific students of Nature awe-struck at the wonderful Mind behind it all.

76

Is it not the essence of practical wisdom to employ every means that will most effectively achieve the goal of the Quest? Is it not being narrow-minded to limit ourselves only to methods that can help Nature yet keep Nature herself out?

77

There are moments when a man may sit alone with nature, when no sound intrudes and all is quiet, pleasant, harmonious. If he will enter into this stillness with nature and enter it deeply enough, he will find that it is associated with what most religions call God.

78

No animal, insect, fish, or bird has ever produced a metaphysical work or written a mystical poem or wondered about its own consciousness. Yet each possesses intelligence within its grade and each, from a bird like the crane to a creature like the chimpanzee, turns instinctively to the sun at certain times, showing its reverence, again within its grade. All of us acknowledge the physical sun as the original source of our physical life. If we humans are so much more advanced than our animal cohabitants of this planet that we alone can produce the three aforementioned things, we cannot all recognize that we owe our spiritual life—what there is of it—to the spiritual Sun, the ever-glorious Sun behind the sun, to our relationship with God.

79

Why do the sensitive find the freedom of an open uninterrupted view across landscape or seascape so appealing? The largeness and freedom of space echo back from outside the body the same attributes of the Spirit within.

80

It is a delight to sit on a terrace or belvedere and stare across a green valley. But it is a spiritual gain to use the moment to pass from the pleasant sight (as if it were a diving board) into a meditation.

81

Nature is his only neighbour: peace and beauty his only friends. Man, with his accompanying evil, is absent.

82

In the quiet woods or green meadows, or hearing the mountain streams bubbling along their downward way, his appreciation of Nature may rise to actual communion.

83

We may take delight in the beauties of this natural world while at the same time remembering poignantly their doom—a fragile brevity that will wither and disintegrate in the end.

84

Some can pass into the inner state through the gate of mere pleasure at beholding a beautiful scene in Nature.

85

When we are disgusted with the pettiness of mankind we may turn in appreciation to the grandeur of Nature.

86

Whether in the sight and presence of the giants of Himalaya or those of the Swiss Alps, massively standing against the sky, the effect on thought is the same.

87

Dawn fills the sky with beryl signals of hope.

88

When his affairs become insupportable a man may escape to the sea, if he can, and there, by its shore or on a ship, find a little respite, that is, peace.

89

There is much difference between a window view which looks out on the steel, wood, stone, or brick artifacts of man and one which looks out on the landscapes of Nature or the gardens growing out of man's cooperation with Nature. We need broad, spacious or beautiful horizons.

90

The artist in me joins with the Nature mystic in demanding a window with a view looking out on open country. Seated at such a window, the writer can be content, too, for this helps thought.

91

The effect of sitting by a lake shore or riverside when the weather is good, the wind absent, the temperature pleasant, for a sufficient length of time, may show itself in a sensitive person as calmness, uplift, or appreciation of Nature's beauty.

92

He may go to the silent forest to take wordless comfort when in distress.

93

Winding rivers, snowy peaks, wooded hills, resting animals, peaceful pasturage, feathery ferns, and rustic sights—this is New Zealand outside the few cities.

94

How furtively the dawn comes into being yet how powerfully it grows into daylight!

95

When the sun slants over the Swiss Alps and glistens on the surface of the lake, men are given a message by Nature suggesting that there is a cheerful, positive side to their situation and experiences however distressing the latter might be at the moment.

96

What man who is troubled in consciousness has not felt in the peace of a forest the healing uplift of mind which it gives!

97

In the beauty which Nature can offer man, he may find a catalyst to bring his feelings toward a loftier plane.

98

The invisible rays of the sun can kill bacteria, give life to plants, heal ailing men under some circumstances or kill them under others.

99

The beautiful in Nature, the singing of birds, the coming of Spring's colours recall the beautiful moods in ourself when glimpses revealed the soul.

100

The Matterhorn is not, as we are usually informed, the highest Swiss mountain. There are a few others in its vicinity which are somewhat higher. But it is the central showpiece, the most striking in appearance, and the most interesting to climbers.

101

I stood on the summit of Mount San Salvatore, looking by turns, at the enormous and glorious protecting circle of the Alps. It was one of those clear crystalline evenings when the sinking sun touched ice and snow with rose or gold, and when the Infinite Spirit touched heart and mind with peace or beauty. I thought of that other superb panorama, the lordly Himalayas, of the different years when I visited their eastern, central, and western parts—2,500 kilometres—from end to end. Salvatore—"Saviour"—the very name instilled hope and promised help, while the mountain itself seemed to whisper support.

102

A sensitive person may be gently influenced by such beauty of Nature to pause and gaze, holding himself still for the while, admiring and appreciating the scene, until he is so absorbed that he is lost in it. The ego and its affairs retreat. Unwittingly he comes close to the delicious peace of the Overself.

103

The travelling Goethe wrote his friends in Germany about a Princess he met in Naples—she was young, gay, and superficial—who advised him to go to her large country estate in Sorrento where "the mountain air and lovely view would soon cure me of all philosophy!" Some of us, however, would only be more incited by them to philosophy.

SUNSET CONTEMPLATION

The two great daily pauses in Nature offer wonderful minutes when we, her children, should pause too. Sunrise is the chance and time to prepare inwardly for activity; sunset to counterbalance it. We do not take proper advantage of the gifts of Nature but let ourselves be defeated by the conditions in which we have to live under our times and civilization.

2

Dusk is my mystic hour. With its soft coming I am drawn again to turn away from the world and recognize the divine presence within me.

3

The diurnal miracle of sunrise and the nocturnal fascination of sunset are worth much more than every minute we give them. This is not only because we owe so much to the great orb, but because we can get so much from the salutations themselves.

4

A profound feeling of reverence for the Sun should be a part of the worship, the visible orb being regarded as the vesture worn by the Great Being behind it.

5

The distant horizon, bathed in a sunset of quivering amethyst light, gives joy to the heart, uplift to the reverent worshipper of the Holy and Benign.

6

How lovely are those reddened evenings when the sun is about to bid us adieu! How the heart is warmed and the mind enlightened as it harmonizes with the hush of eventide. It is then so easy to receive what the poet called "intimations of immortality."

7

The sun's dying touch turned the field to sudden gold.

8

The minutes between light and dark just after the sun's setting are precious to him.

9

Fascinated by the utter beauty of a fiery sunset, held and hypnotized by it, the turning away merely to continue a piece of work, to eat a meal or to go out on some business seems reprehensible sacrilege. And perhaps it is. It is in such moments that a glimpse of God's presence becomes possible. For the consciousness is carried outside the ego, desire is diverted to savouring the mysterious stillness, and thought's constant labour is sub-dued or, if good luck prevails, even suspended.

10

The Incas of South America plainly taught that God was unknown and unknowable and therefore unworshippable, but that his highest creation being the Sun, the latter was the visible God for man and fit to be worshipped.

11

Plato tells us of the Greeks prostrating themselves before the sun at its rising and setting. Hence it is not only an Indian custom but one which other enlightened ancients practised.

12

Consider the tranquillity which comes, either to the mind or the body or both, when men live more in harmony with Nature, at sunset. The orb descends in a blaze of glory in the West. Consider further the Greek idea of the "blessed Western isles" and the Chinese "happy realm of the West" pertaining to the soul.

13

As I watch the pair of cranes, themselves watching with perfect con-centration the sun's last diurnal glow before the coming of twilight, I smile at the thought of what they are able to achieve with such instinctive ease while humans, who are supposedly higher in evolution, struggle vainly for years to achieve it.

14

In those moments of suspense when light is yielding so reluctantly to the dark, there is an opportunity to look within and come closer to the Overself.

15

In this mellow autumn dusk, when the passing sun no longer incar-nadines the fallen leaves and the night's peace is softly creeping up, a man may fitly turn inwards to cultivate his awareness of the Overself.

16

Outside, Nature is beautifully still; inside, consciousness is just as beau-tifully still. The two tranquillities blend into one another.

17

To anticipate the sunset hour or await the break of dawn, with body unmoving and mind absorbed, is one timing of this exercise which allies itself with Nature's helpful rhythm.

18

TO BE USED AS A VARIATION ON THE MEDITATION ON THE RISING OR SETTING SUN (Given in *The Wisdom of the Overself*)

First stage: He should fix his gaze upon the rising sun or coloured sky. All other thoughts should be put away at first and his whole attention concentrated upon the physical phenomenon which he is witnessing.

The rays of light must enter his body through his eyes. In this way alone do they attain their utmost efficacy for the purpose of this exercise.

Second stage: The student tries to partake of the profound inner pause wherein the entire solar system is briefly plunged, to experience within himself what is actually occuring within the greater existence of which he is a part . . . to tranquillize all his thoughts so that personal matters are wholly absent.

The Sun behind the sun, the mystical Light of the World-Mind illumes man's mental world and at the same time penetrates it through and through, provided he is present and passive in consciousness to receive its power.

Third stage: This stage moves with the outspreading or waning light until he embraces the whole planet along with it. For this purpose he has to:

1. picture a great globe growing larger and larger within himself as a formless consciousness mentally dissociated from the physical body, until it assumes GIGANTIC SIZE;

2. make the conception as alive as possible by permeating it with faith and conviction, holding the sense of countless creatures existing everywhere;

3. reverse the process, until it finally encloses his own body alone (globe gets smaller and smaller);

4. exercise the belief that he is mind not matter;

5. strengthen the perception of the true relationship between himself and cosmic life, his physical and vital oneness with the universe . . . and try to realize that his own existence is inter-connected by a beginningless and endless web with all the other existences around him.

6. There must be deep devotion and heartfelt feeling in his thoughts.

Goal: He reaches the goal of this stage when the physical scene vanishes, when he is no longer conscious of it, when attention is turned inward wholly on the beautiful mood or spirit thus invoked, when all form is absent and he feels in complete rapport with the universal being, so complete that he knows he is an integral part of it.

When he *feels* something of this relationship as a loving response, then he should cease trying to absorb support from the All—whose soul is the World-Mind—and begin to pass it out compassionately and share its grace unselfishly with others.

He sees them in his imagination suffused with its warm light and sublime peace.

First, he directs his effort with his love towards those who are near or dear to him and to any special individuals whom he would like to help in this way.

Then, he directs his effort with his love towards mankind in the mass— whom he must regard as unconsciously forming one great family.

Third, he directs it towards individuals who are hostile to him, who hate, injure, or criticize him. He must consider them as his teachers, for it is their business to pick out and make him aware of his faults. He need not send his love, but he must send them his pity.

Close exercise with: Short, silent, personal prayer to the Overself.

19

The loveliest of sights is the sunset's transformation of Himalaya's snowy summits from pure white to pale gold, and then to rosy pink. And then to wait, in the hushed expectant atmosphere, for night!

20

It was one of those lovely summer evenings when I sat far into the night: first, enjoying the sunset, then, the darkening landscape, lastly, the lights alone. The curtains remained undrawn: I could not bring myself to attend to waiting work, and shut out this fascinating scene. For it drew me away, held me, melted me. The "I" was going.

I love these long lingering summer sunfalls. Then I can put duties aside, turn from the activities which life amongst men imposes, and go with all this beauty into Mystery Itself.

21

Thus we let our mind, our life, sink out of activity into rest with the twilight itself. We decline into not only stillness of thought, but also stillness of individuality.

22

The light in the room gets less and less, the shades draw in upon him more and more, as his worship proceeds deeper and deeper to its silence and inwardness.

23

Rich are those possible experiences when one sits and gazes at the western horizon before eventide, the sun going out of sight, the heart open to beauty and grace as it longs for the Overself.

24

Once more when the light starts to fail and dusk takes over, the period of withdrawal from outer activity has come. It may last only a few minutes or, better, an hour, but it will be a beautiful, pacific, and profitable recess.

25

In those long summer evenings when the day lingers on as if loath to withdraw from our world and admit the night, when colours run through the spectrum around the sky, we may find new incentive and fresh sustenance for this meditational practice.

26

How beautiful a sight when the last evening rays shine through the shut window on a seated figure whose face is rapt in listening to inner music, whose thoughts lie in stilled abeyance.

27

About the sunset meditation exercise: The practice itself does not depend on whether the sun is actually shining at the time. For Nature comes to a great but brief pause just then. This cessation of inner activity takes place whatever the outer physical conditions are. It can be felt by sensitive persons. Therefore the meditation need not be abandoned if outer conditions seem undesirable, although the beautiful colouring of the skies when sunshine is present helps those who have aesthetic feeling.

28

Whether the sun sets with or without a display of colours, behind trees or in the sea, obscured by high buildings or urban settlements, it should fix the direction of worship in this exercise.

29

As dusk begins, the sacred call is heard and the mind turns inward to its centre.

30

In the rosy glow of sunset, after a wearisome descent into the world of human affairs, celestial hopes are restored and one can turn around to look within.

31

I remember the long twilights of Scandinavia and the Scottish Highlands, as reluctant to go as I to lose them. Here the brief tropical twilight bursts with colour but is soon over.

32

It is time well used and not lost if, in the presence of Nature's master-piece—the solar beauty at its dawn or declination—he turns his back on personal activity to pause for a few moments or minutes, admiring quietly, even humbly reverent. Such attention is, for the atheist, religion discovered: for the toiler, art appreciated.

33

Yes! let us worship Eos, Greek goddess of sunrise, who accompanies Helios in his sungold chariot. O! sunrise! moving through the most beautiful range of colours in the spectrum.

34

Why is it that sensitive refined souls would rather a hundred times look down on a long mountain valley than on a long city street? Why does the handiwork of Nature rest them but the handiwork of man disturbs? A lovely sunset, with its glowing colours and peaceful landscape, may move them deeply. Whence comes this emotion? It is aesthetic, yes, but it is also mystical at its root. Hence the sunset's gold mauve and grey tints may start feelings which uplift, console, and spiritualize a man.

35

The red beauty and hushed serenity of a sunset affect even the insensitive person and make him pause for a few moments. Why is this? Because in that brief while he does what his extroverted life does not ordinarily permit him to do, he concentrates and quiets himself, and thus receives a dim echo of the beauty and serenity which belong to his own innermost being.

36

To the older Greeks the sun was an emblem of beauty. They looked at it with joy. But to the Hindus it was an emblem of divinity. They looked at it with worship. Both attitudes were right and both are called for today.

37

Men pass it by every day, disregarded, as if it were not there at all. This sacred moment of truth is bestowed upon them in those pauses of life whose higher use and real importance are missed because unknown.

38

However hard-pressed, troubled, or fatigued his day has been, this is the hour which relieves—even saves—it, this pause harmonized with Nature's own pause.

39

These spiritual evenings can serve us Westerners better than the spiritual dawns serve the Easterners.

40

The sunset brings rest to Nature's activities. Man may stop his own activity for a few minutes and come into harmony with Nature.

41

He who rises with the rising sun and dies with the dying one in an act of worship gains greatly on all levels of his being.

42

Exercise: In this exercise the eyes are fixed on the sinking sun, the mind lost in its beauty, and the body kept still on its seat.

43

It is as if the sun gave a last lingering kiss to this earth, a farewell greeting to act as a reminder to hold on to hope.

44

If the rising sun stimulates man and many other living creatures to prepare for the day's coming activity, the descending sun warns him to relax from it.

45

This hour when the sun drops low, glowing with colours as it goes down, is well celebrated by evensong services and bell-ringings of the church.

46

If there is a sun showing on any day of the month let face be turned toward it when it goes down.

47

How soothing to sit in the half-light of early evening and let the mind fall away from the world.

48

When the coming of night brings repose to Nature and silence to the landscaped scenes, we experience a stillness outside the self comparable to the stillness which contemplation brings out inside the self.

49

To let the mind come to rest in love and with concentration on a vividly coloured sunset or a garden of flowers is to invite the glimpse.

50

When the sun vanishes in golden splendour there is a mysterious moment: all is still. This is your chance.

51

The charm of long lingering twilights may be deepened and strength-ened by sustained surrender until it becomes a gateway to the mystically hidden self.

52

Those drowsy sundown evenings which come in the warmer months of the year, so restful and so undemanding as they are, can be used to relax all mental effort and to enjoy the affirmations and mantrams which declare divinity of the human soul.

53

The evening light is a blessed one. It transfigures a landscape or a seascape. The evening pause of Nature is for many the favoured hour of meditation. When alone I arrange matters, work, and meals so that this hour of sunset watching and sun worship is not missed.

54

These twilight periods become a veritable oasis in the desert of ordinary living, a sacred sanctuary in the materialism of modern day existence.

55

How much of his philosophy did Plato owe to that habit of his of watching the sunset from a hillside?

56

One who never tires of watching spectacular sunsets has been turned by them into a sun-worshipper, a votary of the oldest religion in existence.

57

There are some sunsets which inspire ebullient joy and other ones which put us in a cathedral by their grave beauty.

58

Was there an unconscious knowledge of the 365-Day Meditation on the Setting Sun Exercise in Benjamin Disraeli? In his novel entitled *Contarini Fleming*, a psychological romance written in 1832, he makes Contarini sit at a window and watch the westering sun go down, with the consequence that he exclaims, "I felt a disgust for all the worldliness on which I had been lately pondering. And there arose in my mind a desire to create things beautiful."

59

Some magnificent play of sun on earth, ocean, or sky may provide a spectacle to hold sense and mind alike enthralled. The effect on feeling may deepen to the point where a sense of uplift, exaltation, and peace becomes overwhelming. This is rare, memorable vision, where faith in an intelligent Power behind things is restored or fortified. It will pass completely, it may even never recur again, but it cannot be forgotten.

60

The sun sinks and vanishes but his admiration does not vanish: it deepens and sinks into love, till he can repeat the seventeenth-century poet Herbert's lines, "Thou art my lovelinesse, my life, my light, Beautie alone to me . . ."

61

It is not enough to practise mechanically: one should *love* this sunset-watching exercise and never tire of waiting for the sun to go down, never weary of staring at the shimmering fading colours.

62

There are few persons who are not susceptible to the charm of a failing, highly coloured sun towards the end of the day. But there are fewer still who understand how to use this feeling in order to obtain a mystical glimpse. To watch the sun change the landscape from green to rainbow colours as it makes its last glorious splash of rays before the evening folds, is to invite the glimpse, provided the watching is done with intense concentration and tender feeling for the beauty of the scene.

63

My happiest hours come when the sun is about to bid us farewell. Those lovely minutes are touched with magic; they bring my active mind and body to a pause. They invite me to appreciate the radiant glowing colours of the sky and finally they command me to enter the deep stillness within, so that when all is dark with the coming of night all is brilliantly illuminated inside consciousness.

64

In Morocco, Egypt, Sudan, Arabia, India, Malaya, Cambodia, and farther east still, the hour of departure for the sun becomes a conflagration of colours far beyond its Western parallel. The joy it yields or the sadness it suggests never tires a sensitive man, not even the thousandth time.

65

No hour of the day provides a stronger hint of life's tragically passing character than sunset. What reflection tells us through thought, this period—so lovely yet so doomed to perish soon—tells us through ecstatic sight.

66

To revel in the sky's twilight colouring, its translucent gold and purple, to wait further and revel again in the afterglow—this is poetic feeling, artistic development, and semi-mystical experience.

67

It is no waste of time to let activity melt into vacuity when the evening pageant of the sun's departure sets in.

68

The joy of watching the sun pass away in a glow of colour is not entirely unmixed. At some point in the period, towards the end, the remembrance that all this beauty, so intense at that moment, is doomed to vanish very soon, touches the mind with melancholy.

69

The sun which is to be seen is a reminder to blind faithless man of That which is not to be seen (unless the inner sight and the inner life are active)—the glorious hidden royal Sun of the World-Mind.

70

One is reluctant to leave the gorgeous, eye-delighting, heart-satisfying feast of colour.

71

This is the radiant magical hour of sunset when worship is the instinctive mood.

72

To sit on a fine day on a park-bench or at a café-table—watching the late afternoon or early evening sky's light change and the colours of objects darken—provides another setting for this beautiful feeling of inward peace. This has always been the day's finest hour. But it comes to its best with solitude. The company of other people's voices does not help it, only obstructs while their thoughts, vividly felt in that passive mood, may be even worse.

73

A beautiful, colourful, and paintable waning of the sun is an offer of grace to the human beings who take the trouble to pause and notice their parent—Nature.

74

The sun is God's face in the physical world.

75

The uncertain light of sundown, the objects indistinctly seen, helps a little this passing into a half-mystic state; but the primal actuator is his willingness to relax from activities, to let his thought drift back to his aspiration, and wait in patience.

76

This visual adventure with sunset ends in a mystical one.

77

Witness a glorious dawn or a golden sunset and let the feeling of admiration grow into adoration.

78

There is a mysterious pause of nature at sunset, sundawn, and at solstices. The most important is winter-solstice, everywhere celebrated in the ancient world; it is Christmas for us. So the ego-thought should pause and recollect. Just as the visible sun is essential to human bodily life and existence, so the invisible sun of consciousness is essential to its mental, emotional, and spiritual life. It is our Overself and God: give it homage.

79

During that pause in Nature which is so noticeable in very quiet country places, away from the towns, and during the fall of the sun in the evening, we may hear the last sounds and calls of animals and birds from a far longer distance than at other times or in other places.

80

We are part of the life of the cosmos. As such, it is possible for us to commune with it inwardly or to be penetrated by it outwardly. In connection with the Sun Worship exercise, it might be mentioned that since both points of the day are equally sacred—that is, the rising and the setting sun hours—the benefit is not only spiritual, but *could* also be physical. A visitor once told me that having faithfully practised for 365 days the exercise given in this reference in *The Wisdom of the Overself*, deafness suddenly disappeared. And lately I was told of a Japanese writer who, after a long illness with lung consumption, went on the morning of the Winter Solstice to worship the rising sun. He felt a great fervour. He experienced some kind of illumination, and the same day recovered good health. This happened about a hundred years ago.

81

When the pause is greatest—that is to say, when the sun is down so low as to be almost on the horizon—there is his greatest chance to merge with it in a beautiful, smiling harmony.

82

Other men usually worship in the way they are taught; mine came from no outside instruction but from a spontaneous and instinctive reaction of the heart. It is the only religious rite that stirs me, this worship of the declining sun, of its coloured beauty and healing stillness.

83

When the sun has descended to the line from where it rose—the earthly horizon—his thought can descend too and sink back into its quiet source.

84

There is a point where this inner world of divine being intersects the outer world of common existence, and therefore where awakening is possible more easily than at other times: the pause between day and night (paralleled by its counterpart the pause between night and day). Anyone can take advantage of Nature's stillness by willing his own stillness in untensed passivity.

85

One morning a neatly dotted in jacket and trousers, tall and lean man appeared on the doorstep of the little house where I lived in Mysore City (whenever I was not travelling around India). With him, but a short distance away, I then noticed another man standing there, who was shorter, sterner, and stouter. He wore the white robes of a swami. The wiry-figured man addressed me in simple, half-broken but quite understandable English; he introduced himself as a disciple, the other as a guru, and proffered his service as interpreter between us. The guru then addressed me and explained that they had come from the North, that he wished, if acceptable, to teach me a single exercise and talk about certain other spiritual matters, and that he would then depart in the early evening. (They had brought their own food with them.) This is how the knowledge of the Meditation on the Sun exercise in *The Wisdom of the Overself* (Chapter 14, "The Yoga of the Discerning Mind") was literally brought to me. It must be added, though, that I took a writer's license to adapt the exercise to Western culture. Where the guru showed and quoted some obscure Hindu *Veda*, to prove that the exercise was a fully authentic prescription—an authority which did not carry the same weight to non-Hindu Western minds—I saw and seized on the possibilities of appealing to the aesthetic sensibilities, the artistic appreciation of the sun's beauty instead. The guru did not object to this adaptation. It illustrates the mysterious oneness of the mystical life all over the world that what was prescribed in some little-known scriptural text in India of several thousand years ago, was practised personally by a European who had never left Spain, never studied any Oriental text at all. I refer to Saint Juan de Cruz, better known to us as Saint John of the Cross, who lived about four centuries ago (1542–1591). (He was the Spiritual Director of the more famous Saint Theresa of Avila.) Such was the genesis of this lovely and easy exercise among my writings. It used physical act—seeing—to yield an emotional consequence, and then led the practicant into a state of consciousness which transcended both. It is an exercise which has helped many people, if their reports are valid. Certainly it has consoled and comforted the ill-fortuned, actually helped some sufferers of bodily maladies, while those who care for art got artistic treats they might otherwise have missed!

86

It is a quietening experience to sit in the sinking sunlight and let the play of personal matters recede from the forefront to the background of attention.

87

To sit in utter silence, while subdued twilight touches us with peace and the room around and the world outside darken in the dusk, can be a beautiful experience.

88

The falling shadows of eventide worked their ancient witchery on me. I ceased this endless activity and lapsed into a stilled body and a silent mind.

89

Let him greet the new day with a new smile: for dawn is to be welcomed by both body and soul.

90

It is a joy to gaze reverently during a calm evening at a sunset tinting the sky with soft pink, lilac, and green, and then use this mood for entry into meditation.

91

When the twilight hour is at its peak, a spell seems to have fallen over the lake, the fields, and the mountains.

92

It is a lovely countryside experience to let the sunset lapse into a quiet broken only by the croaking of frogs or the shrilling of crickets.

93

Those who pay homage to the sun whether they admire it for aesthetic reasons or revere it for spiritual ones are obeying a right instinct.

94

Was it a time of such a sunset viewed from his Thames-side Chelsea home that Carlyle wrote: "From a small window we can see the infinite."?

95

For evening brings the mild sadness which attends darkness but also the contrary feeling of mild pleasure which attends repose after toil.

96

Soon the lamps will be lit in the darkening room, this holy pause will come to an end, this strange reminder of a Home beyond home will pass into a gentle memory.

97

Yes, it is true, one may be a sun worshipper and love those moments when it lights up the pieces, the furnishings, or the pictures in one's room and this is even more accentuated when the sun has its last burst of glory in the evening.

98

In that mysterious period of the day when the light fades out but lamps are not yet switched on, when the room is half lost in growing shadows, when Nature itself seems to pause for a few moments in its work, lies an opportunity for man. It is an opportunity to create a corresponding pause within himself.

99

What could be more important symbolically or more pleasing aesthetically than to watch the shining sun rise from behind mountains or over seas? What hope it gives, what help it promises to all beings and not only to mankind. What too could be more beautiful and more tranquillizing than to watch the same sun setting in the evening?

100

"It came to be my favourite place. It was there that I usually . . . gazed, as I never could do enough, at the setting sun." —Johann Wolfgang Goethe.

101

The poet Keats knew the richness of this hour, which left "the reader [of poetry] breathless . . . in the luxury of twilight."

102

What is all this reverence for holiness and appreciation of beauty which come of themselves at sunset but an effect of light upon Nature's land or seascapes?

103

The light has nearly gone. The city has become a gigantic silhouette in the dusk. The recession into contemplative peace is almost over. Soon— movement begun, activity resumed—the outward phase of life where the ego has to struggle its way through problems while enjoying its few pleasures follows.

104

As day retreats and night falls, the opportunity enters. When measured in time it stays differently at different seasons of the year, that is, while dusk lingers.

105

Looking out of the little window and across the lake, after glancing at the mountains to the right and to the left, I stared at the vanishing sun, absorbed in its beauty and its mystery.

106

The charming hour of sunset brings its message of repose not only to us but also to most of the birds who flock home to their perches.

107

When the sun dips low and vanishes, when dusk begins to fall and the colours darken and merge, the mind can move with Nature into its great pause. A man whose temperament is sensitive, aesthetic, religious, psychic, or Nature-loving can profit by this passage from day to night and come closer to awareness of his soul.

108

As the dwindling light and increasing shadow bring on dusk's soft melancholy, it is offset by the still-fresh memory of the lovely colours just passed from the sky.

109

In those few moments all Nature seems to hold her breath, to rest and be still. But he seldom hears or listens and misses the chance.

110

The final glimmer of sunlight followed by the closing-in of darkness could be a melancholy event. But the adoration and concentration which preceded it bring enough tranquillity to dissolve all such negative feelings.

Index for Part 1

Entries are listed by chapter number followed by "para" number. For example, 1.52 means chapter 1, para 52, and 7.56, 77, 80, etc., means chapter 7, paras 56, 77, 80, etc. Chapter listings are separated by a semicolon. Please note also that, for the reader's convenience, the first number in the right-hand running heads throughout the text indicates chapter number.

Entries are listed by chapter number followed by "para" number. For example, 1.52 means chapter 1, para 52, and 7.56, 77, 80, etc., means chapter 7, paras 56, 77, 80, etc. Chapter listings are separated by a semicolon. Please note also that, for the reader's convenience, the first number in the right-hand running heads throughout the text indicates chapter number.

ategories from the Notebooks

his outline of categories in *The Notebooks* is the most recent one Paul
.unton developed for sorting, ordering, and filing his written work. The
listings he put after each title were not meant to be all-inclusive. They
merely suggest something of the range of topics included in each category.

1 THE QUEST

*Its choice—Independent path—Organized groups—
Self-development—Student/teacher*

2 PRACTICES FOR THE QUEST

Ant's long path—Work on oneself

3 RELAX AND RETREAT

*Intermittent pauses—Tension and pressures—Relax body,
breath, and mind—Retreat centres—Solitude—
Nature appreciation—Sunset contemplation*

4 ELEMENTARY MEDITATION

*Place and conditions—Wandering thoughts—Practise
concentrated attention—Meditative thinking—
Visualized images—Mantrams—Symbols
—Affirmations and suggestions*

5 THE BODY

*Hygiene and cleansings—Food—Exercises and postures
—Breathings—Sex: importance, influence, effects*

6 EMOTIONS AND ETHICS

*Uplift character—Re-educate feelings—Discipline emotions—
Purify passions—Refinement and courtesy—Avoid fanaticism*

7 THE INTELLECT

*Nature—Services—Development—Semantic training—
Science—Metaphysics—Abstract thinking*

8 THE EGO

What am I?—The I-thought—The psyche